YOU TARZAN

Masculinity, Movies and Men

YOU TARZAN
Masculinity, Movies and Men

edited by
Pat Kirkham and Janet Thumim

LAWRENCE & WISHART
LONDON

Lawrence & Wishart Limited
144a Old South Lambeth Road
London SW8 1XX

First published 1993
Collection © Lawrence & Wishart, 1993
Each article © the author(s), 1993

ISBN 0 85315 778 2

Cover designed by
Jan Brown Designs, London
Photoset in North Wales by
Derek Doyle & Associates, Mold, Clwyd
Printed and bound in Great Britain by
Dotesios, Trowbridge, Wiltshire

244829

CONTENTS

CONTENTS

For Sarah, Alex and Kate
and
Joshua, Nancy and Ella

Acknowledgements

The idea for this book emerged in discussions at the bar at the 1989 British Film Institute Summer School *What is British Cinema?*, where we first met. We are indebted to Jim Cook and Nicky North, the BFI Education team responsible for developing and organising that school, as well as to the participants whose contribution to discussion was so fruitful. Amongst these we should like particularly to acknowledge and thank Beverly Skeggs, subsequently one of the most encouraging supporters of this project.

The book took further shape during the 5th Leicester Annual Film and Television Studies Summer School on masculinity, held at Phoenix Arts and Vaughan College in 1990. We are very grateful to Laraine Porter and Michael O'Shaughnessy, co-organisers, with Pat Kirkham, of that event, as well as to the tutors and students who contributed with such enthusiasm to discussions of masculinity(ies) at that and subsequent schools.

Given that the publication of this book coincides with public confirmation that there will be no more 'Stirlings' we want to use this opportunity to attest the importance of the BFI Summer Schools. Since the mid-1960s these annual schools have offered unparalleled opportunities for broadening horizons and debate, as well as for establishing and maintaining contacts and networks within the increasingly pressurized world of education. The establishment of film and television studies in the UK owes much to the imaginative and dedicated work of the BFI Education department. We therefore offer this collection of essays in the spirit and best traditions of 'Stirling', not least of which are collective, collaborative and exploratory scholarship, a sense of the vital importance of film and television studies and a commitment to their future.

There are many individuals whose kindnesses and practical help during the preparation of this book we should like to acknowledge. They are: Pam Birley; Jim Cook; Peter Groschel; Alan Love; Tim O'Sullivan; Markku Salmi; Judith Smith; Tise Vahimagi; Bob Carter and the staff at Vaughan College, Leicester; Nigel Hinds and the staff at Phoenix Arts, Leicester; Bob Phillips and the BFI Information Service and BFI Stills, Posters and Designs.

We greatly enjoyed working together on this project, and with our contributors, all of whom we thank most warmly. They share our disappointment at the refusal of some film copyright holders to grant permission to reproduce stills. We are, of course, most grateful to those copyright holders who did allow us to use their images, particularly MCA Television. Our final thanks go to Vicky Grut, an engaged, patient and energetic editor, and to the rest of the staff at Lawrence and Wishart. It has been a pleasure to work with them.

Pat Kirkham and Janet Thumim
January 1993

You Tarzan

Pat Kirkham and Janet Thumim

'I've just met a wonderful man. He's fictional – but you can't have everything.' Cecilia/Mia Farrow in *The Purple Rose of Cairo* (Woody Allen, US, 1985).

Reading the essays in this anthology may not completely answer the question posed in Leon Hunt's title 'What Are Big Boys Made Of?', yet the overlapping concerns of our fourteen contributors mark out some of the grounds on which the question may be considered. When we first discussed the project in the summer of 1989 the idea was to gather together (fairly quickly, we thought) some of the research which we knew certain men were undertaking or planning, in relation to masculinity and cinema. The decision to devote the first volume exclusively to men's writing grew out of our belief that it is important for men themselves to write about the construction and representation of the masculine in relation to their experience as masculine subjects. We offer the anthology, and this introductory essay, not as a definitive project but as a speculative and, we hope, enjoyable contribution to debate about the cultural construction of gender.

In the fascinating and stimulating dialectic of the editorial process we have been able to begin exploring the representations of various masculinities as discussed by the writers of these essays. How are these representations achieved, with all their certainties and uncertainties, in the visual and dramatic currency of filmic constructions? What narrative pre-occupations have alerted our contributors, how are signs decoded, what seems clear, what remains ambiguous? Reading through the essays which comprise this volume, certain recurrent sites have become apparent. It is at these sites that various traits of masculinity are signalled; these may be qualities either asserted or assumed in the construction and development of masculine characters, or they may be signifiers of themes quite consciously concerned with an interrogation of masculinity. Broadly these sites are *the body, action, the external world* and *the internal world*.

By *the body*, we refer to the visual representation of the male, to dress, to the spectacle of the male body and the invitation to audience pleasure in this spectacle; we refer also to the actor's presence, his star persona, as an important element of this material construction. *Action* references various manifestations of the physical, including violence, competition, aggression, skill and endurance, in which these attributes are depicted in terms of the male body in action. Thus the filmic construction of *being* (the body) and of *doing* (the body in action) are both sites where assumptions about masculinity are made manifest. *The external world* we use here to indicate filmic representations of the public interaction of male characters with each other and with the conventions and institutions against which they operate. It is here that collective masculinities begin to delineate patriarchal order itself.

Last, but certainly not least, is *the internal world*, which we use to refer to the experience and articulation of being, from the inside, as it were. From the point of view of the female reader the psychic structures of the male can only be read through interpretation of the visible – actions, dress, mise-en-scene – and the auditory. One asset of this particular collection of essays is precisely that here we have access to the articulation, by experienced male movie readers, of a succession of representations of men and masculinities.

In these introductory notes we want to develop the schema outlined above in relation to propositions and ambiguities which seem to us to stand out in the essays which follow. This is, it goes without saying, both an exploratory and a tentative endeavour, one which as editors we are privileged to begin. We hope it will be developed by readers as they use and debate the understandings of and insights into masculinity, masculinities, emerging in their own readings of these essays and the films to which they refer.

THE BODY

The pleasures to be had in consuming the spectacle of the 'perfect' male body are fraught with difficulties, not least because of the contradiction between the vulnerable passivity arguably implicit in the state of being-looked-at, and the dominance and control which patriarchal order expects its male subjects to exhibit. One of the features of films which specifically purvey this pleasure – the adventure, the epic, and the sports film – is the need for (potentially) erotic displays of the male body, for both the intra-diegetic homo-erotic gaze and the gaze of the audience, to be motivated in the narrative. In his essay on the male epic, Hunt, drawing on Steve Neale's work on masculinity and spectacle,[1] suggests that the 'troublesome' eroticization of the male body is routinely motivated by the evidence of suffering and endurance marked on the surface of the body in such signs as bulging muscles and sweat. The bead of sweat, representative of bodily fluids, may allude to *both* vulnerability *and* power. It is the visual mark of the male's power in marshalling and controlling his bodily resources. The slogan 'No pain, no gain', quoted by Garry Whannel in his essay on *North Dallas Forty* (Kotcheff, US, 1979), with its representation of the ritualized combat of American football, directs attention to the attributes of skill and endurance, which in this film justify the visual display of the male body. Both in the cinema and in the wider patriarchal culture of which cinema and sport are both a part, a sustained and frequently erotic attention to the male body is, it seems, allowable only in terms of the demonstration of its qualities of skill and endurance. Only in this way can the suggestion of a feminizing passivity, consequent on being the object of the look rather than the bearer of it, be refuted.

For our purposes it is the marks of these qualities *on* the body of the male, represented on the cinema screen, which are of particular interest. In what ways are suffering, endurance and pleasure visible; how are they inscribed on the surface of the body? Beyond this question lies the meaning of the body itself – not as a signifier of individual prowess, nor even as a pleasurable object for the gaze, but as a cultural icon. Walt Morton in his essay 'Tracking the Sign of Tarzan' suggests that part of the appeal of the Tarzan films is that Tarzan 'offers audiences wish-fulfilment' in the 'naked, melodramatic sign of truth'. Thus the male body (almost) unadorned is offered as an uncomplicated spectacle. Perhaps the appeal of Tarzan lies precisely in the offer of a return to an apparent simplicity, albeit a spurious one. His 'sinuous curves of a Greek god' (Edgar Rice Burroughs) stand for a definition of an ideal masculinity, moreover one untroubled by culture, civilization, or women.

Even Tarzan, however, needs his loincloth and consideration of the male body also entails consideration of how it is clothed and decorated. The question of who keeps their shirt on and who doesn't is an important one, as Andy Medhurst notes in his essay ' "It's as a man that you've failed": Masculinity and Forbidden Desire in *The Spanish Gardener*.' The complex codes of male dress and display have rarely been systematically described: for the thousands upon thousands of words written about Vivien Leigh's dresses in *Gone With the Wind* (Fleming, Cukor, Wood, US, 1939) there are very few about Gable's 'manly' outfits and even fewer about how that famous body filled them to perfection. Clothes can sexualize men just as they can sexualize women. It is surely significant, for example, that Tarzan/Weismuller's loincloth, illustrated on the cover of this book, is slit to the waist at the side thus elongating his already long legs and further objectifying them, and him. Indeed, it is just where there is very little clothing that detail is foregrounded and becomes especially meaningful.

But the ideal physical perfection of the star of sport or cinema, or the epic hero, has a dual existence. Being in part defined by what it is not, it carries opposing meanings. The ideal, presented by Weissmuller in his slit loincloth or in the figure of the 1950s epic hero, is accompanied by the disturbances and distortions of 'anti-heroes' as in 1950s science fiction cinema. The 'perfect' body also implies its obverse, the mutilated or decayed body. These problems, and that of the paradox presented by the male star's passivity, are united in Richard Dyer's discussion of Rock Hudson, particularly of his physical presence in the 1950s films re-read in the light of his subsequent decline and death from AIDS in 1985[2]. Dyer suggests that Hudson's portrayal of the signs of conventional masculinity has the effect of subverting the apparent contemporary security around ideas of gender, normality and heterosexuality. 'Rock – The Last Guy You'd Have Figured?' was first published in 1985 and Dyer is now less certain of the validity of reading back into a film knowledge which was not available to its contemporary audience, in this case knowledge concerning Hudson's homosexuality. Though this practice may invalidate suggestions about the readings made by contemporaries, for subsequent audiences the films can only be read in the light of such knowledge. A similar problem, arising from the development of the star-text[3] subsequent to the film in question, is also germane to discussion of Dirk Bogarde's 1950s films, of which *The Spanish Gardener* (Leacock, UK, 1956), is one example. Nevertheless Bogarde's anodyne masculinity in the popular series of Doctor films (*Doctor in the House* UK, 1954; *Doctor at Sea* UK, 1955; *Doctor at Large* UK, 1957; *Doctor in Distress* UK, 1963, all directed by Ralph Thomas) certainly takes on another dimension when viewed in the light of Dyer's discussion.

But does the 'parade of signs' by which Dyer summarises Hudson's performances call attention to the signifier – that is the visual and filmic construction of the masculine – distancing the signified – the man? Does the distancing of the signified begin to unsettle its meaning? Brecht would say yes. So would the women in *L'il Abner* (Panama and Frank US 1959), whose deformed, disruptive and awkward (but nevertheless 'real') menfolk have been transformed into the appearance of perfect specimens of muscular masculinity. But these flawless ideal men are so narcissistically preoccupied that they have no desire for the women – they don't even see them, so absorbed are they in flexing their perfect muscles. The women's song 'They was mean, they was cranky, but they loved hanky panky, Put them back the way they was' refers directly to the excessive space which this display of perfection has generated between the signifier and the signified.

One of the many useful insights of feminist scholarship is that patriarchal language locates the feminine beyond the boundaries of the masculine. The feminine is all that which the masculine is not. Tom Ryall, in his discussion of successive male stars' performances in the central role of Hannay in three versions of *The 39 Steps* (Hitchcock, 1939; Thomas, 1959; Sharp, 1978) 'One Hundred and Seventeen Steps Towards Masculinity', shows how this particular aspect of popular cinema's function as a 'technology of gender'[4] operates in practice. He suggests that, in some popular cinematic representations at least, masculinity is broadly defined for the audience in its encounter with the feminine. In other words, it is in this ubiquitous encounter that the audience can most clearly read answers to the question 'what kind of man is this?' Ryall further proposes that the nature of the encounter is coded in the features of the stars. Star personae can offer a shorthand history of variants of the masculine in its encounter with the feminine. This proposition may be explored further in reading the essays by Fisher, Medhurst and Page, which also attend to details of star personae.

ACTION

Filmic depictions of the male body in action offer chivalrous deeds, sports, combat and violence, with an emphasis on competition. A variety of strong and well-tuned bodies are presented. The male epic, for instance, offers 'heroes' who are strong both physically and morally, the former frequently offered as the sign of the latter. Peplum movies (which starred male body builders and a former Tarzan actor) as well as the Tarzan films themselves, (the stars of which included a former Olympic swimming champion and a male physique model), leave us in no doubt as to the significance of physical strength in the portrayal of an ideal masculinity. The success of the 1932 *Tarzan the Ape-Man* (Van Dyke) made Johnny Weissmuller as popular a star as Clark Gable whose appeal, Fisher suggests, rested on a 'tough guy' physicality despite the fact that his roles involved a great deal less action than Tarzan faced, and certainly no single-handed crocodile killing. Fisher's account suggests a Gable more crude and ape-like than the aristocratic Tarzan could ever be.

Several essays deal with filmic representations of training for action, and of the acquisition of survival skills. Here it is the process of *forming* a body which will function effectively, to which audience attention is invited. Travis Bickle in *Taxi Driver* (Scorsese, US, 1976), for example, trains his body for action. A solitary male against the world, he does it alone (except for the privileged view of the audience) and he does it voluntarily. The sportsmen in *North Dallas Forty* also train voluntarily, unlike the gladiators in the male epics whose training is enforced, as is that of the raw recruits in *Apocalypse Now* (Coppola, US, 1979) and other war movies discussed in John Newsinger's essay, 'Do You Walk The Walk?'. We should note, however, that all these 'trainees' are depicted as victims of bullying by their respective 'coaches': winning is what all these 'games' are about and the end, it seems, justifies the means. Both sports and war films relate this collective training not only to male bonding but also to rites of passage from boyhood to manhood. Normative channels of masculinity are often highlighted in those films which critique them. Whannel in 'No Room For Uncertainty' suggests that this is the case in *North Dallas Forty* in which another rite of passage, from able bodied player to 'has been', affords the opportunity for an interrogation of the norms.

The paradox of pleasure in 'ideologically unsound' practices (a phenomenon with which many of us can identify) is also explored in Whannel's essay. The nonsense of the game and its rituals are highlighted in the film as the audience is invited to empathise with Phil Elliott/Nick Nolte's dilemma; he yearns for the pleasures of the sport even though he knows 'the game' to be both exploitative and degrading. In the last shot of the film he refuses to play 'the game'. He refuses even to catch a ball thrown to him by a friend. He stands, static and passive, his arms held out to the sides as if nailed to a cross. But the image, like the contradictions of contemporary masculinity, is ambiguous. Is this masochism, or salvation – or is it both?

The question of rites of passage is, it seems, a familiar ordering principle, particularly in films dealing with the socialisation of the young. The triangular relation between the father, his son and the gardener in *The Spanish Gardener* can be understood in these terms, and the question also arises on a somewhat larger scale in Mike Hammond's discussion of *Dead Poets Society* (Weir, US, 1989). The main emphasis of the film, however, is on the transition from boyhood to manhood of a group of schoolboys, in particular one who is torn between two sets of values, both expressed as demands. But when this young man comes to act independently it is not the act of the successful man but that which his society judges a failure, namely suicide.

There is a stark contrast in the ways in which young male bodies are turned into fighting/killing machines in the war film (*Platoon*–Stone, US, 1986, *Full Metal Jacket*–Kubrick, UK, 1987) and the male epics explored in Hunt's essay. Whilst the army trainees are systematically dehumanized and defeminized (their hair is cut and the sergeant in *Full Metal Jacket* aims to transform them from 'queers and women' into 'real men'), the gladiators in *Spartacus* are 'pampered . . . oiled, bathed, shaved and massaged', we might say 'feminized', the better to perform. Though the ostensible performance in all these films is in combat, nevertheless various preparatory cosmetic processes are emphasized: the consequence is the distancing of the male 'object of the gaze' from the socially constructed 'masculine'. In this way the male spectator can enjoy the homo-erotic spectacle without being unmanned by it.

Violent action in the male epic is related to clear codes of honour, as is often also the case in war films. In the case of those 'critical' films about the Vietnam war, however, the violence is shown to be barbaric, meaningless and morally wrong. Newsinger argues that such films dealt with a major crisis in US foreign policy and world domination in terms of a crisis of masculinity: this is in an interesting contrast to those horror and science fiction films of the 1950s which drew on wider issues as metaphors for instabilities within dominant masculinities. But, in the anti-Vietnam war film the subject matter – what we see on screen – is, despite the films' own critique, still wanton killing, systematic massacre, the destruction of villages and the rape of women. Many of the films sexualize violence, not only in rape but also through a sexualization of the weapons themselves. Much is made, in Clint Eastwood's 1992 western *Unforgiven*, of the synonymity of the penis and the gun: apart from the various anecdotes of legendary fights and fighters, Bill Munny/Eastwood himself has not only given up gunfighting but also sex which, he tells his friend Ned, he 'don't miss much'.

Page presents the violence against women in the De Niro/Scorsese characters as the result of the men's inability to contain their aggression. Their inner rage is so great and their social skills so few that their anger constantly disrupts their lives by dictating their actions. Despite the change, over the last decade, in social attitudes towards rape, explored in such films as *The Accused* (Kaplan, US, 1988) and *Thelma and Louise* (Ridley Scott, US, 1991), a great deal remains to be written about cinematic representations of that particular form of violent male action, a subject hardly touched upon in this volume. Fisher's article on Gable refers us back forty odd years to one of the best known scenes in cinematic history, the so-called 'row and rape' scene in *Gone With The Wind*. It is illuminating to consider the choice of Gable for the role of Rhett Butler in the light of his previous roles which had fused his dynamic physical magnetism with violence towards women. The idea of Gable as a 'tamer' of women (he hit them) in his screen persona not only informed readings of him as Rhett but also made him the overwhelming public choice for the role. So great was his particular brand of sex appeal that, as Helen Taylor has pointed out, most contemporary women did not remember the scene as one of rape so much as of passion, and also recalled their own desire for Gable.[5]

Violence and despoliation also act at a metaphorical level in film.

Fisher argues that in *Gone With the Wind* Scarlett O'Hara/Vivien Leigh is a metaphor for the land which man despoils. If Scarlett herself can be read like this, then the land and house, Tara, are also a metaphor for the beleaguered Southern way of life which is coded as domestic, genteel and cultured – feminine – threatened not just by the Yankee army but also by big business, industrialization and modernization, which are coded here as masculine.

Just as strength is frequently used as a yardstick of dominant masculinity, so its opposite, weakness, is used to signify a lack of masculinity. In Indian cinema, however, Sharma notes (in his essay *Blood, Sweat and Tears*), the routine and acceptable co-existence of what in the West would be contradictory signifiers – the sensitive, even tearful, son and the aggressive male rebel. In Western cinematic constructions of masculinity, however, such a co-existence would be unusual and the weak man is, simply, not a proper man, not a whole man. He is demonstrably *less* than a man and frequently feminized to emphasize that point. Most of our contributors have chosen to focus on filmic roles depicting strength rather than weakness, with the exception of Wells and Medhurst, although the latter did set aside a proposed article on 'Strong Men of the 1950s' in order to concentrate on that wonderfully 'soft', though not necessarily weak, man of the 1950s, Dirk Bogarde.

Related to strength and weakness, the hard and the soft, is the question of size – the big and the little, tall and short, fat and thin. There is no doubt that size is an issue, for men, in relation to their masculine identity. Dyer notes how Rock Hudson's size gives him a solidity and strength which his name suggests but which his performance style and his roles often undermine. The essay in which this issue is most clearly addressed, however, is Paul Wells' 'The Invisible Man: Shrinking Masculinity in the 1950s Science Fiction B-Movies' which focuses on anxieties about that taboo subject, impotence. The irony is, however, that excessive size (and, by implication, excessive potency?) is not a solution either. Thus the films comment visually and metaphorically on the dreadful dilemma that constantly confronts us all, namely how to construct our identity, how to get the image we offer to the world exactly, or nearly, right, as well as on the injustice of being the 'wrong' size or shape.

THE EXTERNAL WORLD

Male power is central to any consideration of masculinity; patriarchal order continually attempts to define power and masculinity as practically synonymous. It is therefore no surprise to find that in filmic representations of masculinity, associated issues such as status, hierarchy, knowledge, skill, language and success inform our understanding of the operations of male empowerment and control, whether this be exercised over events, people or emotions. Social status is a significant indicator of power and the most unequivocal 'heroes' discussed in this anthology are either born at the top of their particular social group or have risen to the top through sheer ability and/or special circumstances. Thus it is possible to have both the nobleman born to lead and the low born leader of the slave revolt occupy analogous positions of narrative and moral power within the male epic. As the (noble born) outlaw Robin Hood/Kevin Costner says in *Robin Hood Prince of Thieves* (Kevin Reynolds, US, 1991), 'nobility is not a birthright; it is defined by one actions'. With Tarzan, as with Robin Hood, there is no problem. How could the son of a British nobleman do anything but act in the most fitting and chivalrous way on every occasion? As the 1984 *Greystoke: The Legend of Tarzan, Lord of the Apes* (Hudson, UK) demonstrates, it is all a matter of breeding; Tarzan instinctively knows how to behave like a 'gentleman'.

In filmic representations, as in real life, excessive behaviour is by no means restricted to any particular social group. However, the drives of the rich Rock Hudson character in *Magnificent Obsession* (Sirk, US, 1954), for instance, are given noble foundations whereas the obsessive characters discussed here by Page and by Panayi, in his essay on *One Last Chance* (Gabrielle Beaumont, UK, 1990), are both poor men. Bickle/De Niro is a taxi driver, while Nick/Jackos is a lumpen proletarian gambler, one of whose aims in life is, precisely, to avoid a regular job as a taxi driver. For both, class intersects with their construction of masculine identity. Nick/Jackos' obsession is also rooted in, and relates to, a strong and specific ethnicity. Bickle, by contrast, is a social isolate, yet Scorsese represents his obsession as a tirade against what he (Bickle) perceives as the breakdown of the social order. As Sharma suggests in his discussion of the Vijay/Bachchan character in *Agneepath* (Anand, India, 1990), the question of *dispossessed* social status is important in the Indian film because it lends moral weight to the obsession and offers a narrative context for an avenging violence.

In their different ways, all these films fuse social issues with individual obsessions, but it is only in Panayi's essay that the well worn notion that the social institution of marriage can curb obsessions and excesses such as gambling, criminality and drinking, is raised. The central protagonist, Nick, asserts his masculinity on his wedding night not through his sexual prowess (another topic, like marriage, not dealt with in any detail by our contributors) but by going out on his own to a casino, by returning to his 'old', public, world. It is fascinating, for the female reader, to pursue the notion that marriage, or even a close, regular and routinized relationship with a woman, somehow means the end of a strongly defined masculinity. It is a theme familiar in popular cinema, notably in the western where woman is represented as the domesticator and emasculator of the hero. She appears in both these guises in Eastwood's *Unforgiven* (1992), having, in addition, two other well tested roles: she motivates and instigates action. But, like the classic western it recalls, this film is all about men and the contradictions of masculine identity: women appear only as signs, ciphers, markers of the boundaries of the masculine. Fisher suggests that Gable brought the down to earth qualities of the western hero into films which dealt with the everyday, with contemporary urban experience. The American populist hero might have shifted to the city and be wearing suits but he was essentially the same 'true' man underneath. There was no genuflection to social niceties in the contemporary proletarian roles played by Gable in Depression America of the 1930s. He was in every sense the 'Woolworth Romeo'; 'cheap, cheerful and sexy'. Like De Niro, he was regarded as an actor who could carry off parts in which men were represented as uncouth, hard drinkers, tough fighters, hot tempered and congenitally programmed to treat women badly.

The films of war which Newsinger considers and the male melodramas discussed by Medhurst and Hammond (in which women play little part) allow courageous and/or enlightened (male) individuals from the lower ranks to assume a degree of authority. The leading characters, typically, occupy a position mid-way between the extreme or ultimate authority of institutions such as the school or the army, and the younger or less experienced boys or men in their charge; they occupy the 'liberal' middle ground of sanity, reason and common sense which the films' preferred readings privilege. They do not encourage rebellion but rather offer a different, usually more 'democratic', way of operating within the hegemonic institutions and framework. In short, they are offered as the best possible people to lead young boys or men through their rites of passage to an acceptable version of dominant masculinity. Their power is not the absolute power of the institution within which they have to operate but, since that power is (often crudely) coded as 'bad', the films not only allow them considerable moral power but also focus on their methods of wielding authority.

The difficult question of how men can be affectionate and tender without being read as sexual is also at issue in this context. An example, as Medhurst shows, is the delicate nuancing of the relation between the gardener, José/Bogarde and his employer's young son in *The Spanish Gardener*. The tripartite structure allows a comparison of two different types of male-to-male authority relations, each suggesting differing father-son relationships with all their attendant pains, pleasures, and anxieties. Freudian notions of absent father and 'ideal' substitute father are self-consciously invoked in the case of *Dead Poets Society* as well as in *Agneepath* where the son himself substitutes for the father, with all that that implies for masculinity and the son's relationship to the mother, as Sharma demonstrates.

Sport offers other opportunities for men to rise to glory and altered social status through performance. The sports film discussed here, however, does not follow this trajectory of success, fame and fortune. Instead Whannel, in writing about *North Dallas Forty* emphasizes the equally well worn narrative of the courageous individual fighting against established yet corrupt and immoral power. Once again, the power of the hero is shown to be both provisional and relative. The successful football players might have considerable status with the fans and a consequent standing in the local community, but real power is institutional and structural and resides with those who own and run the team. At the end of the day both Elliott in *North Dallas Forty*, and Keating in *Dead Poets Society* take a beating from 'the system' for proposing a 'decent' (though by no means radical) masculinity as an alternative to the colder more calculating one of big business or the equally cold and ruthless élitism of the upper middle class in its maintenance of social hierarchies.

Not all members of the 'lower ranks', of course, get the opportunity for social advancement on celluloid. There are two discussions in this anthology of a filmic representation of a gardener. Whilst in real life gardening and associated tasks rate amongst the lowest paid manual jobs, in cinema they help position the character as someone in tune with the outdoor life and, therefore, as unproblematically healthy and 'male'. The association with nature is a more complex and ambivalent one because of allusions to growth and fecundity usually aligned with the female, although the natural world is posed as an opposition to a female coded 'civilization' when portrayed as 'raw' or 'untamed', as in some westerns. Care is taken in *All That Heaven Allows* (Sirk, US, 1955) to emphasise Hudson's horticultural specialism, trees (bigger, stronger and more robust than plants), and his status as (college trained) expert but, as Medhurst shows, the Bogarde character proved more problematic. In both, however, strong individuality is suggested by the solitary nature of the job and the associations of ties with the earth are used to enhance the characters' 'rootedness' and solidity. Readers may speculate as to whether it is a coincidence that in the examples discussed by Medhurst and Dyer this somewhat 'feminized' occupation is carried out by actors whose performances frequently destabilized the then normative readings of white, male heterosexuality, each in his own particular way.

THE INTERNAL WORLD

The absorbing question of male anxiety, central to Page's study of Scorsese, figures large in many of the essays. Wells, writing about science fiction cinema of the 1950s, argues that the frequent distortion of the material body is evidence of a deep seated unease generated by contemporary (1950s) gender politics. Certainly disquiet concerning the conventions of heterosexual behaviour is close to the surface in many of the films. *The Incredible Shrinking Man* (Arnold, US, 1957), offers size as a marker of the masculine: as 'the hero' shrinks, it becomes clear that he is not what he (and she) thought he was. Here is male anxiety expressed in material appearance. His (the hero's) disorder results in her (his wife's) empowerment. Does the possibility of 'her' (woman's) empowerment therefore produce his disorder? Anxiety about uncontrollable female power is even more clearly expressed in *Attack of the 50 Foot Woman* (Herz, US, 1958) whose title alone is designed to send shivers down the patriarchal spine. Wells argues that such anxiety not only focuses on gender politics, but is also their consequence. Though he does refer, in his readings, to contemporary fears about nuclear accidents and the Communist 'threat', he suggests that these are narrative pretexts masking more or less overt studies of gender politics. Male anxiety over the politics of gender in this decade is perhaps vindicated by the emergent women's movement of the late 1960s; certainly it is expressed most forcibly in the misogyny which then pervaded British and American popular cinema. It also raises questions about the current 'backlash' against feminism and women's emancipation, arguably evidenced in contemporary movies of male anxiety, such as *Fatal Attraction* (Lynne, US, 1987) and *Blue Velvet* (Lynch, US, 1986).

Whereas in science fiction cinema male anxiety is figured visually through grotesque distortions of form, in horror it is more likely to be signalled by means of an horrific formlessness emerging from that terrifying borderline between the clarity of the masculine and the obscurity of the feminine. Peter Hutchings, in *Masculinity and the Horror Film* suggests that the horror of the monstrous, whose very formlessness recalls the pre-oedipal maternal figure, is in its power to render the (male) reader/spectator passive, therefore helpless. Hutchings speculates about the nature of the pleasure typically derived from such horrific representations, specifically by male audiences. The question, he argues, concerns power: in particular it concerns the spectator's recognition of 'temporary disempowerment'. But this recognition simultaneously conceals the fact that the 'spectator's hold on power is structural and provisional rather than personal'. Thus the experience of vulnerability, of subjection in the face of the formless, the unknowable and the monstrous is enjoyed and used to deny – to disavow, perhaps – a more pervasive vulnerability experienced outside the cinema. Hutchings notes, in this connection, the particular pleasure derived from the horror genre by adolescent males, possibly the most anxious of all male groups.

Anxiety about gender identity is directly articulated in many of the essays which follow, particularly in Page's discussion of Scorsese's characters and in Dyer's discussion of Rock Hudson. Nor is it far from the surface in the male epic, where the role models are not only strong and clear but virtually (and at times literally) impossible to live up to. Several essays (see Page, Panayi, Newsinger, Hunt and Sharma) touch on obsession. In some the fanaticism relates to revenge, gambling, or training the body as a machine and is fused inextricably with the characters' masculine identity. What these characters have in common is proving themselves not only by taking risks but also by taking more risks than anyone else and thus being more 'manly', in a perverse and destructive extension of the competitive ideal. These are the men who cannot say no to a challenge, cannot walk away from a dare. They are in contrast to the (equally obsessive) heroes of the male epic whose masculine identity is often specified by the control involved in being able to say no, being able to deny, precisely in order to prove oneself the greater man.

Such films, structured around the questions 'what kind of man is this?', both conceal and imply the underlying question 'what kind of man am I?' It is this enigma which fuels the narrative. Masculinity, these films suggest, cannot be taken as known but is rather something that men must 'live up to'. It is a condition of which the standards are difficult to define, and which is so structured through competition that it is unlikely ever to be achieved. The male epic's characteristic focus on definitions of masculinity produces, Hunt argues, a tension between an 'heroic' discourse of stoicism, sacrifice, and self-sufficience (signified visually by the bead of sweat) and a melodramatic discourse of emotion, vulnerability and love (signified visually by tears). Put another way, this is also the tension between control and loss of control, central to patriarchal discourse of the masculine. The ultimate image here, the narrative resolution of this tension, is that of El Cid's corpse on his horse, leading his troops into battle. Is this simply another version of 'the good father is the dead father'? El Cid's transformation into 'more than a man' is problematic: does this mean that he 'lives up to' his masculinity? Or does it suggest that by his example he defines it, and sets another task – to go beyond it – offering an impossible model for others to 'live up to'. No wonder Scorsese's heroes are anxious, if masculinity is doomed to be so provisional. It seems that while a woman's work is never done, a man's work *can* never be done.

In De Niro's portrayal of the two Scorsese characters, Page argues, muteness or inarticulacy operates as the signifier of inner emotional turmoil and agony. Speech is displaced onto 'outbursts of violence' or 'acts of self mutilation'. He suggests that, 'if the silent phone call is symbolic of Doyle's failure to communicate his inner feelings to his wife, then his saxophone/phallus becomes the expression of his nature, the force of masculinity'. Both the phone and the saxophone are, in their differing ways, instruments for communication but the phone, of course, entails an 'other' whereas the saxophone is innocent of such intentional connection. This insight touches on the negotiations *between* people – men and women, men and men. Scorsese's metaphor implies that a problem of masculinity is its inability to deal adequately with 'the other'. Men, this metaphor suggests, can't speak. Perhaps the problem is, rather, that men can't hear? Travis Bickle (*Taxi Driver*) is trapped in an impasse of alienation as he poses to his own mirror – in Page's elegant phrase 'he becomes his own pin-up'.

The variants of tortured and silent suffering, which for many contributors seem to be telling signifiers of the masculine, reach their full extent in the classic and potent image of the crucifixion. Page refers to Bickle's 'crucified maleness'; Whannel, as we have seen, draws on the imagery of crucifixion in his account of Elliott's position at the close of *North Dallas Forty* when he has left the game but not yet returned to the outside world and, arms outstretched, refuses a catch in the final image of the film. But the most sustained discussion of this metaphor for man's suffering is in Hunt's essay. The crucified body is contradictory and perverse. In this image are united passivity and control, humiliation and nobility, eroticism and religious transcendence. 'The epic hero', Hunt writes, 'demonstrates his control over his body through his ability to give it up'. This is indeed a perverse ideal. The opposing agendas of duty and emotion, law and love, death and desire are united in sacrifice: this is the crucifixion, offered as the ultimate act of self control, thereby transcending control and producing the ideal. But it is, of course, an ideal predicated on violence and denial.

Violence and denial are fundamental to the alienated inarticulacy of Travis Bickle and Jimmy Doyle. Their violent actions take place in the public arena where violence is, arguably, both legitimated and produced by conventional attributes of masculinity such as muscularity, hardness, and so on. But is their isolation *also* a mark of their masculinity?

The questions of power and disempowerment, of control and lack or loss of control which underpin spectator pleasure in horror (discussed by Hutchings) are central ones in the filmic constructions of masculinity detailed in these essays. We have already touched on the paradox of the star who, in order to represent the masculine ideal must cede control of his body by passively submitting himself firstly to the grooming processes and then to the cinematic gaze, the look of the camera. Newsinger draws attention to the scene in Kubrick's *Full Metal Jacket* where the recruits are having their heads shaved; Hunt references the lavish preparation of the gladiators' bodies in the epic; Fisher recalls the careful building of Gable's body image by the studio and Page notes the central importance of De Niro's *own* 'controlled use' of his body in preparing for his roles in Scorseses's films. In all these events there is a constant tension between control by the individual of his body (hence his identity) and the control by others (by those with access to power) of the individual's body – thus rendering it passive, subject. This tension is played out *on* the body, on its surface, in signs such as shaved heads (Newsinger), bulging muscles, soft sinuous curves (Hunt), or 'the flawless surface of conventional masculinity', to quote Dyer's description of Rock Hudson's 1950s body.

Dyer contrasts the 'security of heterosexuality' promised in Hudson's performance style and image, with the 'inherent neuroticism' of James Dean's much less stable image. Did Dean's apparent confusion over his own sexual identity allow him insight into the contradictions surrounding gender identity? Is it this disturbing knowledge which is referenced by the phrase 'inherent neuroticism'? Is the marker of the stable, 'normal' heterosexuality then an undisturbed ignorance of such contradictions? Developing his discussion of Rock Hudson's 'look', Dyer probes the uneasy terrain of identity and gender. Rock, he says, doesn't deliver the masculinity he promises, to women: 'all he does is look the part'. Apropos Hudson's performances, he writes:

> What women want is a real man, but the only real men are but a promise of fulfilment, endlessly put off, never finally kept. You could see this as a critique of the very idea of the 'natural man', exposed as a sham that women would do well to turn their backs on. But I think the films do believe in the ideal of, even the need for, virility, it's just that they don't really believe that 'real men' exist anymore. The films are thus a tragic, rather than a feminist, view of the situation of women.

Dyer's comments concern the fictional men and women peopling these 1950s films. In the commodity culture developing during this decade 'masculinities', along with other objects of desire, are being 'sold' via these filmic representations in order to contain the unsettling experiences of anxiety and lack. Though Dyer's suggestions are concerned with fictional women, the insights he offers resonate with the experience of actual female subjects. The tragedy for women, as described by Dyer, is that what you want is, by definition, what you can't get. If you can get it, it's not what you want. Is this because masculinity cannot be imaged, or because its terms do not cohere, are in themselves incoherent?

Such speculations about 'real' masculinity return us directly to the promises of the Tarzan figure and to the quotation about the fictional and the real from *The Purple Rose of Cairo* with which we opened this introduction. The exploration of and insight into 'masculinities' – we can no longer use the confident singular – collected in this volume offer rich suggestions for approaches to the study of spectatorship, history and gender. But despite this post-modernist slide towards the plural and the provisional, we are still left with 'masculinities' as organised by patriarchal power into certain structures with their signs, their images and their imperatives. They still produce anxiety and instability in the male subject. Is this because of the impossible gap, signalled by the women in *L'il Abner'*, and by Cecilia/Mia Farrow in *The Purple Rose of Cairo* between the symbolic (the signified, the masculine) and the real (the signifier, the man)?

NOTES

1 Steve Neale, 'Masculinity as Spectacle: Reflections on Men and Mainstream Cinema', *Screen*, vol 24, no.6 Nov-Dec 1983.
2 This is the only essay in the collection to have been previously published. It appeared in 1985 in the Californian publication *The Body Politic*.
3 John Ellis draws attention to the function of the star text in modifying possible readings of the film text: 'the film is one text, the star is another text passing through it. The result is a system in which any film is guaranteed to signify over and above its connotations as a textual system' in 'Made in Ealing', *Screen*, vol 16, no.1, 1975.
4 Teresa de Lauretis, *Technologies of Gender*, Macmillan, London, 1987.
5 Helen Taylor, *Scarlett's Women: Gone With The Wind and its Female Fans*, Virago, London, 1989.

Rock – The Last Guy You'd Have Figured?

Richard Dyer

Near the end of *Lover Come Back* (Delbert Mann, US, 1961) there's a scene where Rock Hudson goes into his apartment block wearing only a woman's fur coat. Throughout the film he's been observed by two older men – everytime they've seen him it's been in some situation where it's looked like he was pursuing or being pursued by every attractive woman around. When the two men see him in the fur coat one turns to the other and says, 'Well – he's the last guy in the world I would have figured.'

The two men in *Lover Come Back* had the same difficulty as much of the world's press when Rock's gayness became public along with the news of his having AIDS. *People* magazine quoted his aunt Lela saying 'Never would we think that he would be that [i.e. gay]. He was just always such a good person'. The British dailies reached for their usual clichés – 'Legend that Lived a Lie', 'Secret Torment of the Baron of Beefcake', 'Rock Hudson's Jekyll and Hyde Existence' – emphasising the 'shock' his homosexuality would be to the women fans who had so 'thrilled' to his 'husky frame'. There was apparently nothing gay about Rock Hudson's star quality or his appeal. One paper even managed a back-handed compliment by suggesting that, contrary to popular opinion, Rock was a good actor after all because he had been such a convincing heterosexual.

The reasons it had been impossible to figure that Rock was 'a homosexual' were revealed by a predictable vocabulary. Rock could not be gay because, on the one hand, he was 'virile', 'muscular', 'square-jawed', 'masculine', and, on the other, he was 'nice', 'good', 'likeable'. The linking term in all this is 'clean-cut', that uniquely US men's style of antiseptic machismo. Difficult for the press (and television) to know how to handle this and at best it could mean acknowledging a shift in the perception of gay men – we can be nice *and* butch *and* homosexual after all. At worst and, in Britain at any

27

rate, more insistently in the months since the story first broke, it could be presented as a monstrous deceit practised on the libido of millions of women. Cross either one of these views with the fact of AIDS and you get both the surge of fund-raising and sympathy for AIDS victims (because after all AIDS sufferers are nice, and real, men) and the reiteration of the idea that gay men cause AIDS (just as Rock deceived women sexually, so gay men have infiltrated a deadly disease on the world through their sexuality).

Whether in the benign or malignant version, and many stages of uncertainty in between, what such approaches share is the idea that it is *surprising* to think that Rock Hudson was gay, that there is a contrast between how he seemed on screen or in public appearances and how he was in private, that there was nothing gay about Rock as performer or image. It is this, rather than the media coverage of Rock in the light of AIDS[1] that I want to focus on here.

One can't altogether blame the media for assuming that their readers would be surprised that Rock was gay. In an obvious way, there was nothing gay about the Rock we saw.

When it became known that Montgomery Clift, James Dean, Sal Mineo and others of Rock's generation were, to some degree or other, gay, it was not such a surprise, even to those who were not already in the know. Clift and the rest do fit a certain stereotype of the gay man – sad, neurotic, confused. Even their appearances – physically slight, with intense eyes and pretty faces – are of a kind that contrasts with Rock's large frame, slow eyes and classically handsome face. The image of gay men as sad young men, pretty and anguished, was a prevalent one in the popular culture of the 1950s and 1960s and Rock does not conform to it. The difference is very clear when you see James Dean and Rock together in *Giant* (George Stevens, US, 1956). Dean's Method style now looks mannered – arched torso, hunched shoulders, shifting eyes, staccato speech and a walk so oddly stiff it reminds me of gay porn star Jack Wrangler (whose walk I used to suppose was some bizarre version of butch though I gather it is in fact arthritic). By comparison Rock is still, straight, unfussy, just *there* in the classic manner of Hollywood stars. Dean's style connotes 'naturalism', an acting convention associated in the period with awkwardness and neurotic emotionality. Rock's style suggests a different sense of the natural, namely normality. His very stillness and settledness as a performer suggests someone at home in the world, securely in his place in society, whereas James Dean's style suggests someone ill at ease in the world, marginal and insecure. Easier, then, to see Rock's image, as carried in his performance style, as one expressing the security of heterosexuality, and Dean's the insecurity of gays' positions in society and/or their inherent neuroticism. (You'd have to work very hard indeed to see anything in the film of the supposed affair between Rock and James that Britain's shame, *The Sun*, said Elizabeth Taylor said was going on during the filming of *Giant*.)

Neither in looks nor in performance style does Rock conform to 1950s and 1960s notions of what gay men are like. But nor does he fit with the images of gay desire that are found in gay picture magazines and short films of the period.[2] I do feel less certain about this than about him not being a sad young man; Rock must in fact have been a pin-up and heart-throb for countless gay men. I well remember seeing *Pillow Talk* (Michael Gordon, US, 1959) when it first came out. There is a scene where Doris and Rock, both in (separate) baths spread across a split screen, are talking on the phone. Doris puts her leg up out of the bath and rests her foot against the wall in a typical cheesecake pose and so does Rock, their feet meeting at the split in the screen. The sight of that sturdy, hairy calf (all, in fact, that you can see) fed the fantasies of this already intensely voyeuristic gay teenager for several months thereafter. Yet Rock never became a favourite source of erotic fantasy for me and he really doesn't fit the gay pornographic imagination of the time.

The physique magazines and soft-core pulp novels centred predominantly on two types of desirable male – the youth and the muscle man. Rock was neither. The 'youth' type was identified above all by his crew cut, but also by imagery of jeans, biking gear, campus pennants or other talismen of what's now called youth culture. Tony Curtis, Tab Hunter, Marlon Brando and others fitted this and belong to gay iconography of the period, but Rock never did. In the *Saturday Evening Post* spread on him in 1952, he is at home, washing the car, listening to Frank Sinatra albums, eating ham and eggs. It's all very wholesome, unrebellious, normal, even a bit middle-aged – and naked. He's in shorts, or an après-shower towel, in almost all the pictures, and he has a really lovely body. But he is not the other desirable type; he is not a muscle man. He has a large, strong physique but the contours are soft, the look sleek; he never had much 'definition', was never 'cut', 'ripped' or 'shredded', to use the repellent vocabulary of 1980s bodybuilding. Even by the standards of the 1950s, Rock was not muscley, not like Steve Reeves or even, say, Jeff Chandler. If many of us did put Rock on our walls (or, more likely, would like to have done), it was because he conformed to more general notions of what an attractive man is; it was not a specifically gay taste, whereas Tony, Tab, Marlon, Steve and Jeff conform closely to 1950s gay imagery.

In terms of its relations to stereotypes of gay men *and* gay erotic imagery of the 1950s and 1960s, there is nothing especially gay about

Rock Hudson's image. Does that mean there is nothing to say about it in gay terms?

We are most used to sensing a star's gayness with people like Montgomery Clift and others mentioned above. Despite the largely unambiguous heterosexuality of his roles, Monty always seems to be pushing at the boundaries of masculinity, his gayness troubling, inflecting, exploring what it means to be a man.[3] This was not Rock's way. He produced a flawless surface of conventional masculinity. Yet it is a surface strangely lacking in force and intensity. It's a sort of parade of the signs of masculinity without any real assertion of it. What's fascinating is the way this quality unsettles the apparently complacent heterosexuality of his films. If Monty seems to be trying out new roles for men, Rock, in effect if obviously not in intention, seems to subvert the security with which ideas of masculinity and femininity, normality and heterosexuality, are held. This is especially exploited in two groups of films that were among his most successful – the sex comedies and the melodramas he made with Douglas Sirk.

Rock's sex comedies, from *Pillow Talk* in 1959 to *A Very Special Favour* in 1965, feature not only the kind of gag which I opened with but also plots that revolve around sexual ambiguity. What often happens is that, for part of the film, Rock (sometimes deliberately, sometimes not) appears not to be full bloodedly heterosexual: he is woman-shy, or impotent, or a milquetoast, as a means of getting, usually, Doris Day to drop her defences. *A Very Special Favour* (Michael Gordon, US, 1965), with Leslie Caron, goes further: Rock actually pretends to have turned homosexual because Leslie has rejected him; she is a psychiatrist and takes up the challenge to 'cure' him of his 'inversion' in the time honoured manner. There is one variation on this pretence motif among the sex comedies. *Man's Favourite Sport* (Howard Hawks, US, 1963), turns it on its head. Here Rock is famous for his expertise in what the film avers is a uniquely masculine activity, fishing, but he has never fished in his life. Although the film winds up with him in the arms of Paula Prentiss, he seems rather uninterested in women, even though, farcically, he appears to be carrying on with three at once. Here it's macho that's the facade, whereas with the other comedies it's various notions of unmasculinity. (The pretending-to-be-gay motif even recurs as late in his career as the TV mini-series *The Star Maker*, where Rock, as Danny Youngblood, allows himself to be discovered by Brenda Vaccaro in bed with another man, so that she will think her daughter Angel is safe with him, thus permitting him to elope with Angel later. My thanks to my friend Charlotte Brunsdon for drawing my attention to this episode.) What is all this about? In his book *The Celluloid Sacrifice* Alexander

Walker suggests that 'the main aim of the sex comedy's sparring partners . . . is to make each other neurotically unsure of their gender, their sex appeal and their potency'. Rock pretending *not* to be a wolf in *Pillow Talk* puts Doris Day in a quandary:

> Yes, he *is* the perfect gentleman, but is that really flattering to her as a woman? When he refrains from kissing her, is it just because he respects her or is she really not his type? Of course, he *looks* virile enough, but can one be quite sure? Maybe he dotes on his mother and collects cook-book recipes. And sure enough, Rock's *alter ego* acts as cissily as predicted, and Doris gets panicky. After making men keep their distance for so long, has she now fallen for one with no urge to come hither?[4]

As Alexander Walker sees it, the main effect of this is at Doris's expense, the comedies being at heart misogynistic. He argues that Rock's pretence does not really undermine *his* heterosexual image, even if it does throw her sexual identity into question. After all, we know he's only pretending. Presumably it was assumed that Rock's image was so indelibly heterosexual that he could get away with such stuff. But the insistent return to this pretending-to-be-a-cissy routine also suggests a more elaborate scenario now that we know (and can say that we know) that Rock was gay. Here is this gay man (Roy Scherer Jnr, Rock's real name) pretending to be this straight man (Rock Hudson) who's pretending to be a straight man (the character in the film) pretending to be a gay man (for the sequence or gag in the film). The hysterical pleasures of confusion, so central to comedy and farce, are perhaps even more deliciously delirious here than in, say, *La Cage aux folles* (Edouard Molinaro, France/Italy, 1978), or *Victor/Victoria* (Blake Edwards, UK, 1982), to which, once you know he's gay, Rock's comedies come so close. These 1960s comedies have a reputation for blandness and safeness, for conventional sexual morality crossed with a complacent view of sex roles. Now they look much more interesting, bristling with sexual hysteria and gender confusion, more aware than they've been given credit for, of the instabilities of heterosexuality and normality.

Rock's other great popular success came earlier in the series of lush, weepy dramas produced by Ross Hunter and directed by Douglas Sirk: *Magnificent Obsession* (1954), *All That Heaven Allows* (1955), *Written on the Wind* (1956) and *The Tarnished Angels* (1957). Originally dismissed as lachrymose tripe by the critics, there has been a considerable critical interest in these films in recent years, aided perhaps by Rainer Werner Fassbinder's enthusiasm for them. One of the characteristics of these films is the extraordinary sense of frustration and dissatisfaction in their central female characters. They move in rich, bland suburban interiors that have all the airless comfort and reassurance of a department store or a mail-order catalogue. They are stifled by the anaemic morality and pat emotional texture of their lives. What they need is . . . well, Rock. In these films, Rock figures as the promise of 'life', through his virility and sexuality certainly, but also by his association with nature. It is perhaps clearest in *All That Heaven Allows*. Here Jane Wyman plays a recently widowed suburbanite whose children and neighbours think she should marry a middle-aged, safe, 'undemanding' man. Rock plays the man who comes to prune her trees; he wears lumberjack shirts and reads Thoreau; he is 'natural man'. Jane falls in love with him and it is clear that what Rock embodies is seen as the answer to her restless, empty life.

Though it is possible to see all this in feminist terms, depicting the inadequacies of life for women in bourgeois society and granting the intensity of female (sexual) desire, still the answer to the woman's problem does still seem to be a tall, dark, handsome male – Rock. It is here, though, that the films become really interesting. For although Rock represents the values of natural masculinity, of 'real men', he doesn't really deliver. Marriage is always deferred, his virility is never really put to the test. We never see him 'saving' the woman from her plight, we only have the promise of it. In *Magnificent Obsession*, he will save her by restoring her sight – but the film ends before we know the outcome of his operations on her, finishing on her plaintive cry of 'Tomorrow!'. *All That Heaven Allows* ends with Jane, still not married to him, sitting by his bed where he lies, a cripple in a coma. Similarly, in *Written on the Wind* and *The Tarnished Angels*, the promise of deliverance he represents for Lauren Bacall and Dorothy Malone can only take place after the film is over, if at all. Casting Rock adds to the intensity of this endlessly deferred gratification. He looks the part so perfectly – big, strong, good-looking – yet in the end all that he does is *look* the part. Had he the force, the heterosexual commitment, of a Clark Gable or a Steve McQueen, we know that, even if the films had ended in the same way, he'd still be up on his feet 'fulfilling' the woman before we'd left the cinema (or rewound the tape). With Rock in the part you can't be so sure and this is what gives the films their terrible sense of desolation. What women want is a real man, but the only real men around are but a promise of fulfilment, endlessly put off, never finally kept. You could see this as a critique of the very idea of the 'natural man', exposed as a sham that women would do well to turn their backs on. But I think the films do believe in the idea of, even the need for, virility, it's just that they don't really believe 'real men' exist anymore. The films are thus a tragic, rather than a feminist, view of the situation of women.

In both the comedies and the melodramas, Rock's presence throws into question the ideas and the viability of heterosexual masculinity. Perhaps the campy possibilities of this were not lost on the makers of *Dynasty* (who knows what they really thought they were doing?) when they cast Rock as a stud farmer and threat to Krystle and Blake's marriage. In the Denverian world where there is nothing but image, Rock brought all the weight and authority of a star image which had already given the game away: that there is nothing but image, that the ideas of heterosexuality and normality that *Dynasty* endlessly gestures towards have always been a sham and a mockery.

Rock shatters the dream of fulfilling heterosexuality but there is a way that the visual treatment of the news of his illness has also shattered some of the dreams of the gay life California-style.

What dominated the press and television coverage were before and after, BA and AA, pictures. Rock healthy, strong, gorgeous in stills from films and in early pin-ups, side by side with Rock tired, haggard, tragic. One of the most fascinating examples was the use of a highly touched-up recent photo of him. Some papers (Italy's *Eva Express* for example) said it had been taken after he'd been to Paris for treatment, while others (Britain's *News of the World* for one) said it had been taken 'just a couple of months' before the AIDS story finally broke. Either way it was put beside a picture of Rock ravaged by AIDS. This mix-up suggests the way the juxtaposition of the 'beautiful' and the 'awful' Rock implies not only chronology (one following another) but also simultaneity, as if the two images were different sides of the same thing, two aspects of the condition of homosexuality.

Such a juxtaposition of beauty and decay is part of a long standing rhetoric of gayness. It is the Dorian Gray syndrome. It is a way of constructing gay identity as a devotion to an exquisite surface (queens are so good-looking, so fastidious, so stylish, so amusing) masking a depraved reality (unnatural, promiscuous and repulsive sex acts). The rhetoric allows the effects of an illness gotten through sex to be read as a metaphor for that sex itself.

If anything, this way of seeing gayness has become even more prominent with the coming of AIDS, even if the style of the surface has changed. Now, as the pecs get bigger, the cadaverous effects of AIDS become ever more familiar. The gay glossies set side by side ever more generously proportioned hunks with ever more detailed, alarming and heart-rending accounts of AIDS sufferers. Jeffrey Weeks notes in *Sexuality and Its Discontents*[5] the bitter irony of AIDS occurring now at the end of a period when the image of gay men as effete was put to rest as a prevalent image:

The cultivation of the body beautiful was a vital part of that (rejection of the effeminate image). But AIDS is a disease of the body, it wrecks and destroys what was once glorified.

This paradox, this contrast between a bland, even sexless, physical perfection and the raddled awfulness of sexual practice is not of course the reality of most gay men's lives. But it is a powerful and deeply-rooted imagery and it is encapsulated in the juxtapositions of Rock BA and AA. If Rock's death has brought attention to AIDS, boosted fund-raising, made people realise that 'nice people' get AIDS, it has also been used to reinforce venerable myths about gay men.

NOTES

1 This subject is excellently treated in Rick Bebout's article in *The Body Politic*, No. 119.
2 Superbly discussed by Tom Waugh in *The Body Politic* No. 90 and 101.
3 See Tom Waugh's discussion of the subject in *Cineaste*, Vol. X, No. 2, Spring 1978, pp58-9.
4 Alexander Walker, *Celluloid Sacrifice*, Michael Joseph, London, 1966.
5 Jeffrey Weeks, *Sexuality and its Discontents*, Routledge, London, 1985.

Clarke Gable's Balls: Real Men Never Lose Their Teeth

Joe Fisher

He had brought his Mercedes gull-wing coupe from California and kept trying to improve his time driving up the mountain road from Reno every morning. Surely his face was as well known as any in world history, he was worth millions and could possess just about anything he wished, but he was not world-weary, not lacking in curiosity, and asked about my life and how I worked, and I thought I saw something like my father's animal simplicity in this interest. Perhaps he so *existed* on screen because he was so fundamental. Great actor-personalities, I have come to think, are like trained bears in that they attract us with their discipline while their powerful claws threaten us; a great star implies he is his own person and can be mean and even dangerous, like a great leader.[1]

In the 1930s and 1940s, Quigley Publications conducted an annual poll among exhibitors to establish Hollywood's Top Ten box office stars. Between 1932, the year after he was signed up by MGM, and 1942, when he enlisted in the USAF at the age of forty-one, Clark Gable was never out of the top ten. Gable's ratings are in the centre of the following table, with each year's top star bracketed on the right:

1932	8th	[Marie Dressler]
1933	7th	[Marie Dressler]
1934	2nd	[Will Rogers]
1935	3rd	[Shirley Temple]
1936	2nd	[Shirley Temple]
1937	2nd	[Shirley Temple]
1938	5th	[Shirley Temple]
1939	2nd	[Mickey Rooney]
1940	3rd	[Mickey Rooney]
1941	2nd	[Mickey Rooney]
1942	2nd	[Abbott and Costello][2]

This unique record of consistency becomes more remarkable when you look at the Number One stars: vaudeville comedians for two years, a 200-pound comedy actress in her mid-sixties for two years, and two children for the other seven. Gable's position as leading male sex symbol, certainly after 1934, was effectively unchallenged; small wonder that he was known as 'The King'.

William Clark Goebel was born in Cadiz, Ohio, on 1 February 1901. His father was a wildcat oil-driller who never struck oil; his mother died young. Gable left school at fourteen and worked in a tyre factory in Akron, Ohio. He saw his first play in Akron, became stage-struck, and began work as an unpaid call-boy and bit-part player. He showed no promise, and his father took him away to the Oklahoma oil fields. At twenty-one Gable began to work in stock (touring repertory) companies, and in 1924 he married the director and drama teacher Josephine Dillon, fourteen years his senior. The couple gave up stock and moved to Hollywood in order to further Gable's career. This produced a handful of appearances as an extra in the mid-1920s, but nothing more. Gable was a notoriously poor stage actor at this period. Photographs show a remarkably old-looking young man, far too thin for his build, cheaply dressed but something of a dandy, with huge, cow eyes, huge ears, widely-spaced, rotten teeth and a distinctive yellow complexion which was probably due to undiagnosed hepatitis (after a Warners' screen test in 1930, producer Darryl F. Zannuck noted: 'His ears are too big, he looks like an ape'[3]). Failing to get enough work in Hollywood, Gable left Dillon, went back into stock and in 1928 made his first Broadway appearance, as a romantic lead in *Machinal* (producer Arthur Hopkins described him as a 'Woolworth Romeo'; cheap, cheerful and sexy). In 1931, after failing screen tests with Warners and MGM, Gable was cast by Pathé as a villain in a William Boyd Western. He married a wealthy Texan socialite, Rita Langham, seventeen years his senior, and later that year was signed by MGM.

Gable's simian features quickly established him as a strong supporting villain, often a gangster. But Gable's 1932 entry into the Quigley chart was unquestionably a recognition of sex appeal, not acting ability. This was not the ethereal, classic profile appeal of a John Gilbert or John Barrymore.[4] Gable's allure was somewhere between savagery and sadism. Next to Gilbert and Barrymore, Gable looked like, and behaved as, a Darwinian throwback. Gable was raw, brutal, uncivilized power. He hit women. If you knew Gable in 1931 (before the Hays office became really effective), you knew him as the man who hit Barbara Stanwyck in *Night Nurse* (William Wellman, US, 1931) and who threw Norma Shearer down into a chair in *A Free Soul* (Clarence Brown, US, 1931), or who posed an ever-present threat of physical violence to Greta Garbo in *Susan Lennox: Her Fall and Rise* (Robert Z. Leonard, US, 1931) and Joan Crawford in *Possessed* (Clarence Brown, US, 1931).

The roles assigned to Gable were tailored to show these 'qualities' to their best advantage. Gable's actual and threatened violence became, at least for MGM executives, an 'acceptable' objective correlative for sex. MGM staff writer Frances Marion was given this recipe for a Gable character: 'He's tough, uneducated, got a hell of a temper, can fight his weight in wildcats – you know, Frances, typical Gable stuff, with sex that drives the women crazy'.[6] As the box office response to 'typical Gable stuff', and his initial rejection by MGM clearly show, this exploitation and partial fusion of sex and violence was a reactive, not a pro-active, strategy. The new film public which had been flocking to 'wholesome' films like Marie Dressler's *Min and Bill* (1930) and *Tugboat Annie* (1933) proved also to have a significant appetite for (working class) men who hit (middle class) women, and Hollywood, naturally enough, responded to the demand.

As far as can be established, Gable's appeal was evenly divided between men and women. Did women watching Gable want to be hit? Did they want a man strong enough to keep them in order? Did they want the *frisson* of threatened violence? Did they accept the unstated convention that the violence was not 'real' because it really represented sex? Or do/did that many people actually want rough sex? Writing about women viewers' responses to *Gone With the Wind* (Victor Fleming, US, 1939), specifically to the sequence of events producer David O. Selznick always called the 'Row and the Rape', Helen Taylor comments: 'By far the majority of women who responded to me saw the episode [in which a drunken Gable overpowers Vivien Leigh, then has sex with her] as erotically exciting, emotionally stirring and profoundly memorable. Few of them referred to it as rape'.[6] Did men identify with Gable because of a similar desire for violent sex? Did they accept that the violence was not 'real' but represented sex, or vice-versa? Did they read Gable's performances as a celebration of men's power over women, of the greater strength of male desire? Did they simply want a surrogate on screen who could hit women for them and keep them in order?

Or are all these simply 'necessary' factors in the kind of sexualized melodrama Gable started out in? Was Gable's box office success with a largely working class audience really a matter of class identification? By 1931 it was clear that the Depression was not temporary. Marie Dressler and Wallace Beery (her co-star in *Min and Bill* (George Hill, US, 1930) and *Tugboat Annie* (Mervyn Le Roy, US, 1933) were working class comic grotesques from an earlier generation. Gable was young, virile, not funny, plainly a grown man, plainly working class and the most powerful, threatening and attractive character on the screen. Perhaps there was also a more complex, in a sense more fascistic, response to the Depression in all this. By long-standing fictional/allegorical convention, the American land was seen as female and its settlers and developers male (think for example of Rhett's money impregnating and re-fertilizing Scarlett's Tara in *Gone With the Wind*). Plainly the question of whether a man is lover or rapist is at the centre of this allegory. By the early 1930s this supposedly authentic 'America' was portrayed as having been betrayed by a generation of effete, European, Wall Street men, men no longer in touch with the land and lacking the ability to tame and control it – the kind of men played by actors like Gilbert or Barrymore or Francis X Bushman. In these terms, there were plenty of 'real' men in Hollywood, but they were marginalized, or at least distanced from quotidian urban 'reality' in the Western.[7] Gable was arguably the first leading man to bring 'real' masculine power – the power to tame and control women and land (and less masculine men) – into pictures which dealt with issues related to audiences' daily lives. He wore suits, but he still looked like an ape.

This produced a remarkably potent combination of elemental man and representative man, of 'extraordinary' and 'ordinary' masculinities. When Gable left Hollywood for World War Two service, Victor Fleming, his director in *Red Dust* (Victor Fleming, US, 1932), *Test Pilot* (Victor Fleming, US, 1937) and much of *Gone With the Wind*, said: 'when this present era becomes as remote as the Stone Age is now, they'll still be talking about Gable . . . He's the representative man of our time. No-one will ever forget him'.[8] Between Gable's first entry into the Quigley ratings and Fleming's comment, Gable had been formally elected 'king' of Hollywood. This regal status began as a joking remark in 1938 by Spencer Tracy, which led to a mock coronation at the MGM commissary (itself a cross between a green room for actors and directors and a royal court). This led in turn to a readers' poll by columnist Ed Sullivan, which gave Gable the title by an overwhelming margin (Myrna Loy was the queen). This represents a significant development from the 'dirty sex' figure of 1931-32, who was plainly anything but regal. So how and why did the raw masculinity of Gable's initial appeal develop into 'kingship'?

A superficial answer lies in changes in the way movies were actually *seen* in the early 1930s. Economic strictures meant that the Graeco-Roman and Art Deco movie palaces built in the 1920s, at least in larger towns and cities, were less fastidiously maintained: uniformed commissionaires and usherettes were laid off; house lights were left up so that patrons could find their own seats; and booths selling candy and popcorn (America's only boom crop in the 1930s) were opened. In the context of this diminished mystique a 'Woolworth Romeo' became a more appropriate representative icon than a Shakespearian Romeo like Barrymore. A more persuasive answer, built on this primary change, lies in the narrative strategies of many of Gable's pictures in the 1930s. By their very nature they amplified, even exalted, the 'masculine' qualities which first made him a national sex object. A single film, *It Happened One Night* (Frank Capra, US, 1934; the year Gable moved from seventh to second in the Quigley ratings and won his only Best Actor Oscar), is largely responsible for the transition.

Oddly, at least on the surface, *It Happened One Night* seems to make a fool of Gable's earlier versions of masculinity. Gable/Peter Warne starts by blowing his job as a newspaperman after a drunken telephone argument with his editor. The scene is played to a small crowd, gathered to watch the spectacle of 'a man biting a dog' in the phone booth. The crowd follows him to the New York bus, clearing space by shouting 'make way for the king'. The label seems entirely ironic. How can you be a king with no job, no money and no status? Gable/Peter's male *braggadoccio* is systematically undercut by Claudette Colbert/Ellie Andrews's calculating exploitation of her femininity, as for instance in the hitch-hiking scene, where Gable's hitching techniques all fail; yet Colbert gets them a ride by simply hitching up her skirt. The whole movie is built on a conflict between the apparently 'ordinary' and the apparently 'extraordinary'; between the ordinary guy who starts the film in a phone booth and the extraordinarily privileged woman who starts the film in the headlines and on her father's yacht. Can a 'real' American he-man bring this money-corrupted 'America' to heel? (Look at the way Gable/Peter rations Colbert/Ellie's money when they are on the road together, as if their break from civilization allows the film to break the realities of cash ownership and power relations in order to play out its allegory.)

Gable never wanted to make *It Happened One Night*, mainly because it was a loan-out from gilt-edged MGM to poverty row Columbia. He turned up drunk ('He was not only boiled, he was *steamed*') to his first meeting with the director, Frank Capra. According to Capra the exchange went:

> 'Well, Mr Gable, I –'
> 'That son-of-a-bitch Mayer,' he cut in. 'I always *wanted* to see Siberia, but damn me – I never thought it would *smell* like this, Blech-h-h!'
> 'Mr Gable, you and I are supposed to make a picture out of this. Shall I tell you the story, or would you rather read the script by yourself?'
> 'Buddy,' he said in his tough-guy drawl, 'I don't give a fuck *what* you do with it.'[9]

(This picture of an off-screen persona offers a sharp contrast to Arthur Miller's dedication of *The Misfits* (John Huston, US, 1961): 'To Clark Gable, who did not know how to hate'; but, of course, that dedication was made in 1961, after three decades of 'kingship'. The 'tough-guy drawl' was taught by Josephine Dillon, who had to work hard at pulling Gable's high-pitched voice down to a lower register.)

It Happened One Night used the familiar formula of a 'bus opera' (MGM and Universal had both just made bus operas which flopped at the box office, which is why Harry Cohn, head of Columbia, insisted that the title was changed from *Night Bus*, and assigned a budget of only $325,000 to the picture) to tell a Princess and Toad romance, which in turn tells a socio-political allegory familiar to readers of nineteenth and twentieth century American fiction. Colbert/Ellie is a spoilt princess at the start of the story, sulking and refusing to eat unless she gets her own way. She already has a 'king': King Westley, the aviator (Jameson Thomas) whom she has secretly married. The name (which can hardly be a coincidence) emphasises his iconic masculine power; he even has a phallic flying machine to prove it. She is running away from her Robber Baron father (Walter Connolly), who is fat, rich and cynical, almost a cartoon of masculinity run to seed. In order to get her own way, and to join her king, Colbert/Ellie has to enter a new world of night buses and ordinary working people. So, by an obvious irony, she ends up on the New York bus with a drunken, jobless man who has just been referred to as 'the king'. This king has neither money nor a flying machine, but he does have a male body in prime condition. Colbert/Ellie thus enters a world of fairytale inversion which is, for her, very much a sensual, as well as an emotional and intellectual, experience. This mirrors the fairytale inversions offered to a Depression audience, who are taken into the world of super-wealth and yachts for the price of a seat, and to Gable/Peter, the audience surrogate whose imagination is allowed to create the wild dream of a romance with Colbert/Ellie because of the misrule he instigates when he gets drunk and gets fired.

Gable/Peter's job as a newspaperman is to find and tell stories. This becomes a mission, a movie-long, identity-structuring device, precisely because he is no longer paid for it. In this film's terms, the business of finding a story (which is, of course, the dramatic mechanism which really manufactures its apparent 'givens' of 'character' and 'identity') becomes 'natural' and 'individual' because corrupt and corrupting money is no longer involved. Until he finds a really strong story, Gable/Peter cannot 'sell' himself back into a world of stable or comprehensible cash values (a fair parallel of living, and trying to work, through a major depression); finding a 'story' is essential to his social identity, and in a larger sense essential to the dangerously disrupted social project of containing masculine power and sexuality in a secure material and cultural framework.

Colbert/Ellie brings with her precisely the story Gable is looking for. Gable/Peter has to sit on a pile of newspapers when he first gets on the bus, which signifies plainly how low he has fallen, as well as what he thinks of the newspaper industry which has just fired him. But sitting next to Colbert/Ellie on the bus will put him right on top of a stack of news. Eventually possession of the story means that Gable supplants the original king and, having begun as a toad, becomes the (initially unsought) king of Colbert/Ellie's fairytale. It's a clear instance of the male turning of a herstory into a history: the sound practice of masculinity gives Gable/Peter all the access he wants to the inheritance and information Colbert/Ellie carries with her.

In *It Happened One Night* the two leading players very plainly 'earn' each other (remember that the initial proposition is Ellie's family money and Peter's lack of it), and attain the final reward of a meaningful relationship in the context of the search which frames the whole story. The search is conducted by the rich and powerful and metropolitan, and by a parent, Colbert/Ellie's father. But the 'real' search here, for 'integrity' and identity, takes place in a proletarian, dispossessed and largely rural environment: the night bus, the coffee shops, the motels, the travelling salesman who sits next to you on the bus. It is as if a departure from main-travelled roads can locate, or re-create, some fundamentally American quality of correct male-female bonding which transcends materialism and power.

This quality is found, essentially, in the nature of Gable/Peter's masculinity: in an 'integrity' which cannot easily be overcome because it represents an independent and incorruptible manhood, big and strong enough to take on corporate America and win; at least in the terms of the parable presented here. Colbert/Ellie is un-spoiled, or in a larger sense un-despoiled, by Gable/Peter, the story-finder who becomes a story-maker. But Gable/Peter can do this precisely because he is a 'real' American he-man who overcomes America/Colbert/Ellie by the force of his sexual power, because he is the man who in some sense *ought* to fertilize and cultivate her. Can you imagine *It Happened One Night* with Herbert Marshall playing Peter Warne?

Gable's kingship carried, genuinely, immense cultural power; but the title was given, and then exploited, in a context which made it contradictory, almost grotesque, from the outset. Creating and crowning a king of Hollywood in the Depression was rather like elevating a Roman emperor to immortality in times of major national/imperial distress. Think what it actually meant to have Gable crowned king in the MGM commissary. The public Gable literally belonged to MGM, who bought his performances and persona at a hefty premium. His job, on a piece-work basis (and later, when his agents negotiated a percentage of box office for him, on a commission basis) was to be served up to the public in whatever picture the studio chose to make and to cast him in. In this sense he was the king, the most representative practitioner, of a medium which depended on the dramatic misrepresentation of individuals, unless, of course, you believe that being created and defined by a bourgeois parable represents you in any meaningful sense. The medium sold, and sells, 'realised' narrative fictions (supposedly less falsifiable than a novel because you can 'really see' 'real' people performing them) to a culture based rhetorically on a notion of inviolable individualism, and politically on the 'democratic' representation of its individual members.

'King of Hollywood' is really a definition of a democracy gone mad (if it was ever sane); of the semblance and execution of something close to absolute power, personified by an individual who remained almost entirely powerless, whose only true power was to be a sexually objectified commodity. The real point is that Gable was *sold* as power by a powerful movie industry which could most easily (mis)represent its cultural and economic authority by means of an iconic figure who represented an ideology of individual integrity diametrically opposed to its own; an industry which could at the same time boast that it owned, had 'made', and could contain, this extraordinary image of virility and danger. This is genuinely frightening: you begin to see *Frankenstein* and the other monster myths of 1930s Hollywood gothic as disturbingly accurate covert commentaries on the system which made them. In many ways the whole Gable story is the history of a real-life Frankenstein's monster; certainly the false fusion of physicality and money and manhood in order to 'make' a democratically elected king is easiest to understand as an act of power-crazed alchemy.

The alchemy worked principally because all the major Hollywood studios were vertical monopolies: production, distribution, exhibition (Gable's 'parent' was MGM, and MGM's parent company was the massive Loew's theatre chain) were all under the same financial roof. That was why the studio system worked. That was why Gable could be made king, and why he could make a living as a film actor. In 1938 F.D. Roosevelt filed a suit against all eight major studios (Loew's/MGM, Fox, Paramount, Warners, RKO – the Big Five; and Columbia, Universal, United Artists – the Little Three) under the Sherman Anti-Trust Laws. It is plainly no coincidence that the rugged and populist individualism of Gable's characters in the 1930s expressed sentiments closer to Roosevelt's than the studios'. The studios effectively made money, and power, by playing a game of chicken

Clarke Gable, circa 1940. (Courtesy of BFI Stills, Posters and Designs)

dares, which was really a flamboyant display of authority over the (relatively) subversive narratives they created. You told a story which ought to undercut everything you stood for, and you let the public, and the government, watch you reap the profits, then boasted about it. It was masculine *braggadoccio* institutionalized. If your mandate for power was essentially Prince John's, the smart thing to do was to make *Robin Hood* (Michael Curtiz and William Keighley, US, 1938; Warners; with Errol Flynn, the poor man's Gable), which articulated exactly the opposite.

This 'daring' process was (according to the Darwinian model which made Gable king because he looked, and could be made to behave, like an atavistic throwback) part of a deeply contradictory process of a culture being manufactured, almost as a by-product and very quickly, by investors who simultaneously maximised short-term returns and did everything possible to retain power in the longer term. So you ended up with the bizarre situation of a neophyte technology marketing reactionary parables (and vice-versa) in order to create a 'natural' justification for conquest. This process depended heavily, indeed fundamentally, on the manufacture of appropriately 'natural' masculinities (and femininities). On this level there was never any denying the 'certainty' of Gable's manhood or, by association, his integrity. Sam Goldwyn said: 'When a person like Robert Montgomery comes on the screen you know he's got balls. When Clark Gable comes on you can hear them clanking together'.[10]

Louis B. Mayer, head of production at MGM, had the job of grooming Gable: 'Talent is like a precious stone. Like a diamond or a ruby. You take care of it. You put it in a safe, you clean it, polish it, look after it. Who knows the value of a star?'[11] This is a remarkably 'feminine' way of perceiving a man; a process of grooming and presentation which effectively describes the 'feminine' passivity of a male star in face of the far more 'masculine' and powerful studio system. It was very much at odds with Gable's off-screen persona, at least as it was designed by MGM. This Gable became a man of action, to whom movies were a secondary interest. In fact Gable was known as an unusually diligent actor, a 'slow study' but a perfect timekeeper on the set who always knew his lines for the first take. But away from the set, he was pictured shooting, or fishing, with and without Carole Lombard (his third wife) or riding his Harley-Davidson in the Hollywood Hills with 'men's men' like Victor Fleming and Ward Bond. When Gable's dreadful teeth (which went rotten under the set of caps Josephine Dillon paid for) were finally removed and replaced by false ones in 1933, MGM reported the operation as an appendectomy; real men never lost their teeth.

Gable's living depended on being the pseudo-active object of a female gaze (in the sense that every 'masculine' action Gable ever made in public further defined him as the studios' dutiful, or 'feminine' creature). Yet Howard Strickling, Head of Publicity at MGM and a close friend, tried to present the 'real' Gable as the opposite, as the looker instead of the looked-at:

> The first thing he always did, you know, he'd look her over. She'd know damn well he was sizing her up head to foot. And he was looking at her eyes and he was looking at her lips, you know, and she'd know darn well that he was sizing her up while he was squinting at her, and she'd wonder what this guy was squinting at, you know . . . But mostly they responded, you know.[12]

As in the first sight of Rhett Butler in *Gone With the Wind*, at the foot of the stairs at the Twelve Oaks barbecue, Gable's all-conquering male gaze is reduced to the level of sexual commodity. At Twelve Oaks, his overwhelming physicality is viewed in a 'safe' context by Scarlett and the other marriageable young women standing in a group, at the top of the stairs, partly hidden (even though, like the Gable Strickling described, Rhett plainly knows what a woman looks like in her shimmy). They can then supply each other with his story ('he isn't received') and thus contextualize and to an extent control their experience of him.

Josephine Dillon later described her first sight of Gable in 1923:

> Clark Gable had the furrowed forehead of a man who is overworked and undernourished. He had the straight-lipped, set mouth of the do-it-or-die character. He had the narrow slit-eyed expression of the man who has had to fight things through alone, and who tells nothing.[13]

In effect she reads the 'real' man in the terms prescribed by his movies, as if every physical characteristic is meant to tell a story. It is as if Gable's rags-to-riches rise, and the force of will by which he overcame his unpromising start, are somehow supposed to prove that the integrity of his film characters is 'real'. What Dillon really says is that nothing happened to falsify her initial decision to read the face in this way. She also chooses to ignore Gable's striking physicality. She always insisted that sex played almost no part in her marriage to Gable, whereas *Gone With the Wind* dialogue coach Susan Myrick described him as 'fairly bursting open with IT'.[14] An extra, 'Sara G.', described what happened if you responded to Gable's squinting and sizing up (surely a more apt expression for a woman evaluating a man's sexual potential?):

Gable had a superb physique, strong arms and legs, big feet, and a solid behind. He transmitted sex like sound waves. The act itself was important to him. That was all he wanted. There was no petting or foreplay. No romancing. No kissing during the act, which lasted less than a minute. When it was over, he asked if he could take a shower.[15]

Again there is a major, and revealing, gap. Here is a man who transmits sex like sound waves, by a process which might almost be described as physical narrative, but who actually has sex without giving anything. He was seldom any slower. This might be read as sexual insecurity on Gable's part, making the one-sided fuck ('I don't give a fuck *what* you do with it') as quick as possible in order to minimize the risk of losing an erection and damaging his reputation as a stud. But the reputation was dubious in any case. Although he had sex with a lot of women, Gable was well-known as a 'lousy lay'. This was Lombard's phrase, which Gable often used to advantage by saying that he needed the practice, which does not suggest any great insecurity. The majority of his short-term partners were significantly older, less attractive or more obscure than he. The habit of taking a shower after sex was usual for Gable, who took five or six showers a day, and changed his clothes as often. It is as if masculinity must be kept inviolate by washing away any trace of the woman. This would account also for the lack of physical contact during intercourse, as if it is not 'manly' to touch a woman.

Actually this is a parallel myth of 'integrity' at work: like Dillon, 'Sara G.' is simultaneously describing a contact with royalty and justifying her own role in the transaction. Both women's accounts of Gable would seem extraordinary if they were not people of low cultural status talking about encounters with someone of very high status. What is missing from both is any sense of either woman's *feelings* about the encounter. On the surface their stories seem to be unmediated narrative, though in fact both are wholly subjective rationalizations, predicating a masculinity which is meaningful only in the filmic context which 'creates' it.

The uneasy and contradictory location of both 'essential' male and 'essential' financial authority in Gable's pseudo-active, untouchable masculinity, reached a climax (in every sense) in *Gone With the Wind*. The sexual objectification of one representative man, amplified by narrative strategy, is placed at the centre of a very direct piece of historical/political analysis. Ostensibly this is about Depression America and the aftermath of the Wall Street Crash and Roosevelt's New Deal. Would the film or the novel have been popular if they had been first encountered in the 1890s or the 1960s? The marriage of (Southern) 'America' to the 'right man' is absolutely at the centre of the film. How is a devastated, raped Tara to be refertilized after the Civil War? Will Leigh/Scarlett marry Leslie Howard/Ashley Wilkes or Gable/Rhett Butler?

The sexless, ethereal Howard/Wilkes is the scion of a successful farming dynasty, who somehow *ought* to propagate Georgia's next generation (if the stabilities of the Twelve Oaks barbecue were not violated by the simultaneous arrivals of war in the outside world and Rhett Butler at the foot of the grand staircase). Gable/Rhett is 'not a marrying man'. He is a sexual and social outlaw like Oona Munson/Belle Watling, Gable/Rhett propagates money, not cotton, and he makes his money by smuggling fancy clothes, the manufactured product of raw cotton growing. Profits have been made, and taken, all along the line. Leigh/Scarlett/Tara/America in some sense *needs* both his money (to pay the taxes on Tara after the carpetbaggers move in) and his sex (after marriages to a boy soldier, Charles Hamilton, and a middle-aged 'corn merchant' Frank Kennedy). It would be contractually transgressive for Leigh/Scarlett to have a non-marital or adulterous sexual relationship with either Rhett or Ashley. But in order to ensure Tara's future, and her own, she somehow *must* break the marital rules which have created American civilization; in a literal sense, monogamous marriage and the synthesis of property and propriety, in a larger sense the bonding of land and people to Washington and Wall Street. Again masculinity has become effete and inadequate and somehow *needs* an atavistic outlaw like Gable to resolve its crisis.

Gone With the Wind might never have been made without Gable. Selznick, by superb instinct, used the casting of the picture as hype, fusing its questionable historical perspective with a very public and contemporary search for the right stars and creating his own cinematic crisis to represent the crises of the book and the film. Scarlett had to be an Everywoman: hence the much-publicized trips all over the South to find an 'unknown' (which produced Scarlett's sisters, Anne Rutherford and Evelyn Keyes) once almost every female star in Hollywood and on Broadway had tested for the role. The search ended with the decision to go with Leigh, who would be known to American film fans as Scarlett and no-one else; but Gable was the overwhelming popular choice for Rhett. The unusual name almost certainly comes from the politician Barnwell Rhett, a hysterical South Carolina States' Rights advocate in the 1850s; so secession from a political contract stands very clearly for the sexual/contractual secession Rhett Butler practises at Belle Watling's. Masculine 'integrity' fused with political 'integrity' (in both senses) avoids marriage. Rhett's dangerous authority over Scarlett expressed Gable's kingship more exactly, in the popular mind, than any other role.

Selznick (working as an independent at Selznick International) was forced into an unattractive distribution deal with MGM, which, in order to borrow Gable for the picture, included the (substantial) price of his divorce from Ria Langham so that he could marry Lombard. This in turn dictated the casting of Ashley Wilkes, the figure of inadequate, but historically validated, masculinity against which Gable/Rhett's greater power was to be measured. Jeffrey Lynn and Melvyn Douglas, the two early favourites for the part, were supplanted by Leslie Howard, who was English (nominally; in fact he was really Hungarian). Howard was forty-six years old and Gable was thirty-eight. In the novel Rhett is at least fifteen years older than Ashley, but even with the new hairpieces made for the film Howard is plainly in his forties. This produced an extra resonance of England (Howard, who never attempted any kind of American accent, or troubled to read either the book or the whole shooting script[17]) as ageing and effete and America (Gable) as younger and more sexually red-blooded.

This casting creates an extraordinarily potent hybrid, in a picture which is the high point of Hollywood's marriage of new technology to reactionary parable: a historical picture which is also a Gable picture (a combination which had previously succeeded at the box office in *Mutiny on the Bounty* (Frank Lloyd, US, 1935) and failed in *Parnell* (John Stahl, US, 1937). The masculinity portrayed by Gable was very much of its time. It was not remotely Southern (Gable refused always to attempt any accent) and was set against an otherwise accomplished attempt to re-create an antebellum South.

The moment of glory passed quickly. Gable's career never regained its momentum after the war. He was older and fatter; Lombard's death in an air crash in 1942 affected him deeply; his drinking and smoking, never moderate, increased radically; in the 1940s and 1950s he often shook so much on camera that his scenes had to be reshot. His position in the Quigley ratings plummeted and in 1954 his contract with MGM was not renewed. Gable's fourth and fifth wives, Lady Sylvia Ashley (better known in Hollywood as 'Lady Ashcan'; 1949-52) and Kay Spreckels (1955-60) were both Lombard lookalikes. He set up an independent production company, Gabco, but it failed. Again this has to be placed in context. Gable was king of a Hollywood studio system and the judgement finally obtained in the Supreme Court against the studios' monopolies in 1948 meant that the their power was effectively over. Gable had represented an image of independence, but it was always *ersatz*, always MGM's idea of independent integrity. By 1950 Gable was a middle-aged 'Woolworth Romeo'. Perhaps more importantly, when the new independent production companies came into being, the Gable persona was too heavily associated with MGM product of the 1930s to offer a significant box office attraction to a new generation of entrepreneurs.

Gable's last performance, perhaps his best, was in *The Misfits*. It was the first time he played a man who was supposed to be old (Montgomery Clift/Perc Howland's 'old elderly Gay'; the character is specified as forty-nine in the screenplay). The casting was very much because Gable was Gable, and in a way this was a tribute to his lack of range or development as an actor, as well as to the strength of his characterizations. The performance worked so well precisely because Gable was the icon created by his own earlier film performances. The public knew exactly what they were going to get: a (or *the*) Gable performance. Like John Wayne, Gable was a notoriously inept player until he began to have films built around him – in Gable's case after *Red Dust* and in Wayne's after *Stagecoach* (John Ford, US, 1939) – then they became compelling leading men precisely because of the inflexible, overpowering qualities which made them barely competent as supporting players. Wayne probably came closer than anyone else in Hollywood to being a second king. You could weave a late fable like *True Grit* (Henry Hathaway, US, 1969) or *The Shootist* (Don Siegel, US, 1976) around Wayne and have a film which was secured by the stability, or repetitiousness, of a Wayne performance (and its absolute, indeed its baroque, masculinity), and by the fact that Wayne simply *was* Wayne. In *The Misfits* Gable was used similarly as an ageing king, his masculinity and integrity intact but his Milleresque, American kingdom of no possessions but self-possession dying around him. Once again a princess (Monroe/Roslyn) finds him under a stone, sitting in Harrah's Bar in Reno with his dog. Here the princess is refusing identity and stable focus rather than making the simpler 'spoiled' reaction of Colbert/Ellie in *It Happened One Night*. Having rejected her successful, car-dealer husband (Kevin McCarthy) because he 'isn't there', the only thing she can focus on is Gable/Gay Langland (lack-land). Monroe/Roslyn has made this narrative transition by the procurative agency of Eli Wallach/Guido (guide), a cowboy/flier turned garage hand. He will recommend the best price he can for her smashed-up car, as he will in another sense for her elemental femaleness.

Once again, a female 'America', no longer with Colbert/Ellie's self-possession but now living on the verge of incompetence and hysteria, comes into contact with the man who somehow *should* fertilize and cultivate her, as Gay does the vegetable patch at Guido's house when he and Roslyn are living there. But Gable/Gay's 'right' to this status is deeply dubious in *The Misfits*; where Rhett Butler is allowed to personify both male and material power, Gay Langland's masculine integrity is undercut by the economic changes which have made him a cowboy who drives a truck and kills horses ('I'm doing the same thing I always did. It's just they changed it around'). Casting Gable as Gay repeats, indeed amplifies, the same contradiction. Gay has no property; his home is all around them as he and Roslyn drive in the station wagon she hired in Reno; but Clark Gable was well known as a rich man and the owner of extensive real estate. He was paid more than any movie star in history, until then, for his work on *The Misfits* ($7418.71, after taxes, for instance, for an extra day's shooting close to the end of the picture[18]). Much of the film's strength comes from Miller's awareness of the fusion between (the equally fictional?) Gable and Gay:

> By now Clark Gable and Gay Langland are one and the same guy. I don't know where one leaves off and the other begins. Clark is a hero in the mythical sense of the word as well as being real. All of the pieces became one strand of emotion. Clark, the picture, have a majesty about them that is deeply moving to me. I felt proud that we could create it.[19]

Gable was dead by the time Miller said this. He died on 17 November 1960, following a major heart attack on 5 November, the day after shooting finished. A posthumous son, his first child, was born shortly afterwards. Gable had had two previous heart attacks (without seeking medical attention either time), had lost forty pounds rapidly (from 230 to 190), on Dexedrine, in order to do the picture at all, had continued to smoke and drink heavily, and had insisted on doing many of his own stunts on *The Misfits*. It seems an almost parodically masculine, filmic way to have died: hard, self-sufficient, dedicated; a man loyal to the job he set out to do, dying only after the film was wrapped. The death seems to have all the combined integrity of the iconic leading roles of his thirty year career; but there is also the sense of a death wish, an unwillingness to accept change, a sense that it was better to die than to look after yourself – especially if that meant giving up the tokens of manhood. But how else would the King of Hollywood have died?

NOTES

1 Arthur Miller, *Timebends*, Methuen, London, 1987, p472.
2 S. Cobett Steinberg, *Film Facts*, Steinberg, New York, 1980, pp57-8.
3 Ephraim Katz, *The International Film Encyclopaedia*, Macmillan, London, 1980, p460.
4 Significantly, Gable replaced Gilbert opposite Jean Harlow in *Red Dust* (Victor Fleming, US, 1932); this was Gilbert's last real chance of a sound

comeback. He died of a heart attack in 1936, aged forty-one, after making only three more pictures.

5 Lyn Tornabene, *Long Live the King: A biography of Clarke Gable*, Pocket Books, London, 1977.

6 Helen Taylor, *Scarlett's Woman: Gone with the Wind and its Female Fans*, Virago, London, 1989, p133.

7 It is significant that Gable's first picture was a Western; and Will Rogers, top box office star in 1934, came into showbusiness from Wild West shows.

8 Tornabene, *op. cit.*, p161.

9 Frank Capra, *The Name Above the Title*, Vantage Books, New York, 1985, p165.

10 Taylor, *op. cit.*, p127.

11 Tornabene, *op. cit.*, p127.

12 *Ibid.*, pp193-4.

13 *Ibid.*, p78.

14 Taylor, *op. cit.*, p123.

15 Jane Ellen Wayne, *Gable's Women*, Prentice Hall, New York, 1987, p118.

16 Although Scarlett has children by both men in Margaret Mitchell's novel, so that their sexual inadequacy is less heavily scored there; this is a significant alteration in the film version.

17 Howard only made the film because Selznick promised that he could produce *Intermezzo* (Gregory Ratoff, US, 1939).

18 James Goode, *The Making of the Misfits*, Limelight Editions, New York, 1986, p331.

19 *Ibid.*, p281.

The Historical and the Hysterical: Melodrama, War and Masculinity in *Dead Poets Society*

Mike Hammond

The film *Dead Poets Society* aroused strong feelings in male viewers when it was released in Britain in 1989. They either loved it or hated it; favourable comments ranged from 'this film is what "its" all about' and 'It's about time someone made a film about the problems of manhood for a change' to 'immensely moving' and 'it made me cry'. Others found it 'mawkishly sentimental' and 'the worst kind of film about the worst kind of teaching'. One man said to me that he went to see this film expecting the pleasure of crying but was disappointed.

The film also appealed to idealistic teachers and would-be teachers as well as to those who have suffered at the hands of authoritarian pedagogy and practitioners. One male applicant for a recent teaching post added 'I've seen Dead Poet's Society' to his form intending, jokingly, to reinforce his credibility as a potential John Keating/Robin Williams style of teacher and 'leader' of young people. The film seems to have touched a chord with scholars outside the usual realm of Cultural Studies and Film Studies, who have focused on the issues of educational practice addressed by the film. Pamela A. Rooks argues that the film reinforces the reactionary pedagogical forces it seeks to subvert:

> Teaching poetry, (in *Dead Poets Society*), instead of empowering both

student *and* teacher to transcend the narrowly personal, becomes a cult of personality . . . I wish that *Dead Poets Society* could have been interested in poetry and in people in the rawness and genuineness of the neverending process of growing up and the challenge of teaching those who are growing while continuing to grow.[1]

What seems to be at work in this critique is a lament that the film failed not only to subvert reactionary teaching practices but also to bring the true spirit of poetry and high art to the attention and edification of a large movie-going public. A similar sentiment comes from Brian Cox in a section on cultural analysis from his book on the Cox Report when he acknowledges that:

> many people's imaginations are dominated by film television and video . . . I have to admit that in my own university tutorials references to Dennis Potter's television series *The Singing Detective* or the film *Dead Poets Society* arouse enthusiasm from students who have little to say about writers such as Spenser, Milton, and Pope.[2]

Cox's suggestion that education at the highest level must now recognise the media as a pedagogical tool with which to lead the students to high art is tempered by the fact that the film has been perceived by the students as high art itself.

What seems to be missing in these responses is a recognition that the issue of education, apart from any connections with 'the real', is essential to the development of the film's narrative, a point not lost on the popular critics; Phillip French writes:

> *Dead Poets Society* raises complex ideas about education, society and citizenship without always thoroughly dramatising them, and the soaring, upbeat ending, goes right for the heart.[3]

whilst Kevin Jackson comments:
> . . . young audiences have found its rather pious view of their emotions appealing; and while adults are unlikely to be particularly moved by it, they maybe able to respect Weir's desire to confront issues too complex for a commercial film to resolve.[4]

The issue that is missing, or displaced in these reviews is masculinity. A trade paper got closest to revealing the film as concerned with masculinity by focusing on the film as a rite of passage . . . for its production company:

> Touchstone was originally formed by the Walt Disney Company to release films with adult-oriented themes, yet more often than not, these projects have consisted of sex comedies and action films. With

Peter Weir's *Dead Poets Society, the label has come of age*.[5] (my emphasis)

This metaphorical play and displacement in the reviews is not surprising since the film itself disguises the fundamental issue of masculinity through its emphasis on poetry and great (male) literary figures, whilst also dealing with the cathartic and uplifting experience of self-realization. The connection between high art and masculinity is most emphatic when Robin Williams/John Keating jokingly tells his students that when he was their age people would 'kick copies of Byron' in his face when he went to the beach, or that women swooned when the *Dead Poets Society* met. The displacement of conflicts around masculinity by the 'artistic', the 'higher ideal' leads me back to one of the comments of a friend of mine who recommended this film to his students because it was what 'it' was all about. This unnamed, and ineffable, 'it' is what I am concerned with in this essay.

The film *Dead Poets Society* takes place in a boys boarding school in Vermont. The year is 1959 and the school has the reputation of being the best preparatory school in the country with over seventy-five per cent of students going to the Ivy League universities. The repressive atmosphere is disrupted by the new English teacher John Keating. He inspires his senior year pupils (seventeen years old) to be 'free thinkers' through reading poetry, mostly 'the romantics', looking inside themselves to find their own voices and referring to him as 'Oh Captain, my Captain'. Seven of his students begin to take his advice and revive his old Dead Poets Society where they read poetry to each other in a dark cave. The clandestine meetings instill the boys with confidence and they begin to pursue their (mostly forbidden) desires. Neil (Robert Sean Leonard) auditions for a part in a play against his father's wishes, Knox (Josh Charles) pursues Chris (Alexandra Powers) a local high school cheerleader, and Todd (Ethan Hawke) starts to overcome his shyness. Things begin to come unstruck when one of the boys, Charlie (Gale Hansen) writes an article putting the argument for admitting girls to Welton and signing it 'the Dead Poets Society'. Charlie is found out and is punished but does not reveal the names of the other boys. Later Knox persuades Chris to accompany him to see Neil in a production of a Midsummer Night's Dream. Neil's father also witnesses his performance and afterward takes him out of Welton, enrolling him in a military school. Neil commits suicide and Keating is held responsible. Each boy is forced to sign a deposition which blames Keating for Neil's death. In the final scene Keating returns to the class which is being taught by the evil Headmaster Mr Nolan (Norman Lloyd). Todd stands on his desk and shouts 'Oh captain, my captain!'

and most of the other boys join him; the music swells and the film ends.

The central concern of this film is with masculinity and in particular with rites of passage, male bonding and the relationships of older authority figures to adolescent males. The film sets out to show how boys become men; its background is an idealised history, the mode of narration is melodrama, and most importantly, it is a film (like the war film) in which women are very much relegated to the background. I would like to suggest some ways in which the film addresses issues of masculinity through its formal properties and to examine how it utilises the generic conventions of the war film and melodrama to resolve the contradictions posed by the narrative.

A GENERIC MIX

In the 1980s Hollywood cinema utilised the narrative and generic traditions developed through its history in order to revitalise the industry and, of course, the currency of its cultural capital in the process. Also the tradition of incorporating (and recuperating) 'other' film practices such as those of the avant garde and the 'art-house' film continued to be an 'active ingredient' in the reworking of established forms. The most significant feature of the post-classical Hollywood cinema however is the way in which generic and formal properties are combined and reworked, often self-consciously, in ways which attempt to deal with the ideological crises and contradictions presented by the Women's movement, the Civil Rights movement and the Vietnam War. This seems to manifest itself particularly through films that concern themselves with history; the time travel film. (*Back to The Future*, Robert Zemeckis, US, 1985; *Peggy Sue Got Married*, Francis Coppola, US,1986), the war film (*Platoon*, Oliver Stone, *Hamburger Hill*, John Irvin, US, 1987, *Full Metal Jacket.*, Stanley Kubrick, US, 1987) and the memory film. (*The Big Chill*, Lawrence Kasdan, US, 1983, *Field of Dreams*, Phil Alden Robinson, US, 1989, *Stand By Me*, Rob Reiner, US, 1986). What is striking about these films is that, unlike period pieces of earlier decades which displaced ideological conflicts onto a wide range of historical moments, they deal with a specific time, the 1950s and 1960s, which is generally within the living memory of their audience (or at least within the 'family memory' of younger brothers and sisters or daughters and sons who have heard the 'tales'). While it is true that the same can be said of popular narratives which followed World Wars One and Two, these generally worked from narratives about returning veterans, families and couples experiencing loss through circumstances beyond their control incurred in a just and humane cause. The films mentioned above, however, are concerned with reorganising history in order to close off the contradictions and conflicts that are brought about by the loss of coherence of notions such as the 'just cause' or the nuclear family. According to Timothy Corrigan:

> . . . this is a nostalgia for an image of a self regressively emptied of traditional symbolic and social definitions (such as the patriarchal family or conventional gender relationships) and thus a self opened to other relationships according to which the individual might be at least *imagined* as an agent of history.[6]

The terrain that these 1980s narratives are built on is cross-generic or involves the self-referential combination of genres. This allows the pleasures offered by the 'traditional' genres while at the same time providing the viewer with the novelty of a revitalised genre. It is precisely this combination of genres that is crucial to the ideological work of the film.

The crisis in the traditional and marketable concept of the nuclear family, what Fredric Jameson calls the crisis in the paternal function, is also a crisis of masculinity. In that these issues have been the subject of established genres, there are territories marked out for the way these contradictions are resolved. In a response, if not to post modernity then at least to market forces, melodrama has been incorporated or 'coupled' with the war film to respond to contemporary issues and anxieties surrounding masculinity in the film *Dead Poets Society*.

THE WAR FILM AND A PLENITUDE OF HISTORY

In an article on mannerism in recent cinema, Will Straw comments:

> . . . it is not so much a nostalgia for a specific lost historical past which is at work as nostalgia for the phantasmatic embodiment by particular styles of the plenitude of historical periods.[7]

This is a particularly apt description of the stylistic features evident in Peter Weir's *Dead Poets Society*. The film is set in 1959 but the iconography and mise-en-scene evoke the period of the pre-1914 English public school. This conflation of time periods, 1950s America and pre-Great War England, offers a plenitude of history that is significant not only for its utilisation as a device for the narrative's formal oppositions (the high culture of the preparatory school opposed to the mass culture of the local high school) but more importantly to the melodrama and war film genres that are brought to bear on and seek to close off the conflicts of social, sexual and gender difference.

Steve Neale has outlined the ways in which the formal properties of the Hollywood mainstream film 'intersect' with the ideological concerns of the war film. Of particular interest here are the hierarchies of narrative knowledge and power which are played out in the war film. He focuses on the way war films represent authority or the high command's 'attitudes to their power and its use; (and) their attitudes to the effects it has on the men subject to it; . . .'[8] Interestingly he uses Stanley Kubrick's *Paths to Glory* (US, 1957) to illustrate his point, a film that has some similarities to *Dead Poets Society* in that the character Dax, a junior officer, tries to use his power to protect his men against the abuses of the High Command who are motivated by career and prestige. *Dead Poets Society* uses a similar technique by placing Keating (Robin Williams) between the boys, who are represented not unlike a group of young recruits, and the principal and other teachers at Welton Academy. The Headmaster passes the 'light of knowledge' in the opening scene of the film and at the same time introduces John Keating as the new English teacher and a former pupil, in this way situating him between the elderly tutors and the boys, since he is both teacher and student. This structuring of hierarchies gives the film the aspect of a 'critical' film in the sense that the oppositions it sets up are between the personal and the institutional in much the same way as those in *Paths of Glory, The Big Parade* (King Vidor, US, 1925) or *All Quiet on the Western Front* (Lewis Milestone, US, 1930).

Hierarchies exist among the boys as a group much as they do in groups of soldiers in war films. These hierarchies are expressed initially in the study group, which functions to introduce us to the characters and their relationship to each other. Neil and Charlie are recognised as leaders while the other boys have their 'specialisms' such as Meeks the intellectual, Knox the future lawyer and 'romantic' and Pitts, the science expert. Like the war film these characters serve to detail the conflicts facing the protagonist, in this case Todd, and his battle to overcome his insecurities and become articulate. These roles as they are apportioned out in an all male environment necessarily create tensions and conflicts around homoeroticism which the war film 'works out' through the excess of the combat scene. Since the threat of violent death in combat is not present in *Dead Poets Society* the film finds other means for the repression of homosexual desire through Neil's death. The presence of death is necessary to legitimise men embracing. The similarity of the war experience of male bonding and that of public school is lucidly described by Paul Fussell in *The Great War and Modern Memory:*

> What we find . . . especially in the attitude of young officers to their
> men, is something more like the 'idealistic', passionate but
> non-physical 'crushes' which most of the officers had experienced at
> public school . . . What inspired such passions was – as always –
> faunlike good looks, innocence, vulnerability and 'charm'. The object
> was mutual affection, protection, and admiration. In war as at school,
> such passions were antidotes against loneliness and terror.[9]

The resolution of these tensions in *Dead Poets Society* can be found in
the excess of formal properties such as mise-en-scene, soundtrack and
camera movement.

Another aspect of the war film genre that Neale outlines is the
'initial event':

> In war films there can in fact be two primary situations (and hence two
> initial events). They correspond to two distinct narratives: the specific
> and local military conflict upon which any one film tends to focus, and
> the general and contextual narrative formed by the chronology of the
> war in which it is set. Although some knowledge of the second
> contextual narrative is always assumed, and although some reference to
> it is nearly always made (if only in introductory title sequences, voice
> overs, dedications and the like), *it tends to remain implicit.* (my
> emphasis)[10]

It is not too great a stretch to read into the opening of the film the
existence of a general narrative event, namely the Vietnam War. The
historical moment 'before the deluge' is represented through the
evocation of the pre-1914 years of 'innocence' signified by the painting
at the beginning of the film, which suggests the romantic vision of
doomed youth. This is, of course, reinforced in Keating's first lecture
where he leads the boys to photographs of earlier graduates from the
Great War period who are referred to as 'fertilizing daffodils', (There is
also reference to a third historical moment, the Civil War, and the year
1859 when Welton's first graduates left for the Ivy League or the
battlefields). The function of this historical reference point is to
provide motivation for the otherwise implausible introduction of
Keating, whose approach to teaching must have escaped the interview
panel's notice, into such a repressive educational atmosphere. Through
his emphasis on romantic poets, stream of consciousness poetry, and
'the dangers of conformity' he is signified as a source of inspiration for
the dissidence that earmarked the 1960s and, of course, formed the
backbone of opposition to the Vietnam War.

Fredric Jameson has described historicity as:

... neither a representation of the past nor a representation of the future (although its various forms *use* such representations): it can first and foremost be defined as a perception of the present as history; that is as a relationship to the present which somehow defamiliarises it and allows us that distance from immediacy which is at length characterised as a historical perspective.[11]

This observation serves a larger argument about the difficulty today in representing history as a reification of the reader's present, the present as a sequel to a past which confirmed the narrative logic of the emergent bourgeoisie. The fact that the 1950s and the 1960s appear as settings for a significant number of recent film and television texts can be seen as an indication of a crisis in the representation of history. Jameson argues that films such as *Blue Velvet* (David Lynch, US, 1986) and *Something Wild* (Jonathan Demme, US, 1986) have aestheticised this crisis by combining the 'high elegance of nostalgia films' with the 'grade-B simulations of iconoclastic punk films'.[12] What is apparent in *Dead Poets Society* however is that the representation of history is presented as unproblematic. It is a nostalgia film in which the conflicts of history are represented as conflicts in male identity and as a rite of passage to an idealised present. This displacement of the historical onto the personal marks the convergence of the melodramatic and the 'real'.

MELODRAMATIC MASCULINITY

If a concern with the specific historical period of the 1950s and 1960s is a new feature of a significant number of 'post-classical Hollywood' films, the reliance on melodrama as a mode of signification, as a wealth of critical writing on melodrama has shown, is a long established tradition. David Rodowick writes:

> [Melodrama] is a structure of signification which may reproduce itself within a variety of narrative forms ... by organising the historically available series of discourses, representations, conceptions, values, etc. which constitute the dominant ideology, into a system of conflict, which in turn, produces the fictive logic of particular texts.[13]

Rodowick goes on to point out that the domestic melodramas of the 1950s were organised by social, psychic, and formal determinations and the type of narratives produced were characterised by three factors; a) the displacement of the social economy and the historical conditions of the text onto familial and personal terms, b) internalised dramas of identification which were self-consciously oedipal, c) 'a system of conflict determined by the figuration of patriarchal authority which in turn mediated the relationship between the social and psychic determinations in the text'. This 'aesthetic economy' was undermined by the:

> contradictory demands of the general ideology which promised, through the acceptance of its authority, a world of economic mobility, self determination, and social stability, but delivered in its stead a hierarchic and authoritarian society plagued by fears of the internal subversion of its ideologies.[14]

The difference in the way that *Dead Poets Society* articulates these configurations lies not only in its historical context of production but also in the way that it utilises the historical moment of the 1950s and the transparent 'contradictory demands' of the ideologies of that time to efface those of the 1980s. Where the 1950s melodrama had to chart a path between arbitrary and formal resolutions of conflicts and letting the 'crises of identification follow their self destructive course'[12] the 1980s male melodrama (*Dead Poets*, *Kramer v. Kramer*, Robert Benton, US, 1979, *Ordinary People*, Robert Redford, US, 1980) dispenses with the latter and, instead of questioning the power of authority, it reinforces it through the production of all-male families and by investing in the masculine the reproductive powers of the feminine.[15] This repression of the 'crises in identification' produces excesses in the text and distortions in modes of objectification and specularity which the films attempt to contain through presenting themselves as 'serious' films, dealing with the very 'serious' matter of masculinity.

Tania Modleski has outlined the film's patterns of excess in the section 'Dead White Male Poet's Society' of her book *Feminism Without Women*:

> ... although it is directed by Peter Weir, whose previous work (e.g., *Gallipoli*, 1980, *Picnic at Hanging Rock*, 1975) is suffused with a lyrical homoeroticism, *Dead Poets* denies this dimension of boarding school life so resolutely that its repression can be systematically traced, the duplicitous meanings emerging after all.[16]

The emergence of the film's ideological failure through its inability to resolve tensions brings to mind the debates about melodrama as a form that reveals the machinery of effacement. One of the properties of melodrama is that both the irresolvable conflict and that which is repressed return in the form of excess in the mise-en-scene and the music. This is certainly evident in *Dead Poets Society* in the shots of the Vermont countryside, the repressive oak offices of Mr Nolan and Neil's father, and, of course, the music throughout, particularly in the final scene.

EXCESS AND ADDRESS

The excesses of the text of *Dead Poets Society* are produced through the anxieties surrounding the sexualised male body. In this sense the subject anticipated by the text is male and heterosexual. There is a double bind presented by the representation of male rites of passage within the tradition of visual pleasure in mainstream Hollywood cinema, as outlined by Laura Mulvey.[17] The narrative agency is given over to certain male characters but they are also caught up in the film's objectifying gaze. In the first instance John Keating, through Robin William's performance, is offered as object of desire and identification. I am concerned here with the montage scene where Keating/Williams is 'lecturing'. The relationship has to be coded through the hierarchy of teacher to pupil but there are also some interesting parallels with codes identified by Klaus Theweleit when writing of the importance of oratory to the early Nazi movement:

> . . . the speaker touched the mass with his 'magnanimity', he was said to have endowed it with a 'soul'. Soul is a term often mentioned in connection with the situation of oratory . . . Soul seems to have more to do with the act of speaking; the activity is more important than the message it conveys.[18]

This is particularly indicative of the films ideological work when recalling the rituals of banner carrying, and flame lighting, which are remarkable in their similarity to fascist rituals. The coding of the institution as repressive in this manner is offset by the oratory of Keating, but both work to reinforce male authority.

In another formulation, Neil's relationship with Todd results, through Neil's death, in Todd's successful entrance into manhood. This relationship is the site of the film's conflict from which most of the excess emanates. The two share the brunt of the films excessive mise-en-scene, particularly in the use of desks and desk sets as symbols of parental indifference and paternal authority. In a scene where Todd is dejected because his parents have sent him the same desk set for his birthday that they had given him on his previous birthday, Neil suggests that he throw it into the lake. The desk in Neil's father's office is the site of paternal authority and of the conflict which ends in Neil's death. The Law and the paternal father come together in the scene in the Headmaster's office where Todd is made to sign the paper which indicts Keating for Neil's death. This scene is marked by the extreme close up of the pen Mr Nolan, the headmaster, hands to Todd in a kind of evil transference of phallic power. These scenes are counterbalanced by Keating's standing on his desk earlier in the film to remind himself to look at the world differently.

Mary Ann Doane in an article on the 'Woman's Film' examines the way that space is used in a 'fairly strict mapping of gender differentiated societal spaces'. While this is common in the family melodrama, she draws attention to the sub-genre which she calls the 'paranoid women's films'. 'In this cycle, dramas of seeing become invested with horror within the context of the home'. Here it is important to note the films incoherence around its depiction of the boarding school as home, the horrible home of Neil, and the indifferent home of Todd (a place we never actually see). In the 'Woman's film' Doane asserts that the mechanisms of voyeurism and fetishism are 'no longer necessary to invest the look with desire' and that the look becomes invested with fear, anxiety, horror because it is free floating and objectless.'[19] In the case of *Dead Poets Society* the look is structured in a way which plays out the passage from boyhood to manhood. Todd's point of view is the one privileged by the film and bears all the hallmarks outlined by Doane. It is linked with fear, hysteria (Todd's silence) and anxiety around the spaces to be filled, i.e. the headmaster's office, the halls of the school or the home of the father. This poses a problem for the text in that, while the trajectory is one from the pre-sexual to the sexual, it is still invested with the mechanisms of voyeurism and fetishism and must find a way to deal with the problem of having adolescent males as its object. In a sweeping gesture of textual fetishization, the film interposes women through the photograph of Keating's girlfriend in London or the one dimensional character of Chris whose entire position is one of objectification. This, however, does not alleviate the problem and the look is drawn to the site of paternal authority: the paternal desk, the punishment of Charlie, the suicide of Neal, and Todd's acceptance of the pen of Mr Nolan. Apart from the framing of Todd's head through the legs of another student, it is of some importance that the act of defiance to one male authority in deference to another is acted out on the 'gender differentiated social space' of the top of a desk.

CONCLUSION

The cross generic combinations and the plenitudes of history which mark a significant number of American mainstream films are powerful elements in attempts to efface contradictions and address anxieties which threaten the dominant ideology. What is significant is the transparency of these structures and the failure of their totalising project. The comments at the beginning of this article suggest that a number of readings are possible which can totalise, or fix, the meaning through issues of educational practice, the injustices within male rites of passage or a romantic pursuit of the ineffable 'it'. Any of these readings do this to some extent but not without leaving a residue of incoherence. For example there is the contradiction between the film's criticism of repressive educational methods of the boarding school and the 'cult of the personality' teaching methods of John Keating, or in the incoherence of a celebration of a rite of passage which must suppress the homoerotic desire between males. These incoherencies produce excesses in the text which cannot be contained. I have argued that these contradictory elements are addressed through the use of the generic structures and conventions of the war film and the melodrama. I have also tried to show a relationship between the way these narratives try to resolve the anxieties produced by those perceptions. *Dead Poets Society* has as its central concern the rite of passage from boyhood to (heterosexual) manhood. Neil fails to make this transition. He is unable to achieve identification with either his repressive father or the liberal (an unswervingly heterosexual) Keating. His sacrifice allows Todd to find his 'voice'; his barbaric yawp is 'Neil'. The forbidden love is given eternal life and remembrance through death.

NOTES

I would like to thank Pat Kirkham for her helpful comments, editorial skill and infinite patience while I was writing this article.
1 Pamela A. Rooks, 'Woo who? Exclusion of otherness in *Dead Poets Society*', *Australian Journal of Communication*, Vol. 18 (2), 1991, pp75-83.
2 Brian Cox, *Cox on Cox: An English Curriculum for the 1990's*, Hodder and Stoughton, London, 1991.
3 Phillip French, *The Observer*, 24 September 1989.
4 Kevin Jackson, *The Independent*, 21 September 1989.
5 *Screen International*, June 1989.
6 Timothy Corrigan, *A Cinema Without Walls*, Routledge, London, 1991.
7 Will Straw, 'The Discipline of Forms: Mannerism in Recent Cinema', *Cultural Studies*, Volume 1, Number 3, October 1987, p369.

8 Steve Neale, 'Aspects of Ideology and narrative form in the American war film', *Screen* 32:1, Spring 1991, p39.
9 Paul Fussell, *The Great War and Modern Memory*, Oxford University Press, London, 1975, p272.
10 Neale, *op. cit.*, p37.
11 Fredric Jameson, *Postmodernism or the Cultural Logic of Late Capitalism*, Verso, London and New York, 1991, p284.
12 Jameson, *op. cit.*, p287.
13 David N. Rodowick, 'Madness, Authority and Ideology; The Domestic Melodrama of the 1950s' from *Home is Where the Heart is*, Christine Gledhill, (ed.) British Film Institute, p272.
14 *Ibid.*, p272.
15 Susan Jeffords, 'Reproducing Fathers: Gender and the Vietnam US in U.S. Culture', Linda Dittmar and Gene Michaud, (eds.) in *From Hanoi to Hollywood, The Vietnam War in American Film*, Rutgers University Press, pp203-217. In this article Jeffords argues that dominant U.S. culture is redefining itself through 'oppositional relations of gender' and through masculine appropriation of reproduction in order to 'reassert the primacy of the masculine point of view in determining definitions of difference', p231.
16 Tania Modleski, *Feminism Without Women; Culture and Criticism in a 'post-feminist' Age*, Routledge, New York and London, 1991, p138.
17 Laura Mulvey, 'Visual Pleasure and Narrative Cinema', from Bill Nichols (ed.) *Movies and Methods, Volume 2*, University of California Press, 1985.
18 Klaus Theweleit, *Male Fantasies* Vol. 2, Psychoanalyzing the White Terror, University of Minnesota Press, Minneapolis, 1989, p117.
19 Mary Ann Doane, 'The "Woman's Film"; Posession and Address' in Gledhill, *op. cit.*, p284-287.

What Are Big Boys Made Of? *Spartacus, El Cid* and the Male Epic

Leon Hunt

'WHAT KIND OF A MAN ARE YOU?' (*EL CID*)

Steve Neale has argued that 'Where women are investigated, men are tested. Masculinity, as an ideal, at least, is implicitly known.'[1] The assumption here seems to be that being investigated and being tested are mutually exclusive, yet in films which concern themselves with the parameters of heroic masculinity 'as an ideal' – westerns, 'rogue cop' films, epics, the Rambo movies – masculinity may well be investigated *by* being tested. In this essay, I shall examine *Spartacus* (Stanley Kubrick, US, 1960) and *El Cid* (Anthony Mann, US/Spain, 1961), two examples of the male epic, a genre which not only explores the spectacle of the male body, but poses the question what are little, or rather, big boys made of?

In considering this question, two concerns will be dominant. Firstly, masculinity as (homoerotic) spectacle and as a world of passionate heterosexual relationships between men; secondly, masculinity as enigma and problem. These films derive much of their fascination from their inquiry into questions of honour, patriarchal law and heroism. In doing so, they do two things. They construct masculinity as something that can no longer be taken as 'implicitly known' and as something almost impossible for men to live up to. In *El Cid*, the question is asked, 'What kind of a man are you?' and later 'What kind of man is this?' This is the question the genre is constantly asking in its probing of the boundaries and limitations of the 'heroic' male. At the same time a dialogue is set up between an 'heroic' discourse of stoicism, sacrifice and self-sufficiency and a melodramatic one of emotion, vulnerability, love and tears.

For my purposes, the male epic is easier to define than the epic. The latter tag has been applied to a range of films that takes in the classically-derived *Quo Vadis* (Mervyn Le Roy, US, 1951), the heroic *Lawrence of Arabia* (David Lean, GB, 1963) and even the purely spectacular *Star Wars* (George Lucas, US, 1977) which, interestingly, claims to take place 'a long time ago '. As a broad-ranging definition, Derek Elley's is as good as any 'the epic form transfigures the accomplishments of the past into an inspirational entertainment for the present.'[2] But the male epic is more specific, I would identity two types, both produced between the early 1950s and the early 1960s: the Italian 'peplum' movies, especially those chronicling the adventures of Hercules, Maciste and Ursus, and those made in Hollywood and as co-productions with Spain or Italy, such as *Ben-Hur* (William Wyler, US, 1959), *King of Kings* (Nicholas Ray, US, 1961, the first Epic produced by Samuel Bronston) and *Barabbas* (Richard Fleischer, Italy/US, 1962). My concern is with the second type, which reveals the following four characteristics:

1. A heroic, central male character, after whom the film is named – *The Fall of The Roman Empire* (Anthony Mann, US/Spain, 1964) is a notable exception – e.g. *Ben-Hur, El Cid, Spartacus.*
2. The hero is somehow 'transfigured' and becomes more than a man. Sometimes this takes on religious overtones, as in *El Cid*, or simply involves the hero becoming a legend, as in *Spartacus.* Either way, this is achieved by taking on/being given/having to live up to a title or name, which in turn involves living according to an almost impossible code or law, which in turn involves, in most cases, the hero giving up his life.
3. The display of the male body. 'I never seen a film in which the hero's bust is bigger than the heroine's,' Groucho Marx is supposed to have said of Victor Mature's performance in *Samson and Delilah* (Cecil B. de Mille, US, 1949). The type of spectacle and pleasure Mature's body offers points to a fundamental feature of the male epic; a generic iconography which functions not only to represent 'ancient history', but to produce what Paul Willemen has called the 'unquiet pleasure' of repressed homosexual voyeurism.[5] As a 'body genre' the male epic features sweat, muscles, shows of strength, tunics and loin cloths (thus its descendants are vehicles for Stallone, Schwarzenegger and Van Damme). Three recurring generic set-pieces are particularly important to its display of the male body – the chariot race (*Ben-Hur, Fall of the Roman Empire*), crucifixion (*King of Kings*, obviously, *Ben-Hur, Barabbas, Spartacus* and *El Cid*) and gladiatorial combat (*Spartacus, Barabbas*).

4. In a manner similar to some westerns, the male epic depicts love stories between heterosexual men – intriguingly soured in *Ben-Hur* and *Fall* (hell hath no fury like a centurion scorned), and particularly intense and passionate in *Spartacus* (Spartacus/Kirk Douglas and Antoninus/Tony Curtis), *El Cid* (Rodrigo/Charlton Heston and Moutamin/Douglas Wilmer) and *Barabbas* (Barabbas/Anthony Quinn and Sahak/Vittorio Gassman).

UNQUIET PLEASURES

El Cid was directed by Anthony Mann,[6] who is important not just because his films include Westerns *and* Epics, two genres with much in common, but also because he is the subject of an essay by Paul Willemen, 'Looking at the Male', which, as its title suggests, has broader implications for the representation of the male body. For Willemen, 'Mann' becomes a way of addressing the inscription of masculinity in certain genres, and the name for the pleasure of watching men being represented in a particular way. His most provocative phrase is 'unquiet pleasure' – the perfect epithet for many epics, not just Mann's – which he elaborates in the following way:

> The viewer's experience is predicated on the pleasure of seeing the male 'exist' (that is, walk, move, ride, fight) in or through cityscapes, landscapes or, more abstractedly, history. And on the unquiet pleasure of seeing the male mutilated (often quite graphically in Mann) and restored through violent brutality. This fundamentally homosexual voyeurism (almost always repressed) is not without its problems: the look at the male produces just as much anxiety as the look at the female.[7]

Willemen characterises Mann's films as 'Spectacular in the true sense of the word,' because they rely so strongly on the 'look at the male figure' and because the 'images always draw attention to themselves, never as fodder for the eye, but always "eye-catching", arresting the look.'[8]

The word 'spectacle' is also part of popular discourses about the epic. The key period of the epic, 1953 to 1964, roughly parallels the cinema's search for strategies to outdo television – cinemascope, casts of thousands, huge set designs – and few genres have been associated quite so closely with sheer spectacle.[9] But while part of this spectacle is provided by huge coliseums and celebrated chariot races, the genre is also associated with the pleasure of watching certain types of male star; Kirk Douglas, Anthony Quinn, Steve Reeves, Reg Park, and, most important of all, Charlton Heston, whose very 'presence' has prompted some striking (male) responses. Derek Elley writes:

> It is hard to imagine (*El Cid*) without the towering presence of Heston – surely *the* epic presence . . . The Cid's visionary side provides many fine moments for Heston's particular brand of heroic intensity.[10]

These sentiments are echoed by David Thomson:

> Heston has sometimes been cited as the clearest instance of the 'monolithic' actor: the man who contributes to a film through his presence and the innate splendour of honest muscle and strong-jawed virtue.[11]

Most breathless of all is the following quotation from *Cahiers du Cinema*, a virtual love poem to Heston from Michael Mourlet. Pleasure doesn't get much more 'unquiet' than this:

> Charlton Heston is an axiom. By himself alone he constitutes a tragedy, and his presence in any films whatsoever suffices to create beauty. The contained violence expressed by the sombre phosphorescence of his eyes, his eagle's profile, the haughty arch of his eyebrows, his prominent cheek-bones, the bitter and hard curve of his mouth, the fabulous power of his torso: this is what he possesses and what not even the worst director can degrade.[12]

All three writers talk about Heston's 'presence' but only Mourlet overtly acknowledges that this has something to do with the representation of his body. Interestingly, the fragmented nature of this account – phosphorescent eyes, haughty eyebrows, torso – becomes quite fetishistic. In cinematic terms, it echoes the way editing often fragments female bodies, yet it infers that, unlike a woman, there is something about Heston which resists any suggestion of degradation. Nevertheless, in this instance, it is spectatorship itself which, to borrow from Willemen again, finds pleasure in mutilating and restoring the male body.

Neale's 'Masculinity as Spectacle: Reflections on Men and Mainstream Cinema' is an attempt to extend Laura Mulvey's work on gender and 'the look' to representations of men. He is concerned in particular with narcissistic identification and, in Mulvey's phrase, the construction on the screen of 'the more perfect, more complete, more powerful ideal ego.'[13] One example Neale offers of such an idealised figure is Charlton Heston in *El Cid*. Heston plays Rodrigo Diaz, the Spanish knight who virtually becomes divine through his inability to waver from a rigid code of honour. He is given the name 'El Cid' by the Moorish Prince Moutamin, whom he releases after a battle: 'Among our people, we have a word for a warrior with the vision to be

just and the courage to be merciful – we call such a man "El Cid".'
Rodrigo is accused of cowardice for releasing the King's enemies;
avenging the honour of his father, he kills the father of his bride-to-be,
Chimene (Sophia Loren), knowing that he risks losing her; loyal to his
King yet insistent on his moral purity (King Alfonso murders his
brother and 'covets' his sister), he is exiled for his refusal to
compromise. Throughout, he defends Spain against the Moors, but
dies just before the final battle, again because of his strict adherence to
what-the-Cid-must-do. In the final sequence, his corpse leads his men
into battle, strapped to his horse, the sun illuminating his armour and
transforming him into a transcendent dead father, more 'the Cid' than
at any other point in the film.

It would be difficult to think of a more 'perfect' male figure.
Rodrigo is presented as being morally flawless – although a subtext
seems to be that this may be, in itself, something like a flaw – and
physically unstoppable even after death. But as Neale suggests, there
are problems in identifying with such a figure. For one thing, this
ideal ego may trouble the male subject with feelings of inadequacy as
much as it impresses him: 'it may also be a source of further images and
feelings of castration, inasmuch as that ideal is something to which the
subject is never adequate.'[14] By raising the question of an increasing
gulf between 'human' Rodrigo and 'ideal ego' Cid, whether or not he
can live up to his name and whether the film requires a live human
subject, Mann comes close to acknowledging the problems of
spectacular narcissistic identification.

What also interests Neale, in common with Willemen, is the
troubled eroticisation of the male body, a process marked by anxiety
and disavowal: 'in a heterosexual and patriarchal society, the male
body cannot be marked explicitly as the erotic object of another male
look: that look must be motivated in some other way, its erotic
component repressed.'[15] He gives as an example the images of
mutilation and death which figure prominently in Peckinpah's
westerns, images which on the one hand repress the eroticism of the
male body but which also transfigure male narcissism through death.
The epic goes even further. Its insistence on violent spectacle, physical
punishment and a contemplation of the male body makes the western
seem restrained by comparison.

To begin with, the male epic shows the body in action. Neale, in
fact, points to the scenes of physical combat in *Spartacus, Ben-Hur* and
Fall of the Roman Empire as striking instances of how the erotic
dimensions of the male body are displaced through violence.

> We see male bodies stylised and fragmented by close-ups, but our look
> is not direct, it is heavily mediated by the looks of the characters

involved. And those looks are marked not by desire, but rather by fear, by hatred or aggression.[16]

Two assumptions need questioning here: that desire and fear/hatred/ aggression are mutually exclusive, and that desire only appears by virtue of its unsuccessful repression. In *El Cid*, for example, Rodrigo is subjected to the ambiguous gaze of Chimene during his fight with Don Martin (a rival King's Champion), a look implying both desire *and* hatred. Elsewhere, he is the explicit object of the admiring looks of other men; as he claims the crown of Valencia for Alfonso, Moutamin watches and comments, 'What a noble subject!'

What I want to suggest is that eroticism/desire *are* present, but are inscribed in a more complex and ambivalent way than Neale seems to allow. Male epics (and other male 'body' movies – Tarzan, Rambo, the Bruce Lee Kung Fu films) make it part of their project to address male narcissism. If one accepts, then, that looks of desire are present, one might usefully distinguish between:

1. 'Legitimate' and 'Illegitimate' looks, i.e. looks of admiration and platonic love versus looks expressing lust, sadism, control and power.
2. Willing and Unwilling objects of the look, How do characters respond to being looked at?
3. Active and Passive objects of the look, involving the distinction, say, between the gladiator and the crucified hero.

It is worth considering these distinctions in relation to the American epic and the 'peplum', which is much less apologetic about its project of celebrating male narcissism, and thus lends itself to the camp appropriation it has generally enjoyed (e.g. the namechecking of Steve Reeves in *The Rocky Horror Show* (Jim Sharman, GB, 1975) but was there ever a time when he *wasn't* camp?) If the male hero in the American epic is frequently conceptualised by critics in terms of 'presence', the 'peplum' is more overtly about bodies, a factor which is reflected in the genres' respective stars. While the former went for stars of a particular dramatic as well as physical 'stature' (Heston, Douglas, Quinn), the Italians entertained no such pretensions and went straight for former body builders and Mr Universes such as Steve Reeves, Reg Park and former Tarzan, Gordon Scott. The latter were more than happy to be looked at; indeed, their former professions had well prepared them for it. In these movies, scene after scene contains 'classic' body building poses which bear little or no relation to the script. Fairly early on in Pietro Francisci's *Hercules* (1957), for example, Reeves is called upon to throw the discus on a particularly transparent narrative pretext; little attempt is made to disguise the scene's purpose in displaying those well-oiled pectorals for a predominantly male group of intra-diegetic admirers. Elley's discussion of this scene acknowledges its erotic dimensions but attempts to reincorporate it back into some 'authentic' classical sensibility:

> The implicit narcissism of the Greek *pepla* – male and female – has rarely been more directly expressed, and is the nearest that film-makers have come to tackling the Greeks' own complex attitudes to sexuality.[17]

Both Neale and Richard Dyer have argued, in different contexts, that where men are presented as objects to be looked at for pleasure, they tend to be in action, never passive.[18] This would apply to both types of epic, although the first section of Vittorio Cottafavi's *Hercules Conquers Atlantis* (1961) is striking for the initial passivity of its hero (Reg Park), would would rather lie in the sun than help his friends, although the very lying and the play of the sun on his body allow the camera to objectify him.

Two motifs in the American epic crystallise the genre's ambivalence towards male narcissism, namely the gladiator and the crucifixion. I shall discuss each in turn, leaving the chariot race, which is not only less frequent but also slightly different, until later.

1 The Gladiator

The figure of the gladiator works in two ways. Firstly, as both *Spartacus* and *Barabbas* make clear, it acts as a focus for a particular kind of relationship. Men are brought together and undergo an ordeal in such a way as to create a camaraderie and affection that must be ruthlessly repressed. Spartacus is the leader of a slave rebellion against Rome which is finally put down by the Roman army led by Crassus (Lawrence Olivier). He spends most of the first section of the film in a gladiator school being prepared for combat, but when he attempts to form a friendship with Draba, an Ethiopian slave (Woody Strode), he is harshly rejected for the following reason: 'You don't want to know my name, I don't want to know your name ... Gladiators don't make friends. If we're ever matched in the arena together, I'll have to kill you.'

More importantly, the gladiator dramatises in a particularly interesting way the tension this genre generates around the male body: he is trained specifically to be looked at, to be a spectacle, yet to be looked at is to die or to kill one's friends. This happens twice; when Spartacus fights Draba in the arena at the gladiator school and later when he is forced to fight his friend Antoninus. Both times he is watched by Crassus, whose bisexuality was alluded to more overtly in the original (recently restored) version of the film but is also signalled in the most widely seen print. The second occasion is a 'private' viewing which generates a particularly ambivalent regime of looks. Throughout the film, Crassus' desiring look is coded as 'illegitimate'. He has had fairly overt designs on Antoninus and displays an ambiguous fascination with Spartacus, but he also wants to see a killing and is placed in a sadistic, controlling position. The gladiator is subjected to a 'bad' look, yet it is also the one constructed for the audience and one which offers the pleasures of the male body to the audience.

The first section of *Spartacus* is quite insistent on the relationship between looking, eroticism and death, and offers a striking variety of angles on this nexus of drives. When we first see Kirk Douglas as Spartacus, he is barely recognisable under heavy beard and several layers of grime. It is the school which transforms him into something we might want to look at (although Peter Ustinov's Batiatus has already observed that he has 'good muscle tone', and we know it is Douglas, the star). This is how the gladiators are introduced to the school:

> A gladiator's like a stallion – it must be pampered. You'll be oiled, bathed, shaved, massaged, taught to use your heads.

Are these men being prepared for battles or to put on their posing pouches? The difference isn't really that great, as it turns out. Spartacus is transformed by the process; in one scene, his oiled body is marked out with red paint to indicate killing, slow kill and maiming areas. But perhaps the key objectifying scene precedes the fight with Draba. Crassus arrives with two women who are invited to choose two matched pairs to fight. The men are paraded for them to look at, and it becomes increasingly clear that the decisions are being made on the basis of physical attractiveness. Displaying the film's idea of decadent Roman lasciviousness, they ogle each of the men in turn, whisper and giggle about an Ethiopian fighter (their gazes indicate where they are looking), choose Spartacus because he looks 'impertinent' and suggest, pointedly, 'Let them wear just enough for modesty.' This is a very anxious scene involving men turned into objects for women (and not even 'nice' women like Jean Simmons' Varinia), men shown to be humiliated by being put on display and men powerless and passive. But it does some interesting manouvring. By the time the (very exciting) fight takes place, the eroticism has been displaced onto the 'bad' women, but they are crucial to setting up the spectacle offered to us. The parading of the men for the women and the actual scenes of gladiatorial combat parallel each other as the 'legitimate' and 'illegitimate' versions of essentially the same spectacle. Certainly, during the fight, our point of view is more closely associated with the small audience than with the other fighters who are forced to peer nervously through the gaps in a wooden enclosure.

2 Crucifixion

If the spectacle of crucifixion seems to be embraced more enthusiastically, it is because its representation of the body is more contradictory at each level: passivity offset by control, humiliation offset by nobility of sacrifice, eroticism offset by religious connotations of transcendence. If the gladiator is unwilling to die, the epic hero embraces crucifixion with some degree of acceptance/willingness; it is the moment where he demonstrates his control over his own body through his ability to give it up. In *Barabbas*, interestingly, it is this control and power that the hero lacks until the final scene. Barabbas is released in place of Jesus, and thereafter, finds himself virtually indestructible. In the male epic scenario, this becomes a source of anxiety, a signifier of powerlessness. Brought before Pilate as a thief, he is told that, having been released once, he cannot be given capital punishment (which, the film suggests, is what he wants). As he is transported to the sulphur mines, he reflects, 'I can't be killed . . . He's taken my death!'

Spartacus actually fights for the right to be crucified. Captured by Crassus, he is forced to fight Antoninus to the death; the winner is to be crucified. Neither is prepared to let the other die on the cross, but Spartacus 'wins'; love, sacrifice and the survival of 'Spartacus' as legend and symbol of freedom are brought together by the final scene depicting his death on the cross, which, like *Barabbas* forms part of a plethora of crosses filling the screen.

While Rodrigo is not literally crucified in *El Cid*, he is associated with its iconography throughout the film. His first appearance forms an objective correlative with a cross full of Moor arrows which he carries on his back. When his former rival Ordonez *is* martyred on the cross, the following exchange with the Moor leader Ben Yussuf (Herbert Lom) points to the transfigurative nature of death:

Ben Yussuf: He is a man like other men. He will die. I will kill him.
Ordonez: He'll never die. Never.
Ben Yussuf: You dare think of him as we think of our prophet?
Ordonez: We do!
Ben Yussuf: Then this will be more than a battle. It will be our god against yours.

Rodrigo's body *is* penetrated, by the arrow which finally kills him, but his body is transformed by death into something else. 'You can't save my life,' he tells Chimene, 'You must help me give it up.' When his lifeless body leads the Spanish army to victory, Miklos Rozsa's score goes into overdrive with a triumphant, emotive organ emphasising the religious spectacle of Cid-as-Law. In this film, in particular, man is placed on a pedestal, something to be worshipped. But a transcendent, glowing phallus is only made possible by the death of the human subject. The ultimate Father is a corpse.

EMOTION, LOVE, OYSTERS AND SNAILS

If the epic, in its male-spectacular form, inevitably produces a visual homoeroticism, it also deals with ostensibly heterosexual love between men, often of a particularly moving kind. However, homosexuality was very much a conscious part of the subject matter of more than one film, particularly *Ben-Hur* and *Spartacus*. When William Wyler was preparing *Ben-Hur* in 1959, he turned to Gore Vidal for advice on how to strengthen the motivation for the conflict between Ben Hur (Heston) and Messala (Stephen Boyd), childhood friends who become mortal enemies. Vidal's suggestion startled Wyler:

> I proposed the notion that the two had been adolescent lovers and now Messala has returned from Rome wanting to revive the love affair but Ben-Hur does not. He has read Leviticus and knows an abomination when he sees one. I told Wyler, 'This is what's going on *underneath* the scene – they *seem* to be talking about politics, but Messala is really trying to rekindle a love affair '[19]

Wyler agreed on the understanding that Heston should not be told that this was what was 'underneath' the scene. Boyd, however, *was* told, and played the scene accordingly. Vidal has commented – and the film bears this out – 'Study his face in the reaction shots in that scene, and you will see that he plays it like a man starving.'[20] This apparent knowingness about what all this honour, rivalry and heroism is 'really' about spills over intriguingly into the film's most celebrated spectacle, the chariot race, which, in at least one other film, becomes a vehicle for both the sort of repressed homosexual voyeurism Paul Willemen is talking about and a repressed homosexual desire alluded to in the text. *Fall of the Roman Empire*'s treatment of the relationship between Livius (Boyd again, and clearly quite used to this sort of thing by now) and Commodus (Christopher Plummer) is strikingly similar. Again, a close friendship turns sour, but the initial depiction of male bonding goes much further than the 'starving' looks of *Ben-Hur*. During their first reunion, they drink from each others' cups, arms crossed, and then fall on top of each other, giggling (this physical contact is echoed in their later mortal struggle: Commodus' stabbing, in an intense clinch, is blatantly sexual). Before too long, they are engaged in a violent chariot race and in the final scene, Commodus emerges from a 'wound' in a giant, stone hand to fight Livius to the death with large spears.

Discussing the *Ben-Hur* story, Vito Russo argues optimistically, 'It was 1959, and the screen was on the verge of a new freedom. Vidal was saying that it *made sense* that the two should be attracted to each other.'[21] However, one would need to remember that the production code forbade overt references to homosexuality well into the 1960s: such 'liberal' British films as *Victim* (1961) and *The Leather Boys* (1963) encountered considerable resistance from censors in the States. In any case, the films seem to suggest more that it 'made sense' that homosexuality 'explained' violent, aberrant behaviour. Structurally, homosexuality in *Ben-Hur* and *Spartacus* occupies the same position and functions in the way that incest does in *El Cid*: 'deviant' behaviour signifying the decadence of a corrupt regime, be it Rome or the Spanish court of Alfonso. What separates these films from an implicit homophobia that was long a part of Hollywood narratives (see Hitchcock, for example) is the way that, in *Spartacus, Ben-Hur* and *Fall*, in particular, the films parallel a 'legitimate', moving relationship between men with both an 'illegitimate' male relationship and a 'legitimate' male/female one. Spartacus is allowed to love Antoninus because it is Crassus who visibly has the hots for him; the Spartacus/Antoninus relationship is presented in a manner not dissimilar to that of Spartacus and Varinia. In *El Cid*, the reunions between Rodrigo and Chimene interspersed throughout the narrative are strikingly similar to moving, emotional scenes between the film's hero and Moutamin. In one memorable scene, the latter pair ride towards each other from either side of a river and embrace in the middle. Rodrigo's question, 'How can anyone say this is wrong?' gives the relationship the dimensions of a forbidden, inter-racial romance.

Spartacus goes furthest, both because it adheres most closely to the 'good' male relationship/'bad' male relationship formula, and because, like *Ben-Hur*, homosexuality was already being smuggled into the script as motivation for the villain's behaviour. The original script made Crassus, the Roman patrician, a bisexual who was quite overtly attracted to Antoninus (Tony Curtis), the androgynous singer/slave who escapes to join Spartacus, and more ambiguously attracted to Spartacus for whom (like Messala and Commodus) he sublimates his desire by seeking his violent death. In a scene which was cut just before the film's British release (and recently restored in a new 70mm print, with Olivier's 'lost' dialogue added by Anthony Hopkins), Crassus obliquely tells Antoninus that he has taken him into his house to do more than prepare his bath. Just how obliquely he does this may be judged from the following:

Crassus:	Do you eat oysters?
Antoninus:	Yes.
Crassus:	Snails?
Antoninus:	No.
Crassus:	Do you consider the eating of oysters to be moral and the eating of snails to be immoral?
Antoninus:	No, master.
Crassus:	Of course not. It's all a matter of taste, isn't it?
Antoninus:	Yes, master.
Crassus:	And taste is not the same as appetite and therefore not a question of morals, is it?
Antoninus:	It could be argued so, master.
Crassus:	Um, that'll do. My robe, Antoninus. Ah, my taste . . . includes *both* oysters and snails.[22]

Several readings of the film have seen Crassus' sexuality as inextricably linked with his pursuit of Spartacus; Elley, for example:

> In the final reels the pull towards their 'reunion' is very strong, the more so for having obtained a complex sexual gloss. The most direct expression of this is Crassus' desire to possess Varinia, 'Spartacus' woman', if he cannot have the man himself . . . When Antoninus flees to join Spartacus and is discovered with him by Crassus at the end, Crassus has been doubly emasculated by Spartacus – rejected by both Varinia and Antoninus for a slave-leader. When the pair come face to face . . . Crassus' behaviour is as much that of a cuckolded lover as a frustrated general.[23]

This is emphasised further by Crassus' desire to *see* Spartacus, a compulsion given a teasing twist by the fact that he *has* seen him fight at the gladiator school but can't remember what he looks like. In their final meeting, Crassus' hysterical blow to Spartacus' face is answered by the slave leader spitting in his face, a suitable climax to this *amour fou*.

If the 'good' Spartacus/Antoninus relationship is set up against the 'bad' Crassus/Antoninus (or Crassus/Spartacus) relationship, it is also compared with that between Spartacus and Varinia. Antoninus and Varinia are both love objects lost by Crassus to Spartacus; in one scene, Varinia sings a song to Spartacus that was first sung to him by Antoninus. But the figure of Antoninus introduces several other important characteristics. If Spartacus, as a gladiator, is ambivalently looked at, Antoninus, a singer, juggler and magician, is presented in a less troubled way. His first meeting with the slave leader follows Spartacus being told off by an old woman for patronising the womens' contribution to the struggle. But Spartacus will place Antoninus, too, in an idealised, 'feminised' and 'nurturing' role, again virtually identical to Varinia's: 'You won't learn to kill – you'll teach us songs,' he tells him, and later reflects wistfully, 'Anyone can learn to fight, but to sing beautiful things and to make people believe them . . .'

The film builds to two emotional climaxes, two tearful farewells. One is Varinia's speech to Spartacus on the cross, where he is already virtually dead and on the point of being more legend/symbol than mere man. But before that, he is forced to fight Antoninus and inflicts the fatal wound that will save him from the cross. As Spartacus cradles his friend in his arms, the following exchange takes place:

> **Antoninus:** I love you, Spartacus, as I loved my own father.
> **Spartacus:** I love you, as my own son that I'll never see.
> (closes Antoninus' eyes) Go to sleep.

At one level, the film's distinction between heterosexually bonded 'buddies' (who really love each other) and predatory homosexuals (who can only express desire through displays of power and violence) seems to conform to a feature Robin Wood identifies in 1970s' buddy movies: 'The overt homosexual (invariably either clown or villain) has the function of a disclaimer – our boys are not like that.'[24] Moreover, the 'father' and 'son' qualifiers do seem to disavow the 'love' relationship a little. But the scene's realisation goes further than any buddy movie, where heterosexual relationships between men and women are usually either absent or shown to be inferior to the repressed camaraderie men enjoy. *Spartacus'* implication is that Spartacus' love for Antoninus is not that different from his love for Varinia but totally different from Crassus' desire for either Antoninus or Varinia. In other words, the 'difference', structurally, is one of power rather than preference. Furthermore, this declaration of love is played precisely according to the conventions of romance: tears, a final kiss, the cradling of his body. By contrast, the final scene with Varinia does not allow this level of physical intimacy – he is already on his painful pedestal, while she clutches his feet and looks up at him adoringly.

HONOUR/SACRIFICE/LAW

I want to return at this point to my other initial concern, namely what type of men are represented, and approach it through the films' discourses around honour, heroism, sacrifice. In their construction of a 'more perfect, more complete, more powerful ideal ego', the films offer homoerotic images and relationships but pursue patriarchal themes and heroic codes. Both films are named after men who live according to rigidly defined codes of honour, and in doing so, become more than ordinary men (legends at least, and in *El Cid* something like a God), but give up their lives in the process. This transcendence, however, takes place within a specific relationship with the law and the father. This relationship is manifested in two ways: in the name that the hero 'becomes' and which lives after his death, and the masculine code of heroism explored not as something 'implicitly known', but as unfamiliar (maybe even uncanny in *El Cid*), contradictory and almost impossible to live up to. In these scenarios, the 'problem' that Steve Neale identifies for the male spectator – that 'the ideal is something to which the subject is never adequate' – is faced by the characters themselves; while the subject dies, the 'ideal' is represented by a transfigured corpse, a name, a legend.

Again, Willemen's study of Mann is relevant, especially when he identifies one of the director's recurring themes as:

> the hero (or villain) pursued by a name. A father's name, or the name the hero wants to make for himself, or merely the name that makes you a target . . . The theme . . . culminates in *El Cid*, whose horrific name wins the battle as he, a corpse tied into its saddle, rides out to meet the enemy.[25]

All three of these names are crucial to *El Cid*. Rodrigo is forced to fight for the honour of his father's name against the King's champion, Count Gormez; but the name-of-the-father is also the 'honorific name' bestowed on him by the Moorish Prince Moutamin. It is his 'merciful' release of Moutamin, furthermore, that brings about the humiliation of his father in the Spanish court. Clearly the name of the 'Cid' is also that which he makes for himself – but is never quite in complete control of – and that which makes him a target; the patriarchal signifier that brings him under an implacable law of honour and duty. When he confronts Gormez, two 'problems' within this code become apparent. Firstly, Gormez is Chimene's father, so to uphold the father's name is also ro risk his marriage, to risk the perpetuation of patriarchy through the family. This rupture in his trajectory is represented as two roads: a patriarchy based on family and lineage, and one based on the living embodiment of a wholly self-referential law that just *is*. After releasing the Moors, he comments to a priest, 'I thought this would be the shortest road to my bride', and is told, 'You did take the shortest road, my son. Not to your bride, but to your destiny.' This renders the Oedipal problematic: killing the father actually jeopardises the marriage; becoming *the* Father involves becoming a dead father. Secondly, this code is defined as a series of negatives, by what men *cannot* do (back down, apologise, admit to being wrong), as this exchange illustrates:

Rodrigo: You shamed my father. I want his name back. But not the way you left it. I want it clean, so he can once more wear it proudly.

Gormez: I *cannot* apologise. It is not that I do not want to. I *do not know how* to.

Rodrigo: People will only esteem you the more for it. Everyone will understand.

Gormez: I have told you no. Go home, Rodrigo.

Rodrigo: I ask nothing for myself. I humble myself. Have pity on a proud old man.

Gormez: I have no pity for those who have outlived the usefulness of their lives.

Rodrigo: Count, I beg you. See? Two words are all I ask. Can you not say 'Forgive me'?

Gormez: *I cannot. I will not.* Now go.

Rodrigo: Don't make me stain my life and Chimene's with your blood.

Gormez: Go home, Rodrigo. No one will think the less of you for not having stood against the King's champion.
(Turns to go)

Rodrigo: (draws his sword) Count Gormez! I will ask you only this last time.

Gormez: I see that courage and honour are not dead in Castille. And now I remember why I once thought you were worthy of my Chimene. Go home, Rodrigo. What glories are for the King's champion in killing someone like you?

Rodrigo: (unsheaths his sword) Can a man live without honour?

Gormez: *No.*

The extent to which 'Honour' becomes a specifically masculine code, an impossible one – you can't live with it, you can't live without it – becomes apparent when Chimene is ostensibly placed in a similar position to that of Rodrigo by her father's death – the same moral imperative, the same clash between love and duty – except that her gender is represented as the barrier to a (masculine) Oedipal resolution. Her father has already said to her, 'You alone can carry my blood – I should have had a son.' Nevertheless, as he dies he asks her to live out a male Oedipality: 'Chimene, avenge me as a son would. Don't let me die unavenged.' In an angry exchange with Rodrigo, Chimene takes up an ambivalent relationship with the 'code of honour', through her awareness that it is responsible for her father's death and of her duty to bear it herself:

> Rodrigo: I did not seek your father's life, Chimene.
> Chimene: No, but you knew he could only answer the way he did. You were prepared to kill him. You bought your honour with my sorrow.
> Rodrigo: There was no other way for me. The man you chose to love could only do what I did.
> Chimene: Why did you come, Rodrigo? Did you think the woman *you* chose could do less than you?

The point is that on the basis of this criterion, she *does* do 'less' than Rodrigo. When he is placed in exile by Alfonso, Chimene gives up her revenge and joins Rodrigo. Only sons are allowed to avenge their real fathers and kill and replace symbolic ones. Chimene gives up duty for love, but at least she lives. Rodrigo appears to have it both ways – killing the father, having Chimene, becoming the Cid/Father – except that his Oedipal 'destiny' is a radically split one. Killing Gormez produces the couple and the family but is also propelled by the 'higher' law embodied by the Cid. Increasingly, the narrative widens the gap between the two, most noticeably in Rodrigo's death – 'You can't save my life,' he tells Chimene, 'You must help me give it up' – but also in an earlier scene where the two 'roads' travel in different directions. Alfonso imprisons Chimene and her children in an attempt to force Rodrigo's hand. It is the Cid's 'destiny' to capture Valencia, Rodrigo's duty and desire to rescue his family, thus leaving Spain unprotected:

> Am I not a man, too? Am I not permitted to think of my wife, my children? Well then, what must I do?

The film can only reconcile this crack in its 'powerful ideal ego' through another character who must hold together the Cid's destiny. Ordonez rescues Chimene and the children, lives up to a 'name' that Rodrigo temporarily falls short of; the film suggests that he is most likely to attempt a rescue and fail in his 'higher' mission. The scene points to why it is not only possible, but maybe necessary for Rodrigo to be outlived by the Cid, a figure untroubled by desire or emotion. The narrator tells us that 'the Cid rode out of the gates of History into Legend'; neither the film nor 'history' can offer a live, human figure who is equal to the rigidity of the Cid.

While *Spartacus* is both less relentlessly Oedipal and more concerned with ideals of freedom than honour, it does allude to a similar distinction between subject and name, man and legend, Spartacus and 'Spartacus'. Crassus explains, for example, that his mission is 'not alone to kill Spartacus – it is to kill the legend of Spartacus.' When the rebel slaves are captured, they are threatened with crucifixion unless they identify Spartacus. Spartacus stands to identify himself and finds his voice just one in a chorus claiming to be, and thus becoming, 'Spartacus'. The emotional effect of the scene derives not only from its bonding/comradeship connotations, but the fact that Spartacus loses his name and his voice to a 'more powerful ideal ego' that is even more abstract than the Cid; not just a mass, but the representation of a populist spirit infusing a mass that takes on the name 'Spartacus'. If the Cid is transfigured into a living/dead phallus, Spartacus' transfiguration (in a less romantically conservative film) is represented by *all* of the crosses lining the road in the final scene; it's an ideal to which the subject Spartacus – uneducated, defeated in the one gladiator battle we see him take part in – is once again inadequate.

MALE EPIC/MALE MELODRAMA

The contradictions within the male epic produce a profoundly melodramatic experience: emotional, hysterical, overwhelming. The films invest in two agendas, one based on heroism, duty, law, death, and one based on emotion, tears, love and desire. It is the theme of sacrifice which unites them. The first produces a drive towards destiny, living up to or becoming more than a man, and invests a great deal in the successful resolution of this meta-Oedipal scenario. The second focuses on family, friends and lovers, emotion and tears – often equally Oedipal in its commitment to heterosexual couples – and often producing a narrative homoeroticism to rival the delirious images of the body. If these often contradictory drives resolve themselves, it is in two types of ambivalently pleasurable highpoint, one emotional and one 'spectacular'. The climax of *El Cid* invites a kind of religous awe – which I always find very moving, its ideological investments notwithstanding – at this transfigured male. But it is also (and this adds to its emotional effect) troubled by a sense of loss, by what the subject gives up in the formation of the 'more powerful ideal ego'. In the second type of climax, the spectacle of the body subjected to danger, pain, destruction is set against a celebration of control over the body through the ability to sacrifice it. In a film like *Spartacus*, which is about freedom and slavery, it is ultimately in the realm of the individual body that battles are shown to be won or lost. Again, what kind of men are these? Can masculinity be taken to be 'known' in an essentially heroic genre which nevertheless explores it as something which, in its 'highest' form, becomes exotic, uncanny, impossible? In her critique of a certain tendency in male, postmodern writers, Suzanne Moore accuses them of what she calls 'gender tourism', namely holidays into and flirtations with 'optional female subjectivity'.[26] One of her targets, the rock critic Simon Reynolds (writing in the first instance about aggressive rap music), later replied, 'if this is the case, my gender tourism is a trip into masculinity', arguing that certain aggressive forms of music offer masculinity as a strange, frightening place to visit.[27] Whether one accepts Reynolds' argument in that particular case, the male epic, in a very different way, seems also to offer men a 'gender tour' into masculinity, which is presented with a mixture of excitement, voyeurism, confusion and anxiety.

NOTES

1 Steve Neale, 'Masculinity as Spectacle: Reflections on Men and Mainstream Cinema', *Screen*, vol. 24, no. 6, Nov-Dec 1983, p16.

2 Derek Elley, *The Epic Film: Myth and History*, RKP, 1984, p13.

3 Anthony Mann's *Fall of the Roman Empire*, the last major Epic, was made in 1964.

4 Quoted in Leslie Halliwell, *Filmgoer's Book of Quotes*, Granada, 1979, p216.

5 Paul Willemen, 'Anthony Mann: Looking at the Male', *Framework*, no. 15/16/17, Summer 1981, p16.

6 Mann worked on *Spartacus* for a while until Douglas replaced him as director with Kubrick. 'I worked nearly three weeks actually directing and all the opening sequence is mine; the slaves on the mountain, Peter Ustinov examining Kirk Douglas's teeth, the arrival at the gladiator's school and the opposition of Charles McGraw. As for the rest, the film follows my shooting script faithfully right up to the escape'; Interview with Anthony Mann, *Framework*, no. 15/16/17, p19.

7 Willemen, *op. cit.*, p16.

8 *Ibid.*

9 'Spectacle,' says Derek Elley, 'is the genre's most characteristic trademark.' *Op. cit.*, p1.

10 *Ibid., p158.*

11 David Thomson, *Biographical Dictionary of the Cinema*, Secker and Warburg, 1980 (revised edition), p266.

12 Quoted by Richard Dyer in *Stars*, BFI, 1979, pp148-9.

13 Laura Mulvey, 'Visual Pleasure and Narrative Cinema', *Screen*, vol. 16, no. 3, Autumn 1975, p12

14 Neale, *op. cit.*, p7.

15 *Ibid.*, p8.

16 *Ibid.*, p14.

17 Elley, *op. cit.*, p55.

18 Dyer is talking about male pin-ups, in 'Don't Look Now', reprinted in Angela McRobbie (ed.), *Zoot Suits and Second Hand Dresses: An Anthology of Fashion and Music*, Macmillan, 1989.

19 Vito Russo, *The Celluloid Closet: Homosexuality in the Movies*, Harper and Row, 1981, p76.

20 *Ibid.*, p77.

21 *Ibid.*

22 Transcribed by Vito Russo, *ibid.*, p120.

23 Elley, *op. cit.*, p111.

24 Robin Wood, *Hollywood from Vietnam to Reagan*, Columbia University Press 1986, p229.

25 Willeman, *op. cit.*, p16.

26 Suzanne Moore, 'Getting a Bit of the Other: The Pimps of Postmodernism', in Rowena Chapman and Jonathan Rutherford (eds.), *Male Order: Unwrapping Masculinity*, Lawrence and Wishart, 1988.

27 Simon Reynolds, *Blissed Out: The Raptures of Rock*, Serpent's Tail, 1990, p151.

Masculinity and the Horror Film

Peter Hutchings

Since the 1970s the horror film has increasingly come to be seen as a 'male' genre, produced largely by men for a predominantly male audience and addressing specifically male fears and anxieties. The pleasures of horror, it has been repeatedly argued, involve the films compensating for feelings of inadequacy on the part of the male spectator, and this process is usually linked with the terrorisation and/or killing of one or several female characters. Many of these ideas about horror have been developed in response to the slasher movie of the 1970s and 1980s, but they can also be applied to the genre as a whole. It is certainly undeniable that in horror cinema most of the monsters are male and most of the victims female, a fact which prompted the following remarks from Linda Williams:

> Whenever the movie screen holds a particularly effective image of terror, little boys and grown men make it a point of honor to look, while little girls and grown women cover their eyes or hide behind the shoulders of their dates. There are excellent reasons for this refusal to look, not the least of which is that she is often asked to bear witness to her own powerlessness in the face of rape, mutilation and murder. Another excellent reason for this refusal to look is the fact that women are given so little to identify with on the screen.[1]

Williams goes on to provide a convincing account of the relation between female spectatorship and the horror film. However, in so doing she makes certain assumptions about male spectatorship which merit further consideration. In particular, in the passage quoted above it is implied that the nature of the male look at horror is self-evident and unproblematic; that men relate to scenes of 'rape, mutilation and murder' (violence nearly always directed against women) through identifying or in some way aligning themselves with the male perpetrators of these acts. This need not necessarily take the form of character identification, which in many recent horror films is fairly minimal anyway. It can also involve an investment in and enjoyment of the power and control (over other characters, over the film's mise-en-scene) which tend to accrue around the figure of the monster.[2] Williams' account of the genre implies that male pleasure in horror arises from the feelings of mastery and power that it induces in the male spectator; although her suggestion – made in passing – that men experiencing horror do so as 'a point of honor' intriguingly implies a degree of unpleasure which has to be overcome.[3]

This view of the genre draws upon a structuring opposition which has underpinned much critical writing, not merely on horror but on cinema in general, namely that between the realm of activity and power which, it is argued, is usually associated with male characters in movies, and the passivity, powerlessness and subjection to the male gaze which is seen to define the cinematic role of many female characters. In the case of horror it is an opposition between male monsters and female victims.[4]

This way of understanding horror has been problematised by Carol J. Clover who, in her study of the slasher movie, notes that in these films the male killer is often presented as 'unmanly' – as childish and/or sexually immature – while what Clover terms 'the Final Girl', that is the female character who conventionally survives and eventually kills the killer, is assigned distinctly masculine qualities. Clover also notes how the male audiences for these films invariably (and vocally) support these 'Final Girls' as they go on the offensive.[5]

While not discarding completely the opposition outlined above and the power relations it suggests, Clover's remarks do indicate that there is clearly a need to attend further to the complexities of the male response to horror. This essay will explore certain aspects of this response. In particular, it will seek to identify what sorts of pleasure are involved for men in the affective powers of horror. It will also suggest ways in which these pleasures might be related to broader social relations of power. An assumption here will be that the male audience response to horror does not emerge spontaneously during the course of any particular film. Instead, horror's effectiveness for men presupposes an already established social position occupied by a male audience and towards which particular effects are directed.

THE POWER OF HORROR

Horror cinema can be characterised by what it does to its audience, that is by the way in which it works on the body of the spectator. Our experience of horror is often felt and described as a series of physical sensations: hair standing on end, muscles tensed, screaming, being made to jump, having the shit scared out of you.[6] Many horror films are in fact marketed in terms of the physical sensations that they promise (or threaten) to induce in the spectator: for example, Bob Clark's 1974 slasher movie *Black Christmas* was sold under the slogan 'If this one doesn't make your skin creep – it's on too tight!'

Horror then can be understood as an experience of subjection, of having things done to you by particular films. Returning to the marketing of horror, we find that this experience is often offered as challenging or punishing. An example to place alongside the *Black Christmas* slogan is the selling line for *Phantasm* (Don Coscarelli, US, 1979): 'If this one doesn't scare you – you're already dead', a line which has many variants in the genre.

One way of thinking about horror is to consider what sort of pleasures are offered by such a challenge. Another connected approach is to see horror as a genre dependent upon a process of victimisation that is apparent both within the films themselves and in the relation between the male spectator and the genre.

Within the various narratives of horror, the victim and the victimiser are indispensable elements, although, of course, the way in which these elements are deployed can change from one film to the next.[7] It is also by no means uncommon for individual characters to combine within themselves the victim and victimiser roles. Many of the classic movie monsters, for example, are rendered sympathetic through their periodic victimisation by the forces of 'normality'. One thinks here of King Kong being strafed by machine-gun fire as he clings to the Empire State Building, or, more ambivalently, of Dracula being forced into the sunlight that will destroy him by an implacable Van Helsing at the conclusion of Hammer's *Dracula* (Terence Fisher, UK, 1958).

It can be argued that the male spectator's response to this situation, this victimisation, is rather more complex than a simple identification or alignment with the victimiser (which, as has already been noted, is a role that can be distributed across several characters, male and female, in the same film). Certainly, as far as his emotional and psychical allegiances and investments are concerned, the male spectator is capable of shifting back and forth between victim (conventionally feminine) and victimiser (conventionally masculine). As Steve Neale expressed it in his analysis of *Halloween*:

> The identifications of the spectator are thus split between the polarities of a sadistic, aggressive and controlling position and a masochistic, suffering and controlled position. These identifications are in turn and simultaneously structured and put into operation across the positions occupied by characters in the film.[8]

I want to suggest here that in fact it is the 'masochistic' (a term which I consider below) or passive elements of this which are most important for grasping the nature of the male response to horror. It seems to me that, inasmuch as horror exists as a punishing, subjecting (but also pleasurable) experience, then 'masochism' is its primary affect. The sadistic point of view of the victimiser – often expressed in the slasher movie through actual point of view shots assigned to the killer as he advances upon his female victim – thus takes on an unexpected significance. It puts the male spectator in the best position to witness and empathize with the victim's powerlessness. To borrow a phrase from Kaja Silverman, 'the fascination of the sadistic point of view is merely that it provides the best vantage point from which to watch the masochistic story unfold.'[9]

Two important questions arise from such a view of the genre and will be considered below. First, why should the experience of passivity/subjection be pleasurable for men; and second, what relation does this pleasure bear to notions of male power and mastery?

MASOCHISM AND MALE PLEASURE

Horror films frequently seek to maximise the opportunities for the depiction of fear, terror and subjection. This does not just relate to the ostensible (usually female) victims in the genre, but also, as has already been suggested, to the monsters themselves. Isolated (although periodic) moments in which a monster is shown as powerless or vulnerable include Dracula cutting open his own chest and being sucked by one of his 'brides' (a scene from the original novel which is repeated in several film versions) or Michael Myers, the killer in *Halloween* (John Carpenter, US, 1979), losing his mask near the end of that film and for a few seconds appearing lost and helpless. More significantly, one can argue that subjection is actually built into the very notion of the monster insofar as the monster's destruction is a generic prerequisite.[10] Hence one of the reasons for horror's fascination with the scene of this destruction is that it provides the male spectator with an opportunity to empathize pleasurably with another's disempowerment, with his or hers subjection before another. In the slasher movies of the 1970s and 1980s the apparent indestructibility of the killer, the need for the 'Final Girl' to 'kill' him more than once, functions in this respect as yet another way of offering repeated images of subjection to the viewer.

The male spectator subjects himself, or is subjected, to the horror experience in two different but related ways; firstly, through a fascination and identification with those objects of victimisation, female and male, with which horror films are packed; secondly, through a willing subjection to the 'mechanical' effects of horror, those associated with mise-en-scene and a play with suspense and knowledge, which often take the form of attempts to make us tense and then make us jump.[11] The archetypal scene here is that which depicts the entry into a dark menacing place of a potential victim. In such a situation (instantly recognisable to an audience steeped in the conventions of the genre) the filmmaker artfully plays with our expectations through an inventive use of shadow and framing, seeking to surprise us with a relatively new variant on the scene of the monster's appearance.

This willing subjection, which I want to argue constitutes a key component in the male spectator's response to horror, can be described as a form of masochism. Freud saw masochism as co-existent with, and inseparable from, sadism: 'The correlation between the two terms of the pair is so close that they cannot be studied in isolation either in their genesis or in any of their manifestations.'[12] This view of masochism is evident in recent writings on horror. For example, in his piece on *Halloween* Neale refers to 'the twin poles of sadism and masochism.'[13]

However, there is another way of understanding masochism, one initially developed by Gilles Deleuze and situated in film studies by Gaylyn Studlar.[14] For Deleuze, sadism and masochism are not complementary but rather work on fundamentally different terrains. Sadism, with its desire for mastery and control over others, is seen as originating in the Oedipal stage of the individual's development whereas masochism is seen as more properly belonging to the pre-Oedipal period, that is the realm of the maternal. The infant's powerlessness before the mother is ambivalently felt by the infant:

> Both love object and controlling agent for the helpless child, the mother is viewed as an ambivalent figure during the oral period. Whether due to the child's experience of real trauma . . . or due to the narcissistic infant's own insatiability of demand, the pleasure associated with the oral mother is joined in masochism with the need for pain.[15]

One can add here that fearful fantasies of absorption by another have also been located in the realm of the oral/pre-Oedipal/archaic mother.[16]

For our purposes, this provides a way of thinking about masochism which sees it as a radically different experience from that of sadism rather than its complement. In terms of applying these ideas to film, Studlar helpfully notes that Deleuze identifies masochism as a condition which 'extends beyond the purely clinical realm into the arena of artistic form, language, and production of pleasure through a text.'[17] I would argue that if we are to locate masochism as a crucial element in the operations of horror, it is most productive to do this principally in terms of the genre's aesthetic identity and its affective powers.

It is useful at this point briefly to consider two horror films in which the monster is given us as feminine, explicitly in one case, in a more coded way in the other. The first of these is the Hammer horror film *The Gorgon* (Terence Fisher, GB, 1964). In this film, which is set in a 19th century, East European, police state, the spirit of the Gorgon has possessed a woman working as a nurse at an asylum. The narrative turns on the attempts of the male romantic lead, in the area to investigate the mysterious deaths of his father and brother (significantly no mention is made of his mother), to establish a relationship with the nurse. His adamant, and within the terms of the film increasingly irrational, refusal to see that she is possessed functions as a sign of his weakness and immaturity. In this situation the Gorgon, the all-powerful figure who waits beyond the desirable woman and is inseparable from her, functions as an image of the archaic, pre-Oedipal mother, before whom all men are rendered helpless infants. Significantly, the Gorgon doesn't actually do anything to any of her victims. The mere fact of her appearance is sufficient to inflict death on others.

Just as the spirit of the Gorgon pervades the town of Vandorf where most of the narrative action takes place, so a sense of helplessness pervades the film *The Gorgon*. All the male characters but one are ineffectual, easy prey to the Gorgon. The main reason behind the somewhat arbitrary introduction of the sole, powerful, male figure (a professor played by one of British horror's authority figures, Christopher Lee) appears to be that without his decisive attack, the Gorgon could not be stopped – a consequence unthinkable within the genre at that time.

For the male spectator the opportunities for sadistic power fantasies within such a scenario are clearly limited. The most likely figures of identification in Hammer horror – the man of knowledge, the young hero – are here either not fully integrated into the drama or completely ineffectual. What we have instead is a persistent terrorisation of the male, something which, according to the argument I am putting forward, should be a potential source of pleasure for the male spectator.[18] That the source of this terror functions in the drama very much as a powerful maternal figure, barely glimpsed and outside language, perhaps makes more explicit than is the case elsewhere one of the possible sources of this pleasure.

Moving from this to John Carpenter's 1982 version of *The Thing*, we find in an Arctic setting a group of men confronting a shape-shifting monster from outer space. The alien is amorphous, without fixed form, and it multiplies through the physical absorption and incorporation of its male victims. In this, it can be seen as exhibiting characteristics of the pre-Oedipal, maternal figure. The male characters' attempts to fight the monster prove largely ineffective. The latter part of the film in particular is full of images of men locked up or tied down in an increasingly claustrophobic research station. Even after the hero has (apparently) destroyed the Thing, he and a colleague (who might be a surviving part of the Thing) face a freezing death together. In this context, death functions as the ultimate passivity or subjection: 'death becomes the fantasy solution to masochistic desire.'[19]

It is a matter of debate as to what extent the maternal figure in *The Gorgon* and *The Thing* acquires its signifying force from its existence as a symbol operative within a patriarchal culture and how much from its plugging into a spectator's archaic memories. What is of concern here is the function of this figure in horror, where it appears to operate primarily as a passivity-inducing device, a means of rendering male characters inadequate and helpless. Inasmuch as ostensibly male monsters exhibit aspects of this maternal figure, they too seem to be serving the same generic function. Seen in this light, *The Gorgon* and *The Thing* become revealing limit-cases, presenting as they do particularly powerful agencies of subjection which other films reproduce in less obvious forms.

The analogy this approach suggests between the infant/mother and male spectator/monster relationships does seem to have a certain explanatory force. However, care has to be taken not to ignore or sidestep the ostensible representation of gender within horror – especially the maleness of the monster and the femaleness of the victim – by marking all monsters as 'really' female and thereby automatically threatening to men (characters and spectators). In order to grasp the sometimes rather tortuous power relations at work in and around horror, we need in particular to consider the way in which male victims in horror are themselves usually marked as 'unmanly', sometimes childish (in both *The Gorgon* and *The Thing*) but most often as feminine.

Tania Modleski has noted how disempowerment in contemporary, horror cinema is often presented as a feminisation of the male body. In particular, she discusses a scene from David Cronenberg's *Video-drome*, in which a vaginal slit opens up in the stomach of a male character (into which a video cassette is subsequently inserted).

In *Videodrome*, the openness and vulnerability of the media recipient are made to seem loathsome and fearful through the use of feminine imagery (the vaginal wound in the stomach) and feminine positioning: the hero is raped with a video cassette.[20]

While agreeing with Modleski's view that such a scene involves a reaffirmation of patriarchal gender roles, I would disagree with her on one point. I would argue that as presented in the film the slit in the stomach is as much a source of pleasurable fascination (for the male character and the male spectator) as it is of loathing. The outcome of this is a masochistic pleasure that characterises the male response to horror. (I would also argue that many of Modleski's ideas about contemporary horror are in fact applicable to the genre as a whole if one considers it in affective rather than thematic terms.)

It follows from this that if the male spectator experiences horror cinema as a series of pleasurable subjections, as multiple fantasies of disempowerment, then, as a subject of a patriarchal social order which insistently identifies femininity with powerlessness, he must also feel it, consciously or otherwise, as a feminising experience. What needs to be thought about now is why such an experience should be pleasurable. This will involve a consideration of male power.

MALE POWER AND MALE PLEASURE

Male characters who are victimised in horror are nearly always marked as unusual.[21] It is as if the presence of a disempowered male poses certain credibility problems and requires special explanation or justification. So, as we have already seen, in *The Gorgon* and *The Thing*, filmmakers provide the particularly effective threat of an archaic maternal figure as a cause for widespread male ineffectuality. Similarly, in *Evil Dead II* (Sam Raimi, US, 1987) lengthy scenes of the male hero being terrorised by supernatural forces are played as high comedy. Female victims, however, require no such justification. In the world of the horror film, the woman is 'naturally' a victim.[22]

The identification of the experience of being victimised as the realm of the feminine is an ideological operation which is not merely a product or an outcome of the horror genre. Rather the genre itself needs to be seen as thoroughly caught up in much wider, ideological practices which support such ideas. Indeed, horror itself is dependent for its effectivity upon an audience (a male audience) already placed in relation to these.

Men who watch and enjoy horror are always already subjects of patriarchy, that is they are located in relation to various institutions, discourses and beliefs which identify, support and perpetuate male power in society. This is the context in which horror operates and it can be argued that, in such a context, the fantasy of disempowerment outlined above takes on a particular significance.

It could be argued that male submission to disempowerment, that is a willing subjection made by someone who already has power, is merely a way of confirming possession of that power. In other words, by temporarily and in a very circumscribed way 'feminizing' the male spectator, horror emphasises the 'normality' of masculinity, thereby reassuring a male spectator.

However, it seems to me that such an approach does not satisfactorily explain the pleasures on offer in the genre. In particular, it does not address the question of why in the first place the male spectator should feel the need for a (re)confirmation of his power and identity. Answering this question necessarily involves a problematising of the relation between the male spectator sitting in the cinema watching a horror film and those patriarchal institutions and belief-systems which provide various positions and role models through which that spectator has identified and continues to identify himself as a man.

Inasmuch as a man is the subject of patriarchy, then he has power. However, this power is not his personal property, it does not emerge from within his own unique being. Rather it appertains to those institutional and ideological positions which the male individual occupies and through which he finds an identity. In this respect, power takes on an alienating quality: it can be used but it can never be owned.

In an article on the male pin-up, Richard Dyer has written of the gap that exists between the mystique of male power (symbolised by the phallus) and the visible reality of men and masculinity: 'Hence the excessive, even hysterical quality of so much male imagery. The clenched fists, the bulging muscles, the hardened jaws, the proliferation of phallic symbols – they are all straining after what can hardly ever be achieved, the embodiment of the phallic mystique.'[23] I want to suggest here that for male spectators horror necessarily operates in this gap, this space between what might be termed the unrealisable ideal or symbolic of masculinity and the real. The pleasure involved in this process for the male audience derives from the way in which the disempowerment of the male spectator doesn't just reconfirm feelings of power, but also, more importantly, serves to cover over the fact that this spectator's hold on power is structural and provisional rather than personal. This arguably provides one of the reasons for the fact that the male audience for horror is predominantly an adolescent one; adolescence being a time when the relation to ideals of masculinity is particularly fraught and problematic.

CONCLUSION

This essay has explored some of the pleasures involved for the male spectator in the horror film experience. However, my discussion of this subject has deployed a rather abstract notion of male spectatorship, one which does not take into account the ways in which variable factors such as sexual orientation, class and race might influence and modify a particular audience's pleasures in horror. It is important to recognise that particular audiences can and will respond to a film in a variety of ways, depending on the social and cultural contexts within which these audiences are located. What this means is that the nature of the male audience's response to, and uses for, horror is undoubtedly more complex and perhaps even contradictory than the model I have outlined suggests. But I believe that this model does identify the framework of affect within which male responses to horror are forged. This framework needs to be seen as itself bound up with the distribution of power within society.

Writing off horror as hopelessly misogynist is clearly an inadequate method for dealing with the genre. At the very least, we need to be aware that the male response is more complex than this dismissive approach suggests. A more systematic account of the genre than can be provided here needs to develop further our awareness, both of these complexities, and of the range of responses and pleasures generated by male spectators. In this way we can gain a clearer sense of the way in which horror, one of the most 'masculine' of genres, can in fact be very revealing – for men and women – about some of the fantasies and the actualities of male power and male identity.

NOTES

1 Linda Williams, 'When The Woman Looks', *Revision – Essays in Feminist Film Criticism*, University Publications of America, Frederick MD, 1984, p83.

2 Steve Neale, 'Halloween: Suspense, Aggression and the Look', in *Framework*, no. 14, Spring, 1981, pp25-29.

3 See Linda Williams, *Hardcore: Power, Pleasure, and the 'Frenzy of the Visible'*, Pandora, London, 1990 for a much more detailed account of male spectatorship.

4 See Laura Mulvey, 'Visual Pleasure and Narrative Cinema', in *Screen*, vol. 16, no. 3, Autumn, 1975, pp6-18 for the 'classic' statement of this opposition.

5 Carol J. Clover, 'Her Body, Himself; Gender in the Slasher Film', in *Representations*, no. 20, Fall 1987, pp187-228, and *Men, Women and Chain Saws*, BFI, 1992.

6 See Philip Brophy, 'Horrality – the Textuality of Contemporary Horror Films', *Screen*, vol. 27, no. 1, Jan-Feb 1986, pp2-13. At a later stage I will suggest that Tania Modleski's work on contemporary horror can in certain respects be applied to the genre as a whole. Similarly here I would argue that if one is concerned as we are primarily with horror's affectivity rather than its thematic structures, then Brophy's ideas have a much wider purchase than his ostensible subject matter might indicate.

7 Obviously there are non-horror films which contain victims and victimisers. When victimisation is figured as a violent or potentially violent subjection, then these other films often exhibit an affinity with the horror genre: see, for example, various Gothic melodramas produced by Hollywood during the 1940s.

8 Neale, *op. cit.*, p28.

9 Kaja Silverman, 'Masochism and Subjectivity', *Framework*, no. 12, 1979, p5.

10 In certain films – for example, the first two *Omen* films – the monster is not destroyed at the conclusion. But here again one can find many images of terrorisation and subjection. It is merely the distribution of these throughout the films which has changed.

11 See Neale, *op. cit.*

12 J. LaPlanche & J.B. Pontalis, *The Language of Psychoanalysis*, The Hogarth Press, London, 1973, p402.

13 Neale, *op. cit.*, p28.

14 Gaylyn Studlar, 'Masochism and the Perverse Pleasures of the Cinema', *Movies & Methods – Volume 2*, Bill Nichols (ed), University of California Press, Berkeley & London, 1985, pp602-621.

15 Studlar, *op. cit.*, p606.

16 Here I am using the terms 'pre-Oedipal', 'archaic' and 'oral' in a more or less interchangeable way. Of course this entails a considerable simplification of these terms. However, I feel that for the purposes of this essay a more rigorous application of them is neither necessary nor desirable.

17 Studlar, *op. cit.*, p604.

18 There are two female victims in *The Gorgon* (three if one counts the possessed nurse, four if one counts the Gorgon herself). In this film, images of men being terrorised sit alongside more traditional images of female terror.

19 Studlar, *op. cit.*, p606.

20 Tania Modleski, 'The Terror of Pleasure: The Contemporary Horror Film and Postmodern Theory', *Studies in Entertainment*, Modleski (ed), Indiana University Press, Bloomington & Indianapolis, 1986, p163.

21 Carol J. Clover notes that while there are numerous male victims in the slasher film, less time is spent on their death scenes than on the death scenes of the female victims: Clover, 'Her Body', pp200-201.

22 It is significant that female horror stars are often referred to as 'scream queens', a term which clearly denotes their primary function in the genre.

23 Richard Dyer, 'Don't Look Now', *Screen*, vol. 23, no. 3-4, Sept-Oct 1982, p71.

'It's as a Man That You've Failed': Masculinity and Forbidden Desire in *The Spanish Gardener*

Andy Medhurst

An intense romantic melodrama, an emotional triangle in which all three participants are male, a complex and anxious exploration of the socially acceptable limits of masculinity – these are not what one would expect to find in a British film of the 1950s, let alone in a glossy, Vistavision, Technicolor, Rank Organisation star vehicle aimed squarely and unapologetically at the box office, but then *The Spanish Gardener* (Philip Leacock, 1956) is an extraordinary piece of work. Extraordinary, but largely forgotten,[1] so a brief summary of the narrative seems necessary. The immediate problem here, however, is that it is a film primarily concerned with interconnecting emotional rivalries, where the key moments are conveyed through look, gesture and nuance, all of which a simple plot outline cannot begin to indicate. Nevertheless, the skeleton of the story is as follows.

A middle-aged English diplomat, Harrington Brande (Michael Hordern), arrives in a small Spanish port to take up the position of British Consul, a post he finds insultingly beneath his estimation of his own abilities. Estranged from his wife, he is accompanied by his young son Nicholas (Jon Whiteley), to whom he is devoted to the point of suffocation. The boy strikes up a friendship with José (Dirk Bogarde), the local man hired as gardener, and the Consul becomes at first irritated, then jealously furious, at the strength of this attachment. His obsession blinds him to the suspicious behaviour of Garcia (Cyril Cusack), another employee, who diverts attention from his own criminal inclinations by framing José for theft. The Consul seizes this chance to expel the rival for his son's affections, and José is sent to Barcelona for trial. He escapes from his guards and flees to the hills, where he is joined by Nicholas, who has been forced to run away from home by Garcia's threats of violence. Harrington Brande, now convinced of José's innocence and desperate to recover his missing son, finds them and reconciliation ensues. The film ends with father and son leaving for a new posting and José cleared of all charges.

Those are the bones, but what matters is the flesh. *The Spanish Gardener* uses that narrative framework to ask a series of searching, difficult and perhaps unanswerable questions about how men can and cannot relate to each other, about male tenderness and sensuality, about what it means to be male in a particular culture at a particular time. Most strikingly of all, it does this openly, not at some buried subtextual level. The dilemmas of masculinity constitute the substantial problematic of the film. Apart from the generically necessary coating of the Garcia plot, it isn't 'about' anything else.

So how could this be? Where did it come from? The film is based on a novel by A.J. Cronin, one of the most successful British middlebrow novelists of the time, published in 1950. Cronin's fiction was well-established as reliable source material for screen adaptations, as witnessed by film versions of *The Stars Look Down* (Carol Reed, 1939) and *Hatter's Castle* (Lance Comfort, 1941) and subsequently by the long-running television series *Dr. Finlay's Casebook*, but there is little in any of those texts, cosily comforting though they were, to suggest the pain and the rage, the confusion and the longing that make *The Spanish Gardener* so compelling. The original novel is worth attention, however, if only to underline the specifically cinematic ways through which the film version achieves its power, and I'll return to Cronin's book where appropriate.[2]

The other context within which the film must be seen is that of British cinema, and British culture more widely, in the 1950s. It was released in November 1956 – note first of all the month, shrewdly designed to capture the Christmas-treat market for both fans of Dirk Bogarde and (rather bizarrely, given the tensions on which the film is founded) the 'family audience' which is invariably targeted by films featuring a child star; note also the year, one of those pivotal points in British cultural history, the year of the Angry Young Man. The impact of the theatrical and literary Angries, however, had not yet been felt in cinema, except perhaps to sow the seeds of a growing dissatisfaction with the predominantly middle-class and generally anti-contemporary films on which the British studios seemed so fixated. Any such dissatisfaction was not felt by the popular audience, however, whose favourite film in 1956 was that apotheosis of retrospective flag-waving, *Reach For The Sky* (Lewis Gilbert). In such a context, *The Spanish Gardener* was neither part of a self-proclaimed cultural vanguard, nor a safe-bet genre film drawing on self-congratulatory notions of national identity.

The Spanish Gardener escapes being caught up in that binary squabble largely through the fact of its location. Difficult as it now is, after decades of package holidays, to see Spain as any kind of 'exotic' setting, the sun and sea undeniably constituted one of the film's major selling points, particularly in the depths of a British winter, with the widescreen and colour underlining this travelogue appeal. The twin central themes of *The Spanish Gardener*, masculinity and Englishness, were unshakeably central to British films of the 1950s – its difference comes with the degree of interrogation and scrutiny under which those discourses are put: the admission of doubt, the acknowledgement of frailty, the realisation that, in stark and shocking contrast to the prevailing ideological certainties of social and sexual identity, being an Englishman was actually a pretty fucked-up thing to be.

The key figure who makes this disclosure possible is not the gardener of the title, iconically embodied by the star whose sunburned and rugged profile loomed over the posters and publicity material, but the diplomat so memorably portrayed by Michael Hordern – the poor, stiff, aloof, buttoned-up, clamped-down, bitter, resentful, hopelessly repressed Harrington Brande. Hordern's performance is a dazzling, if by necessity understated, revelation of a man whose commitment to propriety has left him emotionally barren, utterly unable to open up to his own deeper feelings, his coldness a product of a particular version of masculinity, his emptiness an absolute corollary of his Englishness. He would be a figure of pity, were it not for one thing. Being so helplessly embroiled in his web of repressions, he no longer sees the need for alternatives, and so he is bringing up Nicholas in precisely the same chilly and dessicated way. The tortured has become the torturer – exit audience sympathy, enter José.

Fundamentally a melodrama, *The Spanish Gardener* does not shy away from broad and obvious strokes, so the clash between Harrington Brande and José, the clash over Nicholas' destiny, over what kind of masculinity to pass on, is played out over a series of binary oppositions that, through their very predictability, heighten the intensity of the struggle. So where Harrington Brande stands for and is associated with England, coldness and the inside of buildings, José is the personification of Spain, warmth and the great outdoors. The Consul wears three-piece suits even in the blazing sunshine, while the gardener opens the buttons on his shirt and wears jeans of a tightness rarely seen in British films of the 1950s, where rigorously unsexy, baggy flannels were the trousering norm.[3] The codes of clothing also come into play in their struggle for Nicholas. Harrington Brande has dressed his son in formal, unsuitable clothes, whereas once José has encouraged him to help in the garden, Nicholas eagerly peels off the shirt that symbolises his constriction. The shirt serves as a kind of marker, a border between the two kinds of masculinity which are offered to the boy, which he must negotiate in the rite of passage that forms a crucial part of the film's narrative. When he wears it, he is the delicate semi-invalid cosseted by Harrington Brande; shirtless, he aspires to the lithe muscularity of José.

Harrington Brande is bookish, José vigorously athletic – Nicholas' first mistake, revealing how much he cares for the other man, is to take his father to the pelota game where José is the star player. Harrington Brande insists that they leave, uttering the memorably unmanly phrase 'I've got a splitting headache'. Hordern conveys with delicate skill the scattered clues of femininity that coalesce around Harrington Brande,[4] never resorting to camp, but nonetheless establishing the gulf between himself and José in terms of traditional masculine attributes. His superior in the Diplomatic Service expresses exasperation with him by stating 'It's as a man that you've failed'. In context this is intended to refer to his lack of human warmth, but taking the film as a whole it has wider resonances, indicting him for failing to match up to preferred, masculine norms.

He is, for example, houseproud and fussy, referring to china statuettes as 'friends' before dusting them with a prissily feminised pride, while José reserves his energies for digging and planting, sweat on his muscled torso and soil on his well-worn hands. It would only be slightly fanciful here to invoke an earlier, far more scandalous text which equated a garden worker with an earthy, fertile masculinity that proved irresistible to a pale, domesticated individual of a higher social standing whose passions waited to be unlocked – *Lady Chatterley's Lover*.

Such a comparison is not at all difficult to make when considering Cronin's novel, if only because of its tendency to resort to chain-store Lawrence whenever descriptions of sexual passion are required, but with the film any such claim does run into one fairly sizeable problem, namely this: if we recast José as Lawrence's Mellors, all authentic fecundity and cycles of growth, then we have to see Harrington Brande as Connie Chatterly herself, alone and palely loitering but dying for a bit of horticultural rough . . . which would be to introduce the dimension of undeniable homosexual desire into a British feature film of 1956, surely an anachronistic impossibility.

But why so surely? Just because desires are not spoken does not mean that they are absent, especially in cinema, a medium which would be impoverished beyond recognition if we deluded ourselves that only the literal and the overt had meaning. I should put my cards on the table here: one major reason why *The Spanish Gardener* impresses me as much as it does is that its exploration of the varieties of masculine identity refuses to exclude the question of homosexuality. It never unequivocally labels any of the participants in its convoluted psychodrama as 'gay', but instead, far more suggestively and provocatively, it recognises that tensions between men are rarely free of sexual undercurrents. This is not simply the case in the rivalry between Harrington Brande and José, it is also central to the relationships that both men have with Nicholas.

This, perhaps, is a controversial claim. In an era when child abuse is, quite rightly, an issue of major social concern, any suggestion of erotic desire between individuals of different generations has to proceed with extreme caution. Similarly, adult homosexual men have good reason to want to distance themselves from considering the possibility of children's sexuality, since the insinuation of paedophilia is one of the easiest and most damaging weapons deployed as part of homophobic prejudice. So I open this can of worms hesitantly, but not apologetically. To be matter-of-fact about it, *The Spanish Gardener* is centred on a triangle where three people fight for the affection of the others; all three are male, two are adults, one a child. No sexual activity is seen as taking place between any of them, but the energy and pulse of the film are generated by the anxieties of desire, however half-understood and suppressed. That desire might be for respect, tenderness, devotion, for all kinds of love that need not be sexually expressed. Yet equally, the relay of desiring looks which permeate the film with such electric frequency could indicate more conventionally sexual feelings.

I make (perhaps labour) this point not because I want to make a defence of particular sexual orientations, but because I want to stress how the film operates on a level of ambiguity that is profoundly cinematic. It is precisely because the desires that Harrington Brande feels for José were verbally inexpressible in a mainstream film in 1956, and because desires between child and adult are literally and (to some) metaphorically unspeakable even now, that *The Spanish Gardener* mobilises an interplay of glances, a spiral of inflections, gestures and mannerisms that could mean everything, could mean nothing, and could mean anything in between.

Such an anarchy of interpretation is, of course, untenable for any length of time. Audiences decide, and they decide in part upon the basis of their specific social situation. My homosexuality (and, no doubt, were I considering in detail the film's discourse of national identity, my Englishness) structures and conditions what I see, and what I see in this film, with my skewed and biased queer eyes, is one little gay boy who falls in love for the very first time, with the very same hunk of a gardener that his father is fighting hard not to fall in love with too.

Consider the moment when Harrington Brande first interviews José. It is Bogarde's first appearance in the film, and his fans have had to wait for fifteen increasingly impatient minutes. A long, high shot of the exterior of the Consul's villa shows us the hot, dry landscape with the blue sea beyond. One small figure waits in the garden, another leaves the villa and walks towards him. Harrington Brande asks the newcomer his name and he spins round, in devastating close-up: it's José, and, of course, for all those Odeon-filling fans, it's Dirk, widescreen Technicolor Dirk, as much Dirk as your heart could wish for. The interview proceeds, and we take in the contrasting speech, manner, looks and clothes of the two men. Finally, as Harrington Brande returns to the house, Nicholas comes into shot, and looks José up and down. Very up and very down. It's only a fragment, an instant, far too tiny to bear all the weight I want to load on to it, but it's exactly the kind of shred that queer eyes will identify, memorise and cherish.

I pointed this out, rather less floridly, to some students with whom I was discussing the film, and their response was somewhat startled. They didn't want to see Nicholas as capable of desire because he was 'too young', but I suspect they might not have thought this had Nicholas shot the same lingering, appreciative look at Magdalena the maid. This is the kind of assumption that leads to laws enforcing different ages of consent for heterosexuals and homosexuals, to the gay-men-equals-paedophile paranoia mentioned earlier, and it was there in the minds of my otherwise impeccably left-liberal students too – that you can't be too careful when you're dealing with queer desire. Perhaps, to some people, reading Nicholas' look in the way that I do would be to advocate men sexually preying on little boys,[5] but nothing could be further from the truth. It is the desire coming *from* the boy that thrills me, for it is in that look that I feel the bond of recognition, the memory of discovery, the irreversible moment when desire first descends. You can't see this if you're looking with heterosexual blinkers on, which is why one or two of my perplexed and resistant class of students didn't seem so shocked, because they had queer eyes too.

Besides, if this is all pure speculation, exactly why does Harrington Brande react to Nicholas and José's friendship with such outrage and alarm? Here it is instructive to return to the novel again, since Cronin's treatment of the events differs strikingly from the film's version. In the novel, José is only nineteen (though the film never spells out his age, clearly Bogarde could not have convincingly portrayed anyone so young) and hence his relationship with Nicholas could legitimately be seen as one between two boys, or one adolescent and another about to enter that stage. Although the novel obsessively asserts and reasserts that they have an 'innocent' friendship, the language Cronin employs might for some contemporary readers seem to call this claim into question. Nicholas, for example, 'felt a current of sympathetic understanding – he could not more fully explain it – flowing, flowing gently between the Spanish youth and himself', (p28), while José finds himself struck by 'this new, melting affection for this little boy, which, soft as a southern air, had sprung from he knew not where, filling him with tenderness . . . it made his heart sing' (p106).

Such language is interesting because of its attempt to depict a sensual friendship that stops short of sexuality. On one level, José's warm feelings towards Nicholas are simply a part of the Mediterranean emotionality that the text is schematically eager to contrast with the Anglo-Saxon reserve of Nicholas' father (in the novel, Harrington Brande is American, not English, but much is made of his 'Puritan' heritage, and the contrast with José's Spanishness is still central), and that is not all there is to it. The signs could be read differently, and they are, with spectacular results, by Harrington Brande himself.

Watching the film, the depth and strength of Harrington Brande's loathing for José is somewhat difficult to understand, at least based on the surface evidence. The novel makes things more explicit, though the cost of that explicitness is to usher in a violent hostility towards non-heterosexual desire that is entirely absent from the film. Harrington Brande discovers that on the night when Nicholas stayed with José's family, fearing Garcia's drunken violence, he slept in the same bed as José. His father jumps to one obvious, but unmentionable conclusion: 'a swift revulsion of feeling seized him. No, no, it was incredible . . . he could not . . . he would not believe it' (p142). The unspeakability of homosexuality is shriekingly apparent in those three dots, as again a few pages later, when father is interrogating son: ' "You and he . . ." He whispered huskily, then could say no more' (p149). The film could not even say this much, since the scene in the house of Jose's family not only ends long before bedtime, giving us not even the slightest clue as to the sleeping arrangements, but actually concludes with José kissing and embracing Maria, his girlfriend, a character entirely absent from the novel. Her function in the film is patently ideological, she is wheeled on to quash any doubts about the heterosexuality of José, and simultaneously to underscore the romantic appeal of the Bogarde persona to heterosexual female fans. Her narrative credibility is zero, but her presence speaks eloquently of the sexual tensions surrounding José and Nicholas and the anxious need felt by the film-makers to try and seal them off.

There are two further differences between film and novel which are useful for unravelling the knots of desire that run through *The Spanish Gardener*. The first is the figure of the doctor, the second the conclusion of the narrative. In the film, Dr. Harvey is a fairly minor character, a solidly reliable, decent man played by solidly reliable, decent Geoffrey Keen, one of those supporting actors who populate British cinema with skilfully unselfish performances. The novel instead offers Dr. Halevy, a marauding, French psychoanalyst who has been treating the tormented Harrington Brande for years, and whom the Consul summons to root out the truth about Nicholas and José. The chapters involving Halevy are alarmingly lurid caricatures, as Cronin seeks to score point after scathing point against what he so clearly regarded as the bogus discipline of psychoanalysis.

Halevy is in no doubt that José has corrupted the younger boy, indeed that Nicholas like all boys already has the capacity for deviant desire within him, as he explains to Harrington Brande in a series of ripe metaphors: 'You know that filth exists even in the most unsuspected places. That the sweetest flowers are nourished by the dunghill, that the fairest forest pool, on which pure lilies grow, conceals beneath the surface a bed of muddy ordure' (p157). As if this discourse of anality were not enough, he goes to speak about 'fresh running sores', 'human vileness', 'darker forces' and 'strange obsessions and hidden longings', all of which seems like an excessively circumlocutory way of avoiding the word 'homosexuality'. The novel has one more dubious trick to play: Halevy's analysis scene with Nicholas becomes a sick sexual comedy, as his persistent attempts to persuade Nicholas to 'confess' become revealed as his own sexual fantasies projected on to the boy. By this sleight of hand, drawing on established metaphorical parallels between the scene of analysis and the site of seduction, the novel backtracks on its own dynamic of homoerotic desire to present such an emotion as the lustful dribbling of a predatory paedophile.

Cronin's crowning swipe at Halevy is this: 'In his universe, the world wherein he moved and breathed, normality had no place. Life was a steamy jungle, where unseen forces coiled and writhed in black and bitter mud' (p169). Beyond the risibly feverish imagery, this has a fairly plain meaning – clammy perverts can't help inventing twisted meanings. Call me sensitive, but I'm inclined to take this a little personally, because my project in analysing this film could be seen as analogous to Halevy's in analysing the recumbent Nicholas. After all, a queer critic such as myself also inhabits a world where normality has no place, but for a reason very different from that of the demonised Halevy. In fact, for me, 'normality' has a very important and definite place, as an ideological trope used in the service of maintaining a particular sexual hierarchy, as a fetishised, idealised fiction that cruelly limits the possibilities of human sexual experience, and as such a prime target to be undermined wherever possible. Hence the appeal and potential of a film like *The Spanish Gardener*, since it suggests, however briefly and nervously, that there are ways of living beyond the numbness of norms.

The substitution of Harvey for Halevy is, perhaps, one such suggestion, since it spares us the caricature of the over-zealous, deviant analyst and thus allows us (particularly those of us with deviantly analytical leanings) to continue to speculate on the implications of the relationships before us. These are at their most tense and moving towards the end of the film, where once again the novel's plot and attitudes are radically altered. In Cronin's text, José is killed when trying to escape from the train – two significant details being that it is Harrington Brande's attempt to stop him that results in his fatal fall, and that it is his face which strikes the rails and is dreadfully mutilated, a punishment for his beauty and, in no uncertain terms, the revenge of the repressed. The film's José cannot be allowed to die, especially like that. Firstly, audiences don't go to star vehicles to see the star horribly and unexpectedly dispatched (not until *Psycho*, at least), and secondly, more interestingly, such a punitive solution to the tensions of homoeroticism would be at odds with the film's commitment to sensitive ambiguity.

So José escapes to the hills, to the ruined mill where he and Nicholas had gone fishing, where he is joined by the boy and then his father, both of whom have come through the melodramatically cathartic storm. And there, only momentarily but no less powerfully for that, they forge that most threatening of challenges to normality, a queer family.[6] If one felt the need to slot them into a heterosexual model, then José is the strong but vulnerable father, and Harrington Brande, who loved to dust, who had splitting headaches, who looked with anguished longing at the strapping gardener, gets to play mother at last. He tends the injured hero, even going so far as to tear Nicholas' shirt to dress the wound, the same shirt that had earlier stood for the barrier between English and Spanish, cold and hot, brain and brawn, the barrier that now no longer exists for the few screen seconds when this new social-sexual unit fleetingly constitutes itself and flourishes. The three of them are finally one.

This, of course, cannot be allowed to last. Indeed, it was only allowed to exist in the distant, hidden, ruined mill, a space beyond society, a removed and fantastic location where impossible desires could find completion. They can't stay there, they have to come back to the real world, before going their separate ways. Harrington Brande is off to cool, Northern, Protestant Sweden, where sultry gardeners and the delicious, illicit desires they conjure up will not be on the agenda. Nicholas is bound for boarding school, with the promise of seeing his mother in the holidays, so his socialisation into acceptable masculinity seems secure (after all, homosexuals who go to boarding school almost always marry later, and disavow their real passions as a 'passing phase'). And José stays in Spain, gardening, with the decorative, generically obligatory, but flagrantly unconvincing Maria.

NOTES

I'd like to acknowledge the contribution made towards the completion of this essay by the sharp insights of Linda Rozmovits and the considerable patience of Pat Kirkham and Janet Thumim.

1 It has recently been hailed as 'one of the finest films of the 1950s' (Brian McFarlane, *Sixty Voices: Celebrities Recall the Golden Age of British Cinema*, British Film Institute, London, 1992, p156) but this is an isolated fragment of acclaim.
2 *The Spanish Gardener*, Gollancz, London, 1950. In general I'm very suspicious of criticism which sets out to compare a film and its literary source, since such enterprises tend to be timid, laboured and committed to proving the superiority of the written word. I hope the different emphasis of this essay is obvious enough.
3 Tight, pale blue jeans (as opposed to denim worn as workwear) would have had two meanings to British audiences in the mid-1950s. Firstly, American youth culture, the most shapely exponent of jeans as the emblem of youth being James Dean (there are moments in *The Spanish Gardener* where Bogarde could be mistaken for Dean's older brother). Secondly, though this by definition would not be widely known, homosexuality, since 'American-style' jeans (as they were often advertised in magazines read by gay men) were becoming a key sartorial code in gay subcultures, a fact which might not be entirely irrelevant to the complexities of desire that I see as operating in this film. 'I think the gay crowd took to jeans because of the close and tightness of them, showed up all the essential parts.' (Peter, quoted in *Daring Hearts: Lesbian and Gay Lives of 50s and 60s Brighton*, Queenspark Books, Brighton, 1992, p56). 'I used to go the American import shops . . . I'd search London for a pair of pale blue jeans because I'd seen James Dean wearing them.' (David Ruffell, quoted in *Walking After Midnight: Gay Men's Life Stories*, Routledge, London, 1989, p99).
4 It is, I hope, clear that when I used the term 'femininity' I am referring to certain codes socially associated, often misogynistically, with women's behaviour, not endorsing these as in any way the inevitable attributes of actual women.
5 A difficult question to bear in mind here is whether or not Nicholas is put on display for the gaze of those who find boys of that age sexually attractive.

I'm not qualified to say, but it is worth noting how similar his scrawny body is to the photographs of boys popular in paedophile circles in the 1950s and 1960s. *The Boy: A Photographic Essay* (Book Horizons, New York, 1964) offers over two hundred pages of half-dressed or naked boys of precisely Nicholas' age and build, with a significant proportion involved in fishing, or camping, or other male-bonding activities not wildly dissimilar from those depicted in the film. The text of this book also, in a way that would have given A.J. Cronin several sleepless nights, makes much of boyhood as a period of golden, unrecoverabale 'innocence'.

6 This is perhaps somewhat rhetorical, but it is striking that the idea of the queer family seems to embody a particularly strong affront to those dedicated to preserving normative sexual structures. Witness the carefully orchestrated furore around the book *Jenny Lives With Eric And Martin* (about how a young girl comes to terms with her father's relationship with his male lover) which fed directly into the infamous Clause 28, with its specific forbidding of the representation of homosexuality as a 'pretended family relationship'. Perhaps some gay video workshop should produce a reworked version of *The Spanish Gardener* called *Nicholas Lives With José and Harrington Brande.*

Tracking the Sign of Tarzan: Trans-Media Representation of a Pop-Culture Icon

Walt Morton

Tarzan of the Apes was one of the first novels mass-marketed to the public in a variety of media, a consequence of the growth of mass-media during the first half of this century. The 'pulp' *All-Story Magazine*, published the 95,000 word novel written by American author Edgar Rice Burroughs in October, 1912.[1] Tarzan's story fascinated readers, following in the wake of similar 'jungle' narratives popular at this time.[2] Burroughs eventually wrote twenty-six sequels (*The Return of Tarzan*, etc.), prudently licensing a remarkable number of adaptations of Tarzan to other media.[3] These included: a successful national newspaper serialization (1914), the movies (1918)[4], Tarzan radio shows (1931)[5], and a newspaper comic strip (1929). Burroughs had the foresight to register 'Tarzan' as a trademark in 1913 and made a fortune licensing the name to hundreds of products like: sweat shirts, wrist watches, candy, trading cards, bubble gum, rubber toys, bathing suits, records, coffee and bread.[6] The marketing of Tarzan proves that narrative can be easily adapted between media, and has enduring popularity. Rampant marketing elevated the character of Tarzan to iconic status:

> Duplicating images pries meaning loose from a necessary link to geography, place. The signifier [Tarzan] becomes potentially free-floating, unpinned, ready for exchange within a cash nexus that determines new meaning.[7]

My project focuses on trans-media iconographic differentiation, a study of the differences in the way an iconic figure is represented in various media. The definition of the 'iconic' posits a 'sign' or representation with a strong fidelity to the 'original'. We expect the iconic representation of Tarzan to be motivated by and analogically derived from the Tarzan character created in the novel.[8] But if we look at the marginal differences created in moving the icon from one medium to another, we see the specific devices a given medium favors in communication.[9] The trans-media Tarzan resembles Tarzan in the novel to a greater or lesser degree of correspondence, depending on the way he is represented by artists, actors, and film-makers working in other media. Further, variation in his representation has collateral effects on the audience.

To provide a background for this discussion, I borrow from recent theories of reception and spectatorship.[10] I take as a given that different pleasures exist for readers of a written text as compared to the viewers of a film. What is interesting is to see how the same iconic figure (Tarzan) can be presented in specific ways that cater to the pleasures of the specific medium of consumption. A look at the construction of various 'Tarzans' demonstrates some surprising, even strange, prejudices in the way Tarzan is represented in different media. To demonstrate these biases, I will focus on three inter-related elements of representation: language use, representation of the body, and melodrama.

TARZAN AND LANGUAGE

The majority of the film adaptations show Tarzan as mute, or nearly so. He never speaks English or any language with the sophistication of Tarzan in the novels, rather his portrayal is that of an 'ape-man', a savage. Many male action heroes ('the strong silent type') are reticent with language, as Steven Neale has pointed out with regard to Clint Eastwood, The Mad Max films and Steve Reeves epics.[11]

But the characterization of Tarzan as a mute on film is remarkably striking as the most dramatic deviation from the character of the novels. The novel shows Tarzan the polyglot, a self-taught linguistic genius able to speak English, French, German, Swahili, Arabic, as well as 'Ape-Language' and a number of primitive and pre-historic tongues. Wherever his many novelistic adventures take him – through the genres of Adventure, Romance, War, Science-Fiction, and Western – Tarzan cleverly converses, conveniently articulate in the local dialect.

Tarzan in print media is always portrayed as intimately connected with issues of language acquisition, language use, and the cultural determinacy a given language may impose. The medium of the novel demands audience literacy (the ability to read; knowledge of the semiotic code of language), thus a literate Tarzan becomes isomorphically believable. Self-taught literacy achieved in an intellectual struggle to acquire language is a sub-plot of the novel,[12] as is demonstrated when Tarzan looks at a child's primer in the debris of his long-dead parents' cabin:

> Slowly he turned the pages. Presently, he found a picture of another little ape and a strange animal that went on four legs like a jackal. Beneath this picture the bugs appeared as:
>
> A BOY AND A DOG
>
> And so he progressed very, very slowly, for it was a hard and laborious task he had set himself without knowing it – a task which might seem to you or me impossible – learning to read without having the slightest knowledge of letters or written language, or the faintest idea that such things existed . . . by the time he was seventeen he had learned to read the simple child's primer . . . from then on his progress was rapid. With the help of the great dictionary and the active intelligence of a healthy mind endowed by inheritance with more than ordinary reasoning powers.[13]

Movies do not require audience literacy, and on film, the issue of how Tarzan could acquire language is marginalized, leaving a near-mute Tarzan. The question of whether Tarzan could teach himself to read, while alone in the jungle is never an issue in the films.[14] They present his literacy developing only as a consequence of social contact. The films support the point of view that language is not necessarily innate, but 'begins within a supporting social context without which it does not function, and that the earliest functions of language are interactive, even imitative, rather than detached and personal.'[15] On film, Tarzan learns language from Jane or D'Arnot, in an 'interactive, imitative' manner. The anthropological facts suggest that only limited language acquisition would ever be possible for a feral child, but these facts are not at issue, instead the way the different media portray language acquisition becomes the question.[16] The humanistic Tarzan novels argue that language is an inherent product of Homo sapiens, a function of the individual human mind. The films, when they deal with this issue at all, show language as a result of social contact.

Social conventions of dress also create expectations about language. Tarzan on film is always muscular, fit and (wearing animal skins) connected to nature, suggesting that fur and muscles are biological, hence natural, whereas language and literacy are not natural but acquired through culture.[17] Tarzan's clothing (a loincloth) acts as a signal, indicating how well we expect him to speak. This expectation hinges on the cultural conventions, proper conditions (and dress) for 'conversation'. Conversation typically can be initiated in two acceptable modes among equal-status males in Western culture: first, between equally clothed men, as in the majority of social conversation. Second, between equally nude men, as in locker rooms, saunas, nude beaches, all areas designated by custom as 'nude'. But the third possible combination, conversation between clothed men and naked men, creates such power/status instabilities (awkward feelings on both sides) that conversation is uncomfortable, often impossible.[18] The Tarzan of the novels had 'low status' dress but 'high status' literacy, linguistic ability and lineage. Tarzan on film is displayed as a low-status member of society, due to his dress, hence social norms prejudice his presentation as illiterate and mute. I do not want to suggest that the films have reduced 'content' just because Tarzan barely speaks.[19] Rather my point is to show how the linguistic semiotic code has been subordinated to the visual semiotic code. In place of reading the written word, attention is focused on the erotic spectacle of the body.

TARZAN AND MELODRAMA

One could choose to read Tarzan as novel against Tarzan as film through a number of theoretical approaches, each offering insight.[20] However, reading the narrative as a 'jungle melodrama' is particularly relevant due to the strikingly different ways melodrama is created in the two media (a byproduct of language useage.)

Though Tarzan cannot speak English when he first encounters Jane Porter in the novel, he quickly learns to speak eloquently, even poetically, as when he (after great effort) catches up with Jane Porter in Baltimore:

> TARZAN: I have come across the ages out of the dim and distant past from the lair of the primeval man to claim you – for your sake I have become a civilized man – for your sake I will have crossed oceans and continents – for your sake I will be whatever you will me to be. I can make you happy Jane, in the life you know and love best. Will you marry me?[21]

This sort of over-the-top dialogue (poetic hyperbole) is characteristic of literary melodrama. While there are other devices and constructions used in literary melodrama, poetic hyperbole – dialogue that dares to proclaim the unsayable – is useful to my argument because it is intimately related to speech.[22] Also, poetic hyperbole is a major device used by literary melodrama to engage the reader's interest.

Tarzan in the movies is usually presented within the confines of the adventure-love story, genres frequently associated with the melodramatic. Remarkably, in Tarzan's case, the device used to achieve film melodrama is the polar opposite of the literary: Tarzan as film melodrama resorts to muteness. This is due, in part, to a presentational aesthetic developed in theatre melodrama and later borrowed by cinema.[23] The historical tradition of the power relation between muteness and speech has been discussed by Peter Brooks in *The Melodramatic Imagination*. His view on 'muteness' links it integrally to melodrama:

> Melodrama ... particularly in climactic moments and extreme situations has recourse to non-verbal means of expressing its meanings. Words ... appear to be not wholly adequate ... and the melodramatic message must be formulated through other registers of the sign.[24]

In *Tarzan of the Apes*, the whole narrative falls into the category of an 'extreme situation' where a baby has been raised by apes to manhood, only to encounter his true love (Jane Porter), a woman he cannot speak to but must protect from the hazards (climactic moments) of the jungle. With regard to Jane, Tarzans' actions speak louder than words. No task is too excessively dangerous to prove his love for her, be it killing lions, wrestling crocodiles, or fighting native tribes.

Brooks believes the impetus of melodrama is a striving to locate the 'good' in a Manichean universe, and the good or evil nature of characters is articulated through their appearance. 'The expressive means of melodrama are all predicated on ... the struggle toward recognition of the sign of virtue and innocence.'[25] Beginning in theatrical traditions, 'Evil' wears the cape, the black hat, the vulpine moustache, while 'Good' wears the white bonnet, the fair voice, or more literal symbols (e.g. a crucifix). Conflict between good and evil is the raw stuff of melodrama, as the audience waits to see virtuous characters emerge triumphant. Tarzan on film is marked as 'good' by his 'natural' appearance. Jane has a fair voice, a gentle touch. The villains in the jungle are the snakes in the garden, the hairy uncouth beasts and the black 'savages'.

Brooks elaborates that certain topoi mark the Manichean melodrama, and that 'remarkably prevalent is the enclosed garden, the space of innocence.[26]' Setting the story of Tarzan and Jane in the jungle immediately recalls the innocence of Eden [the biblical garden] with Tarzan and Jane standing in for Adam and Eve. Jane's arrival, like Eve's, ultimately brings Tarzan the knowledge of the outside world, a knowledge that eventually drives him from his Edenic jungle.

One particularly dramatic marker of 'virtue' can be muteness, since it renders the 'good' mute character incapable of defending himself against intimations of evil and false accusations. We masochistically watch Tarzan's suffering, oscillating between contemplation of Tarzan's plight and identification with it.[27] We know his intrinsic 'goodness' because his appearance is an idealization of man in nature (Rousseau's 'noble savage') and he has a 'classy' heredity: a displaced English Lord. But if Tarzan could speak, virtue's Manichean struggle to express itself would be over, because he could explain his identity to Jane.

Tarzan's muteness on film creates melodrama in a way that is the opposite of the literary technique (poetic hyperbole). Tarzan's inability to say what we know to be true, instantly engages a high level of empathy from the viewing audience who wish to see the situation redressed, resolved. The audience can easily feel the awful injustic of his situation: the noble Tarzan has saved Jane from wild beasts, yet he is perceived as a wild beast himself since he cannot communicate his nobility and she, overly civilized, cannot read the 'truth of his nature'. The sign of innocence is concealed, primarily by Tarzan's inability to speak and also in part by his appearance:

> His straight and perfect figure, muscled as the best of the ancient Roman gladiators must have been muscled, and yet with the soft and sinuous curves of a Greek god . . . a personification, was Tarzan of the Apes, of the primitive man, the hunter, the warrior. With the noble poise of his handsome head . . . he might readily have typified some demigod of a wild and warlike bygone people of his ancient forest.[28]

Though Tarzan's hyperbolically male appearance is a masculine ideal, it is not the ideal of civilization.[29] Jane, a product of post-Victorian culture, cannot regress to the level of the primitive to 'see' his virtue. However, when, in the original novel, Jane Porter is kidnapped by Terkoz, the giant ape, she first sees Tarzan as he comes to her rescue and 'to Jane, the strange apparition of this god-like man was as wine to sick nerves.'[30] Tarzan kills the huge bull gorilla in a fierce battle, ending the threat to Jane of the most lurid cross-species miscegenation. Jane rushes to clutch her saviour . . .

> And Tarzan? he did what no red-blooded man needs lessons in doing. He took his woman into his arms and smothered her upturned panting lips with kisses. For a moment, Jane lay there with half-closed eyes. For a moment – the first in her young life – she knew the meaning of Love. But as suddenly as the veil had been withdrawn it dropped again, and as an outraged conscience suffused her face with a scarlet mantle, and a mortified woman thrust Tarzan of the Apes from her and buried her face in her hands.[31]

More literary hyperbole . . . and the ensuing problem for Jane is that though Tarzan has saved her from a wild beast, he is, by appearances, a wild beast himself. Unable to speak his heart, Tarzan is left to demonstrate his chivalry by his actions as when, deep in the jungle, the two of them bed down for the night:

> Then Tarzan rose, and leading Jane to the little bower he had erected, motioned for her to go within. For the first time in hours a feeling of fear swept over her and Tarzan felt her draw away . . . Now in every fiber of his being, heredity spoke louder than training. He had not in one swift transition become a polished gentleman from a savage ape-man, but at last the instincts of the former predominated . . . so Tarzan did the only thing he knew to assure Jane of her safety. He removed his hunting knife from its sheath and handed it to her hilt first, again motionining her into the bower.[32]

Tarzan and Jane spend the night sleeping with the knife between them in the tradition of the codes of chivalry, Tarzan in the role of 'knight-protector' and Jane in the role of 'virgin-maiden.' The scene further demonstrates Brooks' idea that melodrama strives to locate hidden virtue and innocence in an individual.[33] In this case, recognition is accomplished by allusion to the literary-historical codes of chivalry.

TARZAN AS EROTIC SPECTACLE

The power-relations of melodrama take on added dimensions when we consider that Tarzan is not only mute, but nearly naked. This aspect has minimal impact in the novel, but in movie and TV versions, Tarzan's lack of clothes becomes powerfully foregrounded.[34] Richard Dyer, writing in *Screen*, has discussed the presentational aesthetics of the nude male body in cinema, arguing nudity and the spectatorial gaze are 'the fundamental ways by which power relations between the sexes are maintained.'[35] Women – particularly nude or semi-nude women – are frequently presented as the 'sexual spectacle', subject of the masculine gaze of the audience. The positioning of Tarzan in this role of nude sexual spectacle, may cause 'instabilities' in audiences. To place Tarzan thus is a violation of established codes of spectatorship. As Laura Mulvey has noted: 'Traditionally, the woman displayed has functioned on two levels, as erotic object for characters within the screen story and as erotic object for the spectator within the auditorium.'[36] Tarzan's near-nude appearance foregrounds his potential as 'erotic object' and suggests two possibilities: 1)

[handwritten margin notes: "- Violence", "- Fight all, men want to be like this", "- Fight all, holds family"]

heterosexual eroticism by female viewers, 2) homosexual eroticism by male viewers. However, Tarzan has always had phenomenal box-office appeal to a mainstream male audience. A reason for this appeal is also suggested by Mulvey: Pleasure 'developed through narcissism and the constitution of the ego, comes from narcissistic identification with the image seen ... as the spectator identifies with the main male protagonist [his screen surrogate] the power of the male protagonist coincides with the active power of the erotic look, both giving a satisfying sense of omnipotence.'[37] In other words, a large part of the male audience enjoys a narcissistic identification with the power-fantasy suggested by Tarzan's strength and command of nature. This desire to experience a fantasy of greater power can be seen in children, who regularly adopt 'roles' of super heroes, adults, sports figures and royalty in their play. In adults, such fantasy is usually repressed, but film entertainment provides a vehicle for re-activating these fantasies.

The nudity taboos of our 'civilized' (Western patriarchal) culture are more easily broken in a man who lacks speech as well as clothes. This is a further melodramatic component to the presentational aspect of Tarzan: the hyperbolic situation implicit in a 'nude nobleman'. Anthropologist Desmond Morris' ideas on nudity taboos are useful in illuminating this situation.[38] Morris notes that 'the more anti-sexual the society, the more all-covering the clothing.'[39] This becomes interesting when we consider Tarzan as a product of the Victorian age, the most sexually repressive period in British and American history.[40] Burroughs wrote the novel ten years after the death of Victoria, but he set the action in the period 1888-1912, a time when the restrictive influences of the Victorian age were powerful throughout the English-speaking world. *Tarzan of the Apes* offers a narrative that presents a rarely-beheld (hence titillating) spectacle: a displaced Victorian aristocrat in a loincloth. The typical use of clothing to signal status is denied Tarzan, and in this way, too, we have the melodramatic situation of the inability to express the sign of virtue. Tarzan cannot verbalize his nobility, and worse, his clothes suggest just the opposite, that he is a savage.[41]

Another element of the Tarzan power-dynamic is suggested by Dyer's article. He points to a convention of the nude male pin-up which discourages the model from smiling[42], a convention that is almost universally adhered to in Tarzan movies. Tarzan is a serious fellow. The image of the male pin-up as unsmiling and passive is redeemed by the frequent portrayal of 'masculinity-as-activity ... muscularity as the sign of power – natural, achieved, phallic'[43]. The melodramatic consequence of an unsmiling Tarzan is a further concealment of the sign of innocence – the audience doesn't know his internal emotional state – and the portrayal of Tarzan as long-suffering, stoically heroic.

Of the forty-three Tarzan films, I have chosen a representative four
that particularly illuminate the relations between language, melodrama
and the erotic spectacle. These are: the first silent *Tarzan of the Apes*
(Scott Sidney, National, 1912,) the first sound *Tarzan the Ape-man*
(W.S. Van Dyke, MGM, 1938,) *Tarzan the Ape-man* (John Derek,
1981) and *Greystoke, The Legend of Tarzan* (Hugh Hudson, 1984).
Each of these films presents a Tarzan who is the linguistic inferior of
his print-media counterpart and prioritizes the physicality of the male
body in action.

The first screen version was filmed in 1917 by the National Film
Corporation at a time when the use of intertitles to explain the silent
narrative was the norm. Consequently, audience literacy was required
for full comprehension of the story. In this version Scott Sidney
directed an accurate adaptation of the novel featuring Elmo Lincoln, a
muscular character actor, in the role of Tarzan. From the beginning,
the physicality of the actor chosen to portray Tarzan was the central
issue in casting for the role.[44] Elmo appears in the film with a wild
shock of hair (a wig), scanty fur shorts, and a garland of vines over his
shoulder. His near-nudity is all the more striking when he appears
with Jane (Enid Markey) who wears a loose-fitting long-sleeved
mid-calf length dress. Jane's feminine figure is hidden and Tarzan's
physique becomes the object of display. In this version Tarzan learns
to speak limited English (presented in intertitles) from an American
sailor named Binns.[45] This is interesting because the silent film
versions offered a considerably more literate and cosmopolitan Tarzan
than later sound films. In part this was due to the attempt to have the
language of the intertitles approximate the language in the novel. For
audiences of the time, there was no problem in reconciling the image of
a wild jungle man with literate speech, and the film was very
successful, one of the first silents to gross over a million dollars.[46]   In
1929, the trans-media adaptation of Tarzan extended to a newspaper
comic strip drawn by Hal Foster. Comics can be seen as an
intermediary form between print and film, requiring literacy but also
offering the pleasure of graphic images. This medium, as in silent films,
created dialogue for Tarzan that borrowed from the novels.
Consequently, Tarzan's character in comics shows the same kind of
innate intelligence as the novel's Tarzan offers. The artists adapting
Tarzan to comics and newspapers were concerned with the artistic
depiction of Tarzan's image, but also with the re-representation of the
novel's text as it would appear in the comic. Advanced literacy was not
crucial to reading Tarzan as a novel or as a comic strip, however, with
the advent of sound film in 1929, audience literacy was no longer

Elmo Lincoln as Tarzan, circa 1917. (MGM, 1917)

relevant in the consumption of motion pictures. Film consumption moved from the visual-textual (intertitles) mode of the silent years to the visual-aural (sound) mode, emphasizing the spoken over the written.[47]

The 1932 MGM production of *Tarzan, The Ape-Man*, was the first sound version. Louis B. Mayer and Irving Thalberg set director William S. Van Dyke to film the 'biggest, most colossal jungle epic to date.'[48] Their search for a lead in the Tarzan role was again based primarily on physicality, and after interviewing a number of athletes they chose Johnny Weissmuller, the muscular 1924 and 1928 Olympic champion swimmer.[49] Interestingly, screenwriter Cyril Hume and playwright Ivor Novello rendered an adaptation of Burroughs novel that omitted all reference to Tarzan's origin or status as a displaced British Lord, believing that for American audiences, a melodrama involving a nude aristocrat held less thrill potential than the melodramatic jungle love interest between Tarzan and Jane Porter, an American girl. The film was a huge success, one of the top ten grossing films of 1932. Weissmuller had become a box-office draw of the order of Cooper, Harlow, and Gable.

Weissmuller portrays Tarzan as a savage. His only apparel is a thong waistband and buckskin loincloth, considerably more revealing than the costumes worn by previous Tarzans, many of whom wore an over-the-shoulder leopard-skin tunic. Jane (Maureen O'Sullivan) wears a short-sleeved shirt and knee-length skirt, making Tarzan the focus of bodily display. Initially, Weissmuller's Tarzan speaks in grunts with apes and other wild animals. Jane is the vehicle whereby he learns English in a memorable scene where she reveals the function of proper nouns and names herself: 'Jane'. Quickly gasping this abstraction, Tarzan points to Jane and himself while saying 'Tarzan-Jane, Tarzan-Jane, Tarzan-Jane, Tarzan-Jane, Tarzan-Jane . . .' until Jane is reduced to tears of frustration. Weissmuller's Tarzan never passes much beyond this rudimentary level of spoken English. One reason for Tarzan's limited dialogue was undoubtedly a desire on the part of the producers to leave the neophyte actor Weissmuller unburdened with dialogue, but he did not really need to speak, since he was there to be seen, not heard. The unprecedented success of this version of the film had a side-effect:

> In this film Tarzan changed from an intelligent well-spoken English Lord into an unintelligent white ape. The sophistication . . . of the silent era . . . was lost, nonexistent to Metro's crude jungle man who was on the same level with beasts . . . Weissmuller's portrayal became the prototype for later Tarzans.[50]

Johnny Weissmuller as Tarzan, circa 1932. (MGM, 1932)

The fact that the first *sound* version was a box-office hit goes a long way toward explaining subsequent adaptations depicting Tarzan as a near-mute ape-man. However, this historical perspective does not completely explain why the audience reacted equally strongly to an iconic representation of Tarzan that is, in certain aspects, the antithesis of the character presented in the novel. Certainly a mute and savage Sherlock Holmes would not be of equal interest to an audience accustomed to the intellectual Holmes. And part of Tarzan's struggle in the novel is an intellectual one, a point rarely pursued on film.[51] Is the audience appeal of Tarzan in films centered solely on physical spectacle?

A paradox seems to emerge: the melodramatic novel (hugely popular) shows a castaway English aristocrat while the melodramatic film (also hugely popular) presents man as wild jungle beast. In each case, melodrama is achieved via different means. The popularity of the novel can be explained through the emphatic appeal of transformation, the change from savage to civilized as a consequence of learning combined with the thrilling conceit that man can conquer nature. Tarzan becomes an icon of change, literally a 'swinging signifier'. Everyone wants to believe they can fulfill their potential and gain mastery over their environment. Tarzan, as presented in the novel, provides an extreme example of social mobility.

The popularity of the second, 'crude jungle man' iconic representation is fixed to the primitive appeal of man in nature (a la Rousseau), combined with the visual spectacle of male physicality. In part, Weissmuller's Tarzan gained popularity because he embodies nature:

> Naturalness, a fame for inner qualities, for what one is without the overlay of social forms. It is a fame of feeling, a 'natural fame', that is held personally without forbears or tradition, and rejects any honor or virtue that must be validated by social position.[52]

Weissmuller's Tarzan is an 'American Tarzan', classless, ruggedly individual, stoic: the visual-aural Tarzan. Attention centered on Tarzan's appearance (sleekly muscled, 'natural') but not what he says ('Hungawa!') Visual form is elevated beyond verbal content. Moreover, the prioritization of what is seen over what is said continues in Tarzan films up to the present.

In 1980, for instance, John Derek was looking for a vehicle for his wife, Bo, who had been elevated to pop-culture icon status by Blake Edward's comedy *10* (1979). He discovered that MGM still had legal claim to both the title 'Tarzan, The Ape Man', and the story as scripted in the MGM 1931 version. Derek's *Tarzan, The Ape-man* (1981) is not a re-make of the novel, but a re-adaptation of the earlier film. This version's Tarzan is Miles O'Keefe, male physique model with a stunningly muscular form and a beautiful face. Remarkably, O'Keefe actually manages to say absolutely nothing. His only utterance is an occasional 'Tarzan yell'. His loincloth is very similar in design to Weissmuller's, but fractionally more revealing. Though the film's plot is very similar to the earlier version, the story now focuses on Jane 'Parker' (a revision from Porter), a repressed Victorian girl who travels to Africa in 1910 in search of her father only to find liberation and sexual freedom in an Edenic jungle. This film was the first Tarzan film that attempted to shift the role of sexual spectacle from Tarzan to Jane. Bo Derek as Jane wears a diaphanous dress that becomes virtually transparent when wet (and it gets wet frequently).

Offended by this version, the Burroughs estate sued the Dereks, trying to prevent the release of the film because it showed 'too much nudity and not enough of the apeman and was, therefore a violation of the 1931 licensing agreement between the estate and MGM'.[53] The studio submitted the film to District Judge Henry Werker who ordered that the film be edited, and then re-edited, to comply with the intent of the 1931 agreement.[54] The film was released without Bo's nudity, but gained publicity on the censorship issue and by a concurrent *Playboy* magazine photo-essay on the film.[55] However, the court-ordered effect of keeping Bo in clothes was only to heighten, by contrast, the striking male beauty of Miles O'Keefe. This version of Tarzan supports Richard Dyer's arguments on male spectacle and power relations. Consistent with the prevailing conventions of male nudity, O'Keefe's Tarzan *never* smiles, an issue directly addressed in a scene where Jane unsuccessfully tries to teach him to do so. Despite the attempt in this version to foreground female sexuality, the spectator's gaze (and Jane's gaze) keeps returning to the near-nude Tarzan as object of beauty. In one scene Jane tells Tarzan: 'Do you know you're more beautiful than any girl I know? Oh, you're a *lot* more'. In another example, after Tarzan is rendered unconscious by wrestling a comatose python, Jane comes to his side and takes advantage of the opportunity to caress and examine Tarzan's body in a series of close-ups. The viewer, positioned as Jane, cannot avoid eroticizing the male body. Steve Neale has suggested that when the male body is the object of the erotic look in cinema it is often 'feminized', to avoid the problem mainstream cinema's 'masculine gaze' typically has in coming to terms with homosexuality.[56] Neale's example is narcissistic male dancer John Travolta in *Saturday Night Fever* (John Badham, US, 1978). Tarzan, though eroticized, is not feminized, and his hyperbolically male actions (i.e. wrestling gorillas) prevent any considerations of homosexuality.

In 1981, director Hugh Hudson, fresh from a 'best picture' academy award for *Chariots of Fire* (1981) planned to make the definitive Tarzan through a return to the novel and the central nature-nurture controversy, i.e. the novel's idea of man (particularly the British aristocracy) as genetically superior to beasts, able to triumph in any situation because of innate virtue, Tarzan, though nurtured by apes will rise above his environment because of his inborn nature. Even the title: *Greystoke, The Legend of Tarzan* (1984), articulates the pro-aristocratic agenda, foregrounding the lordly 'Greystoke' rather than the exotic 'Tarzan'. 'The legend of . . .' suggests the legendary dimension accorded British aristocracy from Arthurian times. *Greystoke* portrays Tarzan first as natural and wild, later as civilized and aristocratic. The key markers of this change are speech and clothing. As Tarzan moves into the civilized world by acquiring literacy and language, he also begins to wear European clothes which mark his status. Putting Tarzan in clothes removes the pleasure the audience derives from the spectacle of the 'natural, jungle' animalistic male that has been hidden by 'civilization'. Spectators may feel the loss of Tarzan's beautiful body as an object for contemplation.[57]

Accordingly, with the introduction of speech and culture, *Greystoke* moves toward literary melodrama, specifically the tradition of the Gothic novel where a heroine in a mysterious house falls in love with a mysterious man.[58] The end of the film seems more like a strange version of *Jane Eyre* with Tarzan playing the tormented (by etiquette) Lord of the manor and Jane the sexually frustrated governess fascinated by the danger of a relationship. In representative scenes, Jane teaches Tarzan to conjugate the latin verb 'to love', while later the two exchange a torrid midnight kiss on the stairs and declare their forbidden desire.

TRANS-MEDIA FORMATIONS OF TARZAN

The evidence reveals a marked tendency for the movies to represent Tarzan as an erotic spectacle. The long-term success of this representation suggests that the pleasure of the erotic spectacle has been a factor in maintaining audience interest in an otherwise familiar narrative.

The novel cannot offer 'erotic spectacle', which may explain why so few people read *Tarzan of the Apes* anymore. The novel's focus on Tarzan's transformation from savage to civilized elicits a visceral appeal as well as intellectual interest. It shows the transformation from illiteracy to literacy, ignorance to knowledge, jungle to civilization, poverty to wealth, orphan to family, nudity to clothing, nature to culture. No film adaptations focus on this transformative element, preferring instead to fix Tarzan in the jungle mode where he can be exploited as erotic spectacle.

In summation, it becomes clear that a major factor in the representation of the iconic figure of Tarzan is the nature of the medium – novel, comic-strip, or movie – and that different media prioritize different pleasures for the consumer. Consequently, different pleasures require the iconic figure to be represented in different ways. The novel uses devices of melodramatic literature to popularize a story of one man's climb up the evolutionary ladder to civilization. Comic-strip versions walk a 'middle-path', remaining primarily faithful to the language of the novel but offering dramatic artwork of Tarzan in action.[59] The films borrow from the conventions of theatre melodrama to present a mute Tarzan, offering the audience the wish-fulfilment of an idyllic return to nature and the chance to abandon the civilization of writing; to see the naked ape, Tarzan revealed.

NOTES

I would like to thank Marsha Kinder, David James, Pat Kirkham, and Majda Anderson for their comments on drafts of this article.

1 'Pulps' were mass-produced magazines printed on the cheapest 'pulp' paper. They were an immensely popular medium from 1890 until WW Two. Burroughs and many other famous authors read and were first published in this medium. For a good overview, see Peter Haining's *The Fantastic Pulps*, Random House, New York, 1975.

2 Burroughs' Tarzan was influenced by (among others) Stanley's *In Darkest Africa*, Kipling's *Jungle Books*, Haggard's *Nada the Lily* and *SHE*, The Romulus and Remus myth, Prentice's *Captured By Apes; or how Philip Garland became King of Apeland*, possibly Swift's *Gulliver's Travels*, and Defoe's *Robinson Crusoe*. See Gottesman, Ron and Geduld, Harry. *The Girl in the Hairy Paw*, Avon Books, New York, 1976.

3 For a complete biography of Burroughs see Richard Lupoff, *Edgar Rice Burroughs: Master of Adventure*, Avon Books, New York, 1968. This is a laudatory history of Burroughs' life, works, adventures and literary endeavours.

4 Gabe Essoe, *Tarzan of the Movies*, Citadel Press, Syracuse, N.J., 1979. Read this for a good and heavily-illustrated historical overview of the Tarzan films made between 1917 and 1968; contains primarily history, production data, and business-oriented information.

5 364 fifteen-minute records that pioneered the pre-recorded radio show were broadcast widely in the USA, South America, and Western Europe. See Essoe, *op. cit.* p6.

6 The 'Tarzan' name was leased for advertising to consumer-oriented industrial concerns like the H.J. Heinz, Reed Tobacco Co., Royal Baking

Powder Co. and the Signal Oil and Gas, Co. which applied Tarzan to their point-of purchase advertisements at roadside gasoline stations with signs reading: 'The POWER of Tarzan ... Signal Gasoline.' See Essoe, *op. cit.* p9.

7 Bill Nichols, *IDEOLOGY and the IMAGE: Social Representation in the Cinema and Other Media*, Indiana Univ. Press, Bloomington, Indiana, 1981, p51. Nichols' definition fits in with Fredric Jameson's notion of a 'postmodern late capitalism' characterized by recycling stories and images across media. See *Postmodernism: the Cultural Logic of Late Capitalism*, Duke University Press, Durham, North Carolina, 1991. See Chap. 1, 'Culture', for a thorough discussion of how aesthetic production has become integrated with commodity production. Also, see p123 of *Playing with Power*, University of California Press, Berkeley, 1991 for Marsha Kinder's discussion of marketing 'supersystems': the networks of intertextuality that can be constructed around figures (from Tarzan to Teenage Mutant Ninja Turtles) in popular culture.

8 See Nichols, *op. cit.* p11, on the nature of digital, iconic, and indexical signs.

9 My approach can also be read in support of certain ideas of communications theorist Marshall ('The medium is the message') McLuhan.

10 In literary studies, 'reception theory' explores the way readers read and comprehend literature. The central argument is an epistemological one, exploring the way readers use their critical and intellectual capabilities to unravel the semiotic code of language into an intelligible narrative whole. e.g. the work of Wolfang Iser (*The Act of Reading*, Johns Hopkins Univ. Press, Baltimore, 1978), Stanley Fish and others. In film studies, 'spectatorship' theory describes how viewers get pleasure from watching movies. The goal is 'positioning' the spectator – sexually, politically, psychologically – to understand viewers empathic response, and concomitant pleasure. Examples are found in the (often feminist/ psychoanalytic) work of Laura Mulvey (*Visual Pleasure and the Narrative Cinema*) Christian Metz, Mary Ann Doane, Gaylyn Studlar (*Masochism and The Perverse Pleasures of the Cinema,*) Daniel Dayan (*The Tutor-Code of Classical Cinema*) and Jean-Louis Baudry (*Ideological Effects of the Basic Cinematographic Apparatus.*)

11 Steve Neale, 'Masculinity as Spectacle', *Screen*, Vol. 24, no. 6 Nov.-Dec. 1983. Neale re-reads Laura Mulvey's work and relates it to male representation on the screen.

12 As developed primarily in chapters 6, 7, 12 of the novel. See Edgar Rice Burroughs, *Tarzan of The Apes*, Ballantine Books, New York, 1977. Authorized, complete and unabridged reprint of the 1912 text.

13 Burroughs *op. cit.*, chap. 7 'The Light of Knowledge'.

14 See James C. Raymond (ed.), *Literacy: As A Human Problem*. University of Alabama Press, 1982. A collection of papers presented at the 6th Alabama Symposium on English and American Literature, 1979.

15 Arthur N. Appleby, *The Child's Concept of Story*. University of Chicago Press, Chicago, 1989, p30.

16 In 1800, Dr Jean Itard raised the Wild Boy of Aveyron. In the 1920s Dr

J.A.L. Singh raised two feral girls, aged two and eight. In 1970, Genie, a two year old kept in a closet by her demented father for eleven years was released. None of these children ever acquired more than rudimentary linguistic skills.

17 Richard Dyer, 'Don't Look Now', *Screen*, Vol. 23, No. 3-4, 1982, p71. Dyer makes the 'biological equals natural' point in his article.

18 Think of the last time you saw a naked man – phallus visible – speaking dialogue in a Hollywood film. Never? This may well be the case. Even in the arena of the pornographic film, conversation is usually at a minimum.

19 Critic Roland Barthes has suggested that: 'At the level of mass communications, it appears that the linguistic message is indeed present in every image . . . we are still, and more than ever, a civilization of writing'. Barthes is *literally* correct, for the message that comes across in the novel, but not in the films is that *CIVILIZATION = WRITING*. See Roland Barthes, *Image-Music-Text*, Noonday Press, New York, 1977.

20 For example, one might look at John Newsinger's 'Reader, He Rescued Her: Women in the Tarzan Stories', an interesting feminist reading of Tarzan in *Foundation*, Number 39, Spring 1987, pp41-50.

21 Burroughs, *op. cit.* chap. 29, 'Conclusion'.

22 The other devices and constructions that might be mentioned as emblematic are Manichean conflicts between one-dimensional heroes and villains that are conveniently resolved at the last moment, with good triumphant. Further markers are: little internal story logic and sensational or exotic locations (boudoirs and dungeons). When the exotic location is a castle or estate, the genre may blur with the Gothic. See F. Rahill's *The World of Melodrama*.

23 Numerous writers have discussed the history and nature of this connection between the theater and the development of the movies. See David A. Cook's *A History of the Narrative Film*, W.W. Norton & Co. New York, 1981 or Susan Sontag's revisionist essay 'Theatre and Film' in *Styles of Radical Will*, Farrar, Straus & Giroux, New York, 1966.

24 Peter Brooks' *The Melodramatic Imagination*, Columbia University Press, New York, 1985, p56.

25 *Ibid.* p58.

26 *Ibid.* p29.

27 Masochism in viewer identification has been discussed by D.N. Rodowick in 'The Difficulty of Difference', *Wide Angle*, Vol. 5, No. 1, p8.

28 Burroughs, *op. cit.* chap. 13, 'His own Kind'.

29 A 'masculine ideal' as promoted by Western culture, in the mode of the nature-conquering heroes ranging from Hercules to James Fenimore Cooper's Natty Bumppo, and depicted in robust muscular condition in countless renditions of art from old masters to fantasy illustrators (i.e. Superman).

30 Burroughs, *op. cit.* chap. 19, 'Call of the Primitive.'

31 *Ibid.*

32 *Ibid.*, chap. 20, 'Heredity'.

33 Brooks, *op. cit.* p28.

34 Various film theorists have struggled to find a semiotic method that would

reveal the 'language of cinema', the way spectators 'read' meaning out of movies. This is no easy task, as noted by Christian Metz's conclusion that a 'cinematographic language' per se does not exist in the sense we commonly understand language. For Metz, 'cinema' is composed of several semiotic 'systems' operating together. For Metz's full discussion, see 'On the Notion of a Cinematographic Language' in *Movies and Methods*, V. I, Bill Nichols, (ed.), University of California Press, 1976.

35 Dyer, *op. cit.* pp61-72.

36 Laura Mulvey, 'Visual Pleasure and the Narrative Cinema', *Screen* 16, no. 3, 1975.

37 *Ibid.*, under 'C Sections II'.

38 Desmond Morris in *Manwatching*, Cape, London 1977, p213 noted that clothing has three functions: comfort, modesty and display. Comfort hinges on utilitarian uses of clothing while display describes the use of clothes to signal social status. Modesty refers to the use of clothes as a device which conceals sexual signals.

39 *Ibid.* p216.

40 Victoria (1837-1901), of the House of Hanover, reigned for 63 years.

41 The melodramatic device of a nobleman in pauper's clothes has been used in literature regularly, e.g. *The Prince and the Pauper, The Prisoner of Zenda, Star Wars*, etc.

42 Dyer, *op. cit.*

43 Dyer, *op. cit.*

44 Prior to Tarzan, Elmo Lincoln had already established himself as an icon of physical strength with roles as a blacksmith (*Birth of a Nation*), soldier (*Brute Force*), and bodyguard (*Intolerance*) in D.W. Griffith's films.

45 This differs from the novel where Tarzan learns French from Lt. Paul D'Arnot. In all likelihood, the French into English change was a concession to the public, since a French-speaking, English-literate, jungle lord was beyond the conventions of literacy in intertitles.

46 And spurring two silent sequels, Essoe, *op. cit.* p15.

47 In the words of theorist Bela Balazs: 'The sound film struck the first blow at the visual art of the silent film . . . it would destroy the already highly developed culture of the silent film.' Bela Balazs, *Theory of Film*. Dennis Dobson Inc., London, 1952, p194.

48 Essoe, *op. cit.* p67.

49 Walter Benjamin in 'The Work of Art in The Age of Mechanical Reproduction' (*Illuminations*, Harcourt, Brace, Jovanovich, New York, 1968) quotes Rudolf Arnheim: 'The actor [is now] a stage prop chosen for its characteristics and inserted at the proper place.' Thus, the authentic Olympic champion's 'aura' of physical mastery is used as a basis for the filmic Tarzan character.

50 Essoe, *op. cit.* p27.

51 A part of the novel deals with Tarzan groping to understand his own 'human' nature and his struggle to acquire and understand culture.

52 Leo Braudy, *The Frenzy of Reknown: Fame and its History*, Oxford Univ. Press, Oxford, 1986, p. 372.

53 Peter Boyer in the *L.A. Times*, 7/11/81. Burroughs had the foresight to

retain ownership and control of nearly all of his literary properties, including Tarzan, and even after his death, the Burroughs estate has sought to keep Burroughs' work within the vein it was originally written.

54 John Derek said: 'The Judge ordered out, on every frame of the film, Bo's nudity . . . 90% of Bo's nudity will be cut out. If that's not censorship, I don't know what is . . . my Darling little Bo is not going along with [the decision] and I pray to God that MGM doesn't.' Boyer, *Ibid.*

55 The film earned a respectable $30 million at the box office. *Playboy* magazine featured Bo on the cover and an intertextual photo-feature of Bo inside (nude scenes missing from the film).

56 Neale, *op. cit.* p15. Critic Steve Tropiano has made an interesting response to Neale's piece, questioning the definition of a 'feminizied' male, and suggesting the dynamics of representation and the gaze are more complex, particularly in other genres as represented by the masochistic males in 1950's films (Brando, Clift, Dean).

57 Pam Cook in 'Masculinity in Crisis', *Screen*, Vol. 23, No. 3-4, 1982, makes the same point about the demise of Robert DeNiro's physique in *Raging Bull*.

58 For an excellent explanation of the workings of the gothic novel see Tania Modleski's *Loving With a Vengeance*, Methuen, New York, 1982, chap. III 'The Female Uncanny:Gothic Novels for Women'.

59 Thorough development of my ideas on Tarzan in comics and the image-text connection will be presented in the book I am currently writing.

'Do You Walk the Walk?': Aspects of Masculinity in Some Vietnam War Films

John Newsinger

All war films are tales of masculinity. They are stories of boys becoming men, of comradeship and loyalty, of bravery and endurance, of pain and suffering, of the horror and the excitement of battle. Violence – the ability both to inflict and to take it – is portrayed as an essential part of what being a man involves. What is interesting about a number of recent popular films concerned with the Vietnam War, however, is the extent to which they go beyond this to reveal a fractured masculinity, a masculinity that is under pressure, that has been found wanting. There are a handful of important films, beginning with *Apocalypse Now* (Francis Coppola, US, 1979) and continuing through *Platoon* (Oliver Stone, US, 1986) and *Full Metal Jacket* (Stanley Kubrick, US, 1987) to *Casualties of War* (Brian de Palma, US, 1989) that have called American masculinity into question. These films have shown it as unable to cope with the problems and dilemmas, the stresses and horrors that confronted it in Vietnam. This questioning is one of the consequences of a lost war against a Third World people although it does not yet amount to anything like a critique of American Imperialism. What it does indicate, however, is the presence of a radical distaste for colonial adventures and their conduct that certainly has no equivalent in British popular culture. This study will look at the way in which the American male is shown at war in Vietnam in a small sample of films, some of which question, and some of which validate, American masculinity in its martial guise.[1]

Our starting point is Francis Coppola's *Apocalypse Now*, the story of Captain Willard's journey up river to find and kill Colonel Kurtz, a Special Forces Officer, who has gone 'native', surrendered to 'the heart of darkness'. Willard himself is clearly a tormented man, a younger version of what Kurtz has become, a man with a desperate need for the jungle and combat. Every minute that he stays in his hotel room, away from the war, he gets weaker, while his faceless enemy out in the jungle, 'Charlie', gets stronger. Willard is at last given a mission, a mission that takes him on an exploration of the American experience in Vietnam.

Willard's journey provides the opportunity for an examination of a number of aspects of American culture from the perspective of the war: surfing, rock and roll, *Playboy* magazines and, inevitably, the Western. All are implicated in the conflict. Young Americans are shown water-skiing, rock and rolling, surfing, having a beach party and living out reality through the myth of the Western. The film introduces the Air Cavalry and their contemporary Colonel Custer, Colonel Kilgore, who are to assist Willard in proceeding on his way. The appalling Kilgore ('I love the smell of napalm in the morning'), complete with cavalry hat, leads his heavily-armed helicopters in a devastating attack on a Vietnamese village in order to use their beach for surfing. This wholly manic operation takes place quite simply because one of the crew of Willard's boat is a celebrated surfer and Kilgore wants to see him in action. The exigencies of American culture meet the exigencies of war and the accompanying pyrotechnics are appropriately spectacular.

From this almost comic atrocity, Willard and his boat proceed to the Hau Phat base and depot, a brightly lit American nightspot set down in the middle of the hostile jungle. Here they see the *Playboy* show, with its giant, phallic bullets in the background, sent to entertain the troops. A male fantasy is brought to Vietnam and staged before hundreds of soldiers who proceed to run riot. The young women barely escape from their audience: the whole incident is portrayed as one of men out of control, of men driven mad. This is Coppola's vision of the conflict, at least in this film: *Apocalypse Now* is the Vietnam War as madness. Here all the symbolic attributes of American masculinity have become part of the madness: surfing under fire off a blazing village, the 'Playgirl of the Month' teasing in the jungle, the western-style heroics of the Air Cavalry; they are all symptoms of a masculine culture that cannot cope with this particular war.

This theme is explored further as the boat proceeds, through a nightmare landscape, up river. The crew, 'mostly kids, rock and rollers with one foot in their graves', as Willard describes them, are ordinary, pleasant young men, completely out of their depth. They are put to the test when they stop and search a Vietnamese family's sampan.

Obviously terrified, the men's fear manifests itself as bullying and brutality; a sudden movement by a young girl to protect her puppy and they massacre the whole family in a crescendo of gunfire. This scared, trigger-happy slaughter then develops into an attempt to save the life of the young girl who is severely wounded. Willard ends this charade by delivering the coup de grace, no humanitarian concerns must be allowed to interfere with his mission. These young men are not equipped to fight the kind of war they have been thrust into. None of their cultural references are appropriate; they veer from brutality to sentimentality. In the aftermath of the massacre the crew disintegrate. They are driven mad.

As the journey up river proceeds it becomes clear that Willard is following the same route as that earlier taken by Kurtz, not just geographically but also experientially. For him, as for Kurtz, the logic of the war is to embrace ruthlessness, to regard it as a kind of clarity, as the ability to see what has to be done and then doing it quickly, effectively and with full awareness. What he finds, however, is not clarity but a complete surrender to barbarism. Willard arrives at a veritable charnal house, the camp where Kurtz, surrounded by the heads of his Vietcong enemies, rules over his Montagnard followers, mercenary tribesmen in the pay of the US Special Forces. The warrior king has not found clarity: instead he has exchanged the American way for the barbaric madness of what is presented as an older and more 'primitive' culture.

What we see in the controversial, final section of the film is the supplanting of American cultural references by a barbarism that one suspects owes more to Sir James Frazer's *The Golden Bough* than to Montagnard culture.[2] Kurtz tests Willard to discover if he is fit and then proceeds to offer himself up to be sacrificed like a bullock by the new warrior king (Willard) who has come to succeed him. This confrontation at the heart of darkness is, of course, very much an exclusive, masculine affair. The ways of killing and war are the ways of men, but Kurtz has gone too far. Where Kurtz's journey ended in surrender to this barbarism, Willard, we are led to believe, might be able to find his way back. He survives to bear witness to the horror.

The notion that the logic of the Vietnam War involved a descent into madness and barbarism was a very powerful one but it was not to inform the work of other directors. The aspect of *Apocalypse Now* that was drawn on in subsequent Vietnam War films was its juxtaposition of American culture with the brutal realities of a war in a Third World country. The madness remained recognisably American rather than being a journey into some existential, barbaric heart of darkness. Coppola's images of apocalypse were replaced by more domestic concerns: the effects of the war on young American males, how they coped with the experience of the conflict and how well their masculinity was able to survive this particularly grim rite of passage.

The film that was to make the Vietnam War a viable commercial proposition, at least as far as Hollywood was concerned, was Oliver Stone's *Platoon*. This is very much a boys-into-men war story, but it asks an additional question that Vietnam often seems to have posed, namely, what kind of men? The film offers two alternative masculinities, the Jekyll and the Hyde, represented by the two Sergeants Elias and Burns. Both men are 'good' soldiers in the sense that they both try to look after their own troops and to kill the enemy. Burns, however, is scarred, twisted, tortured and has become the embodiment of the war with all of its cruelty and murderous brutality. He is 'reality', or so he tells Elias's adherents among the troops; there is no escaping him. Elias, in stark contrast, has retained his humanity, his humour, his sympathy for his fellows, his capacity for tenderness and love. The film shows the developing conflict between these two men as a struggle for the soul of the new arrival, the 'cherry', Chris Taylor.

Taylor finds himself with a choice of peer groups: the 'red-necks', all eaten up with hatred, violence and machismo, or the 'heads', the laid-back, drug-using rock and rollers, both black and white, who refuse to let the war take over their whole being. The first group is characterised by an aggressive competition for power and status between its members with Burns as top dog; the second adopts a sensual hedonism that makes affection between men possible and legitimate. While Burns is feared, Elias is loved.

In a remarkable 'bordello' scene, Taylor is seduced into the ranks of the 'heads' by Elias. When he first enters their dug-out to the accompaniment of Jefferson Airplane's psychedelic 'White Rabbit', he is confronted by a half-naked Elias draped provocatively over a hammock. The Sergeant asks him if this is his first time, then tells him to 'put your mouth on this' and gets Taylor to inhale marijuana smoke through a rifle barrel. The scene is charged with sexuality and homoeroticism; it ends with the stoned soldiers all dancing with each other. It is cut with a comparable scene of the red-necks relaxing, biting chunks out of beer cans, throwing knives, playing cards, being tough.[3]

The conflict comes to a head when the unit occupies a Vietnamese village and comes near to massacring the inhabitants. One of their number has been killed and they are out for vengeance. In the grip of a madness orchestrated by Sergeant Burns, Taylor is swept along by the fear and the hatred and almost gets to the point of murdering an unarmed Vietnamese civilian. He fires hysterically at the man's feet, making him dance, before backing off, emotionally drained. As he backs away, another soldier, Bunny, one of the red-necks, steps forward and beats the man to death with his rifle butt.

All the villagers are assembled and Burns attempts to question the head man, threatening to shoot a child and making clear that this will only be the start. He kills an old woman who protests too much and is only prevented from turning the village into another My Lai by the arrival of Elias. The two men fight, and the villagers are saved from massacre but their homes are nevertheless torched and the village is destroyed. Some soldiers are shown helping the villagers carry away their belongings, others are shown gang raping a young girl. This dualism is personified in the two sergeants.

The whole episode is tremendously powerful and shocking but it is shown from the point of view of American anguish rather than from the point of view of Vietnamese suffering. The question asked is how American soldiers could come to behave like this, rather than why this is happening to defenceless Vietnamese peasants in their own country. The audience is shown the war from an American point of view, even if it is one critical of the atrocities committed by American troops.

Having said this, it was, nevertheless, unprecedented for a Hollywood war film to show American soldiers as capable of behaving like this and Stone deserves considerable credit for it. It is still inconceivable that a British feature film would show the Batang Kali massacre in Malaya, the Hola camp massacre in Kenya, the behaviour of the Argylls in Aden or the Bloody Sunday massacre in Northern Ireland from a similarly critical standpoint.

Burns gets revenge by murdering Elias. For the time being the dark side of American masculinity has triumphed. The personification of war as rage, brutality, murder and rape, treacherously shoots his rival and leaves him to be finished off by the Vietcong. The American soldier as knight errant, the bearer of the soldierly virtues, is sacrificed – dying in a final, Christlike pose – while a horrified Taylor looks helplessly on. Of course, Taylor eventually restores balance and order and kills Burns, although he only secures the right to do this after having proven his manhood in the last climactic battle of the film. As Taylor observes, 'we did not fight the enemy, we fought ourselves and the enemy was in us'.

From this perspective the film can clearly be seen as an exploration of American masculinity under stress in Vietnam rather than being concerned with the actual politics of the War. It recognises that some soldiers committed atrocities and tries to show what kind of men succumbed to this temptation, but the atrocities do not amount to a condemnation of the War as such. Indeed, in other ways the film is a relatively conventional celebration of the warrior, of masculine bravery, of comradeship. There are, for example, interesting thematic similarities with the *Star Wars* trilogy where Luke Skywalker is confronted with a similar choice between the light and dark sides of the Force. Taylor and Skywalker might seem unlikely brothers, but their relationship is clear: young American males confronted with the choice of different paths to manhood.

Alongside the struggle for Taylor's soul, the film attempts to show the War in a realistic way. Great emphasis is put on dramatising the hardships experienced by the troops – the rain, the discomfort, the insects, the exhaustion – and on showing their fear of death or mutilation. Nevertheless the conventions of the genre demand that the film ends with a last, Alamo-style battle. The American base is overrun by the Communists and a strike on their own positions is called down. The pyrotechnics of modern warfare provide a colourful, exciting display as Taylor fights it out in the dark with his faceless enemies. His skill and courage establish him as a man very much in the same mould as Elias and hundreds of Hollywood heroes before him. He is the chivalrous warrior. It could be argued that the piles of corpses left at the end of the battle and revealed in the morning are themselves a mute condemnation of the war, but Taylor's survival and triumph over Sergeant Burns is the more lasting image. The War has served as his rite of passage from boy to man, and the man who has emerged has retained his humanity, his integrity; he has not surrendered to the madness, against all the odds.

Other films attempted to repeat *Platoon*'s 'realistic' portrayal of the war as experienced by the ordinary soldiers, but without Stone's anguished display of American atrocities. A good example is John Irvin's *Hamburger Hill* (US, 1987), an account of an actual attack by American troops on Hill 937 in the Ashau Valley in May 1969.[4] It is very much the story of young Americans, black and white, going through Hell and emerging victorious. The rain, the mud, the physical exhaustion, the killing and dying – including some particularly brutal hand-to-hand fighting – are all graphically portrayed. Here, being a man is all about endurance: the stoical bearing of suffering is as much the hallmark of masculinity as is the ability to inflict violence and death. The film exults and celebrates the loyalty of soldier to soldier, the solidarity of the small unit and, rather optimistically, shows racial tension becoming racial harmony in the cauldron of combat. The experience of battle is shown as binding men together in a way that no other experience can and, of course, it is an experience that only other men can share. Men die in other men's arms, combat is what being a man, being a warrior, is all about. Accompanying this discourse on masculinity, is the full panoply of gun-fire, explosions and air-strikes.

Another 'realistic' film, *The Iron Triangle* (Eric Heston, US, 1988), is of interest because it attempts to show what kind of men the

Americans were fighting against. The American Captain has an alter ego, the young Vietcong guerilla fighter, Ho, who is 'a man like me'. On one level, this recognition can be seen as a step forward from films that at best leave the Vietcong unseen and at worst portray them as sub-human. But the reality is that there were differences between the Americans and the Vietcong. The latter were not turning the urban areas of South Vietnam into 'red light districts', they were not killing, burning and raping in someone else's country, they were not bringing the full weight of a modern war machine to bear on towns and villages in America. They were a resistance movement fighting against an army of occupation. This is quite a difference – but one that the film fails to deal with in its attempt to depict a universal, cross-cultural masculinity.

The way in which young, American males were transformed into soldiers capable of waging the Vietnam War is explored most successfully in Stanley Kubrick's *Full Metal Jacket*. The film opens with young men having their heads shaved, being ritually de-feminised by having their relatively long hair cut, before being introduced to the Sergeant who will conduct them, at the double, through Marine Corps training. Sergeant Hartman is a monster and he subjects his charges to a regime of personal and physical abuse that is intended to transform them into killers. They are not men yet, as far as Hartman is concerned; they are queers and women, but they will become men. Hartman defines masculinity in crude, heterosexual terms, as being superior to and dominant over people who are 'less-than-men: women and gays. The richness of his catalogue of insults and threats is phenomenal: to Private Cowboy: 'I bet you're the kind of guy who would fuck a person in the arse and not even have the goddam common courtesy to give him a reach around'; to Private Pile: 'I will gouge out your eyes and skull fuck you'. The new recruits are nothing and will remain nothing until they have been re-made in Hartman's image. They are made to sleep with their rifles and to give them women's names: becoming a man and becoming a warrior are the same thing. Violence is a sexual act within this militaristic universe.[5]

The first section of the film is an horrific portrayal of the brutalisation of these young men and the story of the destruction of one of their number, Private Pile. He is overweight and useless at soldiering, so Hartman makes him his scapegoat: whenever Pile does anything wrong, everyone else is punished. The pity and contempt of his fellows are in this way turned to anger and hatred. The end result is a savage, night-time assault on Pile. Among his attackers is the film's main character, Private Joker, who otherwise maintains a position of good-humoured cynicism about it all, remaining a detached observer. Pile retreats from this hell into madness, eventually killing both Hartman and himself.

The film goes on to show the 'new men' in action in Vietnam during the Tet Offensive in January 1968. Their masculinity is demonstrated in a number of ways: they are continually being offered sex by Vietnamese prostitutes (to which they respond with a casual misogyny), they challenge each other for dominance, and in combat they pack enormous fire-power. Instead of joining a fighting unit, Joker becomes a combat journalist with *Stars and Stripes*; he is still the sympathetic cynic, standing apart from it all, 'seeing both sides' as it were, with 'Born To Kill' on his helmet and a peace badge on his jacket. He attaches himself to a Marine squad that includes his friend from boot camp, Cowboy. His entry into the squad involves him in a confrontation with the biggest, the most macho and aggressive of his fellow soldiers, Animal (whose status in the squad is confirmed by the fact that he also has the biggest weapon). The confrontation does not go beyond a display of male aggression where Joker succeeds (just) in holding his own. But, as Animal puts it, while he can 'talk the talk' can he 'walk the walk'? Joker has not yet become one with his fellow 'grunts' (marines); he has not yet killed and therefore is still less than a complete man.

In the last, climatic episode of the film, the squad is ambushed by a lone sniper in the ruins of Hue. Despite all their aggression and fire-power they are pinned down and shot to pieces, losing three of their number. When they eventually find and shoot the sniper, they discover that it is a young, slight, scared, pony-tailed woman. The irony is magnificent: these tough, macho fighting men to whom all Vietnamese women are apparently available, these products of the American war machine, have been put through the grinder by a young woman. This is the most radical statement of any of the Vietnam War films. Kubrick challenges the whole ethos of the masculine warrior, calls into question their mastery of the world. The reconstruction of their masculinity at boot camp is shown to have been in vain, to have been an exercise in masculine vanity, now that it is confronted by the reality of close combat. The marines, for whom killing is an act of sexual prowess, an assertion of gender identity, are beaten, tormented and humiliated by a young Vietnamese woman. She has no need of the masculine solidarity that is all that sustains the grunts. She stands alone.

But what of Private Joker? While Kubrick's indictment of the American military machine and of the kind of masculinity that it manufactures has been triumphantly concluded by this final irony, what becomes of Joker? Here, the film's personal conclusion contrives to undermine its thematic conclusion. Goaded on by his fellows, Joker finishes off the badly wounded young woman, proving his masculinity, becoming one of the 'hardcore'. It is as if his killing of her is a pornographic performance, cheered on by other men. Really hardcore! Their appreciative remarks contrast with the look of horror on his face. Suddenly he is the 'Joker' no more. He might well be in 'a world of shit' but now, at the film's end, together with his comrade-in-arms, singing the Mickey Mouse Club song, he is no longer afraid, he can now 'walk the walk' with the rest of them.

This brings the discussion to what is arguably the grimmest Vietnam War film, Brian De Palma's *Casualties of War*. This is another film about an actual incident: the kidnapping, repeated rape over a five day period and eventual murder of a young Vietnamese woman, Phan Thi Mao by an American patrol in November 1966. De Palma does not even change the names of the men involved (why protect the guilty?) and shows at least something of the horror of their crime.[6] Any portrayal of rape runs the risk of celebrating this particular exercise of male power, of presenting it as titillating, erotic, or exciting. But on this occasion, the controversial De Palma manages to avoid the danger. The reluctance of the military authorities to take any action, thereby effectively condoning such behaviour, is also dramatically portrayed: 'what happened is the way things are', remarks one officer.

The film's main character, Private Eriksson takes part in the kidnap but cannot believe that the patrol's leader, Sergeant Meserve actually intends what he says he will do. Eriksson has no intention of taking part in any rape and one of the other patrol members, Diaz, agrees to refuse along with him. Participation, however, becomes the hallmark of masculinity, the condition for entrance into the band of brothers. Diaz backs down under pressure, but Eriksson still refuses. He is abused and threatened. Meserve makes the position clear when, with his rifle in one hand and his penis in the other, he tells Eriksson: 'The Army calls this a weapon, but it ain't. This is a weapon . . . This is for fighting. This is for fun'. Then he rapes the young woman: she is 'better than nothing'. The order in which the patrol members take their turn reflects their relative status. Having refused, Eriksson now has no status as far as the others are concerned. From this point of view, male status can be seen as being derived from participation in the oppression of women. Eriksson is not a man and therefore is seen by the rest of the patrol as being no longer fit to kill the enemy. He is left with the woman while they go to fight.

While the film shows, with heart-breaking sympathy, the terrible state that Mao is reduced to before her murder, it is nevertheless primarily concerned with the conflict within the patrol between Meserve and Eriksson, with rival masculinities. Meserve is a brave soldier (he has actually saved Eriksson's life) but as far as he is concerned, in the combat zone anything goes. The rape and murder of young Mao is as much a demonstration of his masculinity, of his need to exercise power over others, as is his military prowess. Indeed the film is a relentless indictment of this warrior ethos: 'Just like Genghis Khan man . . . Its fantastic!' exults one of the rapists.

For Eriksson, the lonely defiance of his comrades is an act of conscience. He is a Christian soldier refusing to indulge in the barbaric excesses of his fellows only to find that the military hierarchy endorses their behaviour rather than his. As far as he is concerned his masculinity is not compromised by his refusal to take part in the rape but rather by his failure to save Mao from her fate. Despite official obstacles and an attempt on his own life, he at least partially redeems himself by standing up to his persecutors and ensuring that the other members of the patrol are eventually brought to trial and sentenced to terms of imprisonment. For their part, they cannot understand what it is that they are supposed to have done wrong.

What De Palma does in this film is show masculinity in extremis without any ambiguity or special pleading. The crime that Meserve and his fellows have committed is unreservedly condemned. What De Palma does not do, however, is show the rape and murder from the Vietnamese point of view, from the point of view of Phan Thi Mao. In this sense, the film is an exploration of masculinity rather than of the oppression of women or of a colonial people. The film's focus is primarily on rape as something that happens to men as victimisers rather than to women as victims. This is not to deny the film's powerful indictment of the crime and of the men who committed it, but is rather to insist that it is condemned from a masculine point of view. Moreover, the film makes it quite clear that, as far as the military authorities were concerned, the crime was perfectly acceptable as one of the inevitable side-effects of the War; all that stood in the way was Christian conscience.

There have been many films about the Vietnam War that have shown men engaged in conventional heroics, winning bloody battles in a war that was nevertheless somehow lost. What this study has attempted to show is that there have also been a number of films that have recognised at least something of the politics of the War. This was not a remake of World War Two, with American troops liberating the world from German and Japanese occupation. Rather, it was a war in which American soldiers found themselves acting as the army of occupation, commiting atrocities against civilians, waging war against a whole people. Hollywood has not so far been able to deal with this politically. Instead, what we have are a number of films that portray the War as a crisis of American masculinity. Interestingly, the nearest that Hollywood has come to an explicit statement regarding the politics of the War is Oliver Stone's *Born on the Fourth of July* (US, 1990), the story of Ron Kovic, a Vietnam vet who became a leading campaigner against the conflict. Kovic is paralysed from the chest down: he left his 'prick' in the jungle. It is almost as if the removal of his masculinity was necessary for him to be able to come out against the war. Once that difficult and messy question was out of the way, the 'real' issues of 'proper' politics could be addressed.

NOTES

1 For a good history of the Vietnam War see Gabriel Kolko, *Vietnam: Anatomy of War 1940-1975*, Macmillan, London, 1986. For 'cultural studies' views of the war see the collections: Jeffrey Walsh and James Aulich, *Vietnam Images: War and Representation*, London, 1989; Alf Louvre and Jeffrey Walsh, *Tell Me Lies About Vietnam*, Open University Press, London, 1988 and John Carlos Rowe and Rick Berg, *The Vietnam War and American Culture*, Columbia, New York, 1991.

2 The literary anthropology of Sir James Frazer's *The Golden Bough*, Macmillan, London, 1990, arguably provides the inspiration for Coppola's primitive culture rather than the Montagnard tribesmen who for a time allied themselves with the Americans.

3 For a discussion of this episode in the film see Gilbert Adair, *Hollywood's Vietnam*, Heinemann, London, 1989, pp156-157.

4 The actual battle of Hamburger Hill, so named because the hill turned men into hamburgers, lasted ten days and cost the Americans seventy men killed and another 372 wounded. This was not a large-scale engagement but the significance of the casualty list was magnified by the apparent pointlessness of the war. One suspects that if the war had ended in victory then the battle would have been viewed differently. See Samuel Zaffiri, *Hamburger Hill*, Presidio, London, 1988.

5 For a discussion of sex and combat see Richard Holmes, *Firing Line*, Longmans, London, 1985, pp56-57.

6 For an account of the episode and others see Susan Brownmiller, *Against Our Will*, Penguin Books, London, 1976, pp86-113.

Going Solo: Performance and Identity in *New York, New York* and *Taxi Driver*

Ken Page

Scorsese's male protagonists have much in common. They combine restless energy with a penchant for violence. They hurt themselves and others in their obsessive need to perform and to be recognised as somebodies. As Peachment states 'they are all marked down by the overbearing hunger for celebrity.'[1] In this essay I examine *New York, New York* (Scorsese, US, 1977) and *Taxi Driver* (Scorsese, US, 1976) in the context of the Robert De Niro characters' obsession with performance as a way of defining their identities. As a performer, De Niro invests each characterisation with his star image, which itself includes the notion of obsessiveness. De Niro's body language is a dominant feature of his performances, whether it is the tense muscularity in *Taxi Driver* or obesity in *Raging Bull* (Scorsese, US, 1980). His acting and method testify to a controlled use of the body in performing his roles.[2] De Niro uses his body to project his character's inner turmoil and lack of control. Often, emotions are articulated irrationally in outbursts of violence or dumbly in acts of self-mutilation. Whilst Travis Bickle is taciturn in *Taxi Driver* and Jimmy Doyle talkative in *New York, New York*, both seem more at ease when they allow their bodies to take over and do the talking.

New York, New York is a musical with a vengeance. Set in the period following the heyday of the big band, it tracks the careers of two musicians who collide at a demob dance, get involved, marry and split in the space of two years, and who subsequently achieve success in separate ways. In this film, happy families are out. The pursuit of happiness is sought but rejected because the giving is as one-sided as the taking.

But *New York, New York* throbs with music whose different styles combine, conflict and collide. Jimmy and Francine are both soloists in the sense that their musical voices are foregrounded. When together in the band Francine sings her heart out but Jimmy's tenor sax playing is as obsessively aggressive and over the top as its creator.

The expectations of the musical genre are used and subverted by *New York, New York*. The narrative structure is neither reassuring nor utopian, though these idealistic aims are noted and referred to. The musical numbers are integrated into the narrative structure in a mode which is in contrast to the artificiality of the classical musical. Yet, with its own brand of artificiality, *New York, New York* sets up a dynamic of oppositions which releases the dramatic antagonism between the central couple. As soloists, Jimmy and Francine represent different musical styles and, by implication, ideas of creativity. Blues, jazz and bop are uneasily combined with, and finally opposed to, a mainstream of the type exemplified by Judy Garland, Jo Stafford and Peggy Lee. In addition, the traditional happy ending of the Hollywood musical is propelled into a site of conflict centring on the relationship between De Niro/Jimmy and Minelli/Francine. For both De Niro and Minelli, their star images are conflated with the star roles they assume in the fictional text.[3] They perform as actors and act as performers in ways which conflict with and underpin the inability of their screen characters to function as a couple. Francine and Jimmy's opposition is marked by the differences in their musical approach and appeal. Francine works to perfect her art, complementing and working with other musicians, whilst Jimmy's music is individualistic, sexual and aggressively creative. Their musical numbers release very different emotions: fractured, plaintive and savage or lyrical and controlled. Jimmy's audience bop and sweat, whilst Francine's sit and applaud wildly. Jimmy's are moved, whilst Francine's are transfixed. Francine's music gives pleasure; Jimmy's *is* pleasure, being in essence self-expressive and challenging.

The utopian ideal that Jimmy aspires to resides, symbolically, in the major chord which is an image he explains to Francine in the back of a cab. It is an image full of ironies. The triad of happy fulfillment – music and pleasure; money and freedom; love and sex – is both vindicated and mocked. It is a set of ideals whose interrelationships become discordant and slip out of a major harmony into a minor key associated with the Blues. It is Jimmy's concept and therefore unworkable. The major chord is emptied of meaning by being overfilled with masculine savagery and selfishness. In public, his approach seems to be vindicated by success, but in private it is mocked by the agony of rejection and loneliness. Jimmy's ideal chord of happiness is transformed into bright lights that signal not only pleasure and success, but a failure in terms of a human relationship. But the brightness is brittle and artificial. The lights belong, as Jimmy does, to the night, when problems can be blown away by music, excitement and excess.

The tone of collision between private and public worlds is set from the beginning. Jimmy emerges from the crowd. His Hawaian shirt is gaudy and loose. He is vibrant, active and wants to lay some ass, any female ass will do. His gaze fixes on Francine sitting demurely in army uniform at a side table. Their positions are reversed in the film's final musical sequence, when it is Francine who is performing, and Jimmy who is the passive spectator – a member of the audience rather than the focus of attention as in his initial appearance. At the demob dance, Jimmy's charismatic machismo is overpowering. He improvises chat-up angles with the rapidity of tenor sax riffs. His refusal to accept that no means *no* is reminiscent of La Motta in *Raging Bull*, with his refusal to lie down, or in the case of Rupert Pupkin, to go away, in *King of Comedy* (Scorsese, US, 1982). But Jimmy's exasperating vitality also makes people smile.

Francine smiles, and eventually succumbs to his charming persistence, which becomes increasingly charmless as the narrative unfolds. Jimmy uses people as he uses hotel rooms. He enjoys giving orders, whether to the band, Francine or hoteliers. But he's always like this, he's lovable. Francine loves him and writes poems for him. This is a sufficient reason for Jimmy to decide on marriage; he wants and demands exclusive 'property' rights. If marriage is the termination of Jimmy's singular courtship and proposal, then Francine's pregnancy signals Jimmy's disenchantment with what he considers to be her selfishness. He cannot admit that she is the heart of the band, but he does complain that she is letting him and the band down.

The threat Francine poses is amplified by her growing independence and domesticity. It coincides with Jimmy's best gig and his worst behaviour. Jimmy's first response to Francine's attempted reconciliation in the Harlem nightclub is to leave the table abruptly. There follows an enigmatic phone call in which silence is the dominating factor. If the silent phone-call is symbolic of Jimmy's failure to communicate his inner feelings to his wife, then his saxophone/phallus becomes the expression of his nature, the force of masculinity, his mouthpiece and statement to her and the rest of the world. After the silence, Jimmy plays. Francine, very drunk and very pregnant, weaves her way towards the stage, apparently with the intention of joining in, but Jimmy, upping the tempo and taking the combo with him, erupts into a defiant, savage and piercing solo. His tenor shouts 'Fuck off – I can make it without you.' As a performance it echoes King Kong's roar, and the jungle connotations of the backdrop emphasise an extreme form of masculine insularity, fear and power. The episode is deeply humiliating for Francine who is 'blown' off the stage and effectively out of Jimmy's life and plans. The ferocity is maintained in the car outside.

The hysteria displayed by Jimmy pounding the dashboard, and by his physical attack on Francine, is expressed through a horrifying montage of shots and distorted camera angles. Their argument terminates, not in a rush of blood but water – the birth signal. The tone of separation is clearly delineated in the hospital sequence. Jimmy is in a world in which his nervousness and lack of control is manifest. He is surrounded by women and babies and cannot cope. The film pauses on a blank wall and here the narrative jumps forward some six years.

When we see him again, Jimmy's raw masculinity has been pacified by artistic success and recognition. A reconciliation seems possible with his wife and son, but this is rejected. By once again subverting the generic expectation, *New York, New York*'s closure poses fascinating questions. Does Francine reject Jimmy because she values her independence and fears a repetition of his possessive jealousy? Or, has his success and growing maturity erected a barrier against the passionate antagonisms they once shared? It seems possible that Francine is still 'in love' with Jimmy, but cannot forgive him for the person he used to be.

The transformation of Jimmy, motivated by his own rage and by Francine's rejection, is paralleled by that of Travis Bickle in *Taxi Driver*. However, there are differences. Whilst Travis will drive anywhere and at any time, his work, unlike Jimmy's, is neither gregarious not pleasurable. Travis is a loner who desires to be a man who counts, a man who stands up. Whilst Jimmy plays in clubs, Travis goes to the cinema to watch porn. Doyle has been involved in a long term relationship, whereas Travis' liaison with Betsy is short lived.[4] After his disastrous and socially inept courtship of Betsy, and her rejection of him, Travis buys an arsenal of weapons and retreats to his den with its clutter of fractured maleness. In his apartment Travis broods . . . and plays with his weapons.

The conflation of sexual imagery, misogyny and violence is pervasive and perverse throughout *Taxi Driver*. Male sexuality is displaced. The taxi drivers swap dirty work stories. Wizard relates an incident in which he 'whips it [his penis] out'. When Travis seeks his help, Wizard delivers inarticulate homespun philosophy and urges him to get his head sorted out by getting laid. In the porn cinema Travis listens and watches as a woman's voice intones, 'look at the size of that, it looks so good, it's getting harder and harder . . . it's throbbing now. Sport is a pimp who details the anal and oral sexual services his 'baby' will perform. From the back seat of Travis' cab a fare (Scorsese) invites Travis to 'Imagine what a forty four magnum can do to a woman's face – and her pussy. Travis invites Sport to 'suck on this' before shooting him in the stomach. Easy Andy deals in '44' Magnums, drugs and pink cadillacs. He describes the weapons he is selling to Travis in terms of endearment if they are small, or admiration if they are large. In a lingering pan, the camera slides over the encased guns as if they are jewels or erotic baubles.

The physical and emotional relationship which grows between Travis and his weapons both underlines his status as an ex-marine, and evokes uneasy resonances of childhood. In the hotel room Travis trains the guns on cars passing in the street below. In his room he watches television, Magnum in hand. He cocks and points it at images of women on the screen. In the porn cinema he shapes his fist into a mock gun and 'shoots'.[5] Although there are indications that Travis is troubled by his behaviour, he enjoys the pleasure he derives from possessing 'gun power'.

In his apartment, the mise-en-scene of unmade bed, scattered papers and food cartons, packing-case furniture, gas ring and television set, reveals the sordid mess of Travis' deranged mind. It is here amidst the debris, that Travis, in his own warped way, undertakes the process of repairing the damage done to his sense of masculine identity. He drinks, pops pills and eats junk food. He abuses his body and knows it.

> June 29. I gotta get into shape now. Too much sitting has ruined my body, too much abuse has gone on for too long. From now on it'll be fifty push-ups each morning, fifty pull-ups. It'll be no more pills, no more destroyers of my body. From now on it'll be total organisation . . . every muscle must be tight . . . the idea's been growing in my mind for some time . . . true force . . . all the king's men cannot put it back together . . .

The oblique reference to the nursery rhyme, Humpty Dumpty, suggests Travis' fragility and his desire to regress. He disavows himself as a person, who, 'once overthrown cannot be restored' and at the same time he desires to put himself 'back together again'.[6] His response to Betsy's rejection is focused on his body. Not only does he work out, he also begins to adapt his body to fit his weapons by improvising a sliding mechanism to attach to his arm. He is absorbed and at ease in his work. It is as if he has rediscovered the pleasure of play. The poster on his wall, showing the letters of the word ORGANISED thrown out of kilter, reminds us of Betsy's incomprehension at his joke in the cafe. He re-organises himself by transforming his body into an armoury and his thought processes into those of an assassin.

In public, Travis had adopted the unarmed combat position when confronting Tom. However, in the privacy of his room, confronting his own image in the mirror, Travis rehearses and seeks to perfect his gun draw reflexes. Homi Bhabha argues that the

> image of human identity and, indeed, human identity as image . . . are inscribed in the sign of resemblance.

Citing Rorty, he continues:

> This . . . is part of the West's obsession that our primary relation to objects and ourselves is analogous to visual perception. Pre-eminent amongst these representations has been the reflection of the self that develops in the symbolic consciousness of the sign, and marks out the discursive space from which the *Real Me* emerges initially as an assertion of the authenticity of a person and then lingers on to reverberate – The REAL ME? – as a questioning of identity.[7]

In this confrontation, Travis challenges his image to a dual/duel. Interspersed with muttered obscenities, he says aloud:

> I'm standing here . . . You make the move . . . You make the move. You talking to me? You talking to me? You talking to me? Well I'm the only one here . . . who the fuck do you think you're talking to?

In addressing himself in the mirror Travis Bickle is asserting, questioning and reshaping his identity and masculinity. He wants to be hard. Like Jake La Motta in *Raging Bull*, he rehearses in private to prepare for a performance.[8]

Travis Bickle's words reinforce the make-believe image which he is presenting to himself. He combines his loneliness and his crucified maleness into a play-acting performance that connotes an obsessive and narcissistic fixation. The gunslinger/tough cop pose, drawing on movie imagery, is both text and test of his will to act. He becomes his own pin-up. The mirror image presents Travis both as his own antagonist and as his ideal other. Although on his own in the room, Travis is not alone in his imagination because he shapes both images which are under his control and gaze. Each image reinforces the other and they become the identity that he desires to realise, the image that he desires others to see and recognise. However, whilst the mirror serves to complete him, it also divides him. His identity is split, his 'real me' is fractured.[9]

This subjective/objective interplay of representation is carefully constructed. In these sequences, the intensity of Travis' performance in front of the camera/mirror is intercut with shots which observe him from a greater distance, and from angles which disconcert. At one point, a second take of the same action is used. This not only denotes rehearsal, but also disturbs realist convention, because it draws attention to acting itself. After speaking aloud to himself, a series of dissolves show Travis standing – posing – alone. Simultaneously, the diegetic sounds give way to Hermann's music[10] and Travis' disembodied monologue. As he intones the words: 'Listen you fuckers, you screwheads, here's a man who would not take it anymore . . .' the action freezes and, with an edit, the scene is replayed and the words repeated. This time, on the word 'screwheads', the action cuts from Travis' dominant pose in front of the camera, to an overhead shot of Travis lying on his bed.[11] (Although fully clothed, Travis seems vulnerable, naked and exposed.) The voice over continues, 'a man who stood up against the scum . . . Here is someone who stood up'. Like a child, Travis turns and curls up in a foetal position. The line 'here is' is repeated and shown as a scrawl in his diary. A shock edit returns the spectator to a position in front of Travis who repeats his gun routine. Casting a final glance, and again speaking aloud, the sequence ends with Travis uttering 'You're dead'. Travis as killer and victim? The scum? The spectator? It is a chilling ambiguity. Travis sets out to kill and to die.[12]

In these sequences, Travis manufactures himself into the kind of person he has previously rejected – I don't believe a person should devote his life to morbid self-attention'. The morbidness shifts from Travis' mind to his body as he works out. His muscularity becomes the 'sign of power – natural, achieved, phallic',[13] and through this process his masculinity becomes grotesquely disturbing.[14]

Obsession and performance lie at the heart of the social construction of masculinity in the roles De Niro plays in Scorsese's films. For these characters it matters little whether their performances occur on stage or not; apartment or car, ring or public square, their stage is wherever they happen to be. Alone or in public, they perform under the gaze of a real or imagined audience.[15] Travis Bickle and Jimmy Doyle are violent men and frightened little boys. They are beset by anxieties. Their fears are nurtured within their imaginations. In acting out their desires they perform within a structure of violence and obsession. Both characters are prepared to relinquish self-control to satisfy their need to dominate, even if it is at the cost of their humanity. They are trapped in a state of maleness that is neither stable nor desired. They are tormented and vulnerable. It is in these bleak characterizations that the instability of contemporary masculinity is given expression and identity in *Taxi Driver* and *New York, New York*.

NOTES

Thanks to Anne Webb, Duncan Webster, Andy Medhurst, Val Hill, Pat Kirkham and Janet Thumim for their valuable comments on this essay.

1 Chris Peachment, 'Scorsese: Movie Martyr', *Time Out*, No. 671, July 1971, p11.

2 See Lez Cooke, 'New York, New York: Looking at De Niro', in *Movie*, Double Issue 31/32, Winter 1986.

3 Three differences in the star images of De Niro and Minelli are of interest. Liza Minelli's parents, Judy Garland and Vincent Minelli, are famous Hollywood figures. Liza's 'private' life has been highly publicised. Some of her film roles have stressed her identity as a performer/entertainer. In contrast De Niro was brought up in New York by parents who were artists. His qualities as an actor are foregrounded and he maintains a low profile in his private life.

4 Travis Bickle worships Betsy. He puts her on a pedestal and describes her as an 'angel'. After she rejects him, he associates her with the 'scum'. He refers to her as just another 'whore'. In many Scorsese films women are either idealised or denigrated by the male characters. The virgin/whore dichotomy is a recurring motif in his films.

5 In *Mean Streets* (Scorsese, US, 1973) Charlie shapes his fist into a gun after making love with Teresa. In *Alice Doesn't Live Here Anymore* (US, 1974) Ben uses the same gesture after his advances have been rejected. After the massacre in *Taxi Driver*, Travis points a bloodied finger to the side of his head in a mock gesture of suicide.

6 The Humpty Dumpty nursery rhyme is heard in *Who's That Knocking at my Door?* (Scorsese, US, 1969) when J.R.'s girlfriend has told him that she is not a virgin. He is devastated.

7 Homi Bhabha, 'Interrogating Identity', in Lisa Appignanesi, (ed.), *ICA Documents 6*, ICA Projects, London, 1987, p6.

8 Although the rehearsal motif is similar, there is a reversal in that Jake La Motta's body has been hard and is, at this point in *Raging Bull*, soft and flabby.

9 The use of mirrors is an important motif in Scorsese's work. In *New York, New York* Francine sees Jimmy's image reflected in a mirror when he returns from a long tour. Again, towards the end of the film, after years apart, she first sees him in the mirror when he enters her dressing room. On several occasions in *Mean Streets* Charlie gazes intently at his reflection. In the final scene of *Taxi Driver*, Travis' haunted face is reflected and fractured in a series of mirror images, suggesting that, in spite of his newly acquired status as a hero, he remains psychotic.

10 According to Marion Weiss, the final four chords of *Taxi Driver* are from

'Norman Bates's musical score in Hitchcock's *Psycho* (US, 1960) [which suggests] Travis Bickle's lingering psychotic tendency'. Marion Weiss, *Martin Scorsese*, G.K. Hall & Co., Boston, 1987, p3.

11 The image is reminiscent of the Creature's body lying on the table in Baron Frankenstein's laboratory in *The Curse of Frankenstein* (Terence Fisher, UK, 1957).

12 See Rafferty, T., 'Martin Scorsese's Still Life', *Sight and Sound*, 1983, p188. 'Travis has risen from the dead and been reborn in public.' Marion Weiss argues that the epilogue of *Taxi Driver* may be read as a dream – 'If the spectator accepts the fact that the film's events have been seen through Bickle's eyes, why is it not possible that the ending is an externalization of a distorted mind, pushed to the extreme in the form of pure imagination?' *op cit* p37.

13 Richard Dyer, 'Don't Look Now', *Screen*, Vol. 23, No. 3/4, 1982, p68.

14 Equally disturbing is the film's epilogue where Travis Bickle is represented – by the press cuttings, the letter, the taxi drivers and Betsy – as a hero.

15 cf. Rupert Pupkin in *King of Comedy*, rehearsing in the basement of his mother's house, surrounded by cardboard cut-outs of stars.

One Last Chance: Masculinity, Ethnicity, and the Greek Cypriot Community of London

Panikos Panayi

In societies without clearly delimited spheres of competence, each male individual finds it constantly necessary to assert his superiority or his *isotomia*, that is his right to be treated as a person entitled to equal esteem. Hierarchical relations are resented and resisted as, whenever the superior stresses his rank, the inferior stresses his manliness. *Ki' esy moustaki ki' ego moustaki*: we both have a moustache, we are equals in our manliness. When spheres of influence are not clearly delimited each actor fears an encroachment on his area of insecure prerogatives and he asserts them against all comers. This insecurity is one of the reasons for self-assertion. The Greek-Cypriot ... in all novel situations is not antagonistic but agonistic, parading round the assertion of honour, the social rank, or the knowledge to which he is laying claim like a bird round his mating ground. Prompted by this constant need for a situation in which to prove himself from ancient times to now the Greek who does not find opponents of honour commensurate with his own pits himself against Fate or the Gods. This is the sin of *hubris*. A true man is one who is prepared to stake everything on the one throw of the dice. The Greek is a keen gambler attracted more powerfully by the risk than by the gain more, that is, by the opportunity of proving himself than by the prize.[1]

The film discussed here, *One Last Chance* (Gabrielle Beaumont, UK,

1990[2]) takes gambling as its central theme. This is an important preoccupation amongst Cypriot males in London, varying from the occasional flutter on horses to the self-destructive spending of Saturday nights in London casinos. The central character of the film, Nick (played by George Jackos), aged thirty-five, has spent his entire adult life gambling. He has no other career, no other life, and, at the beginning of the film, no wife. He is like a child who has never grown up. Nick picked up his obsession as an adolescent: he cannot let go of it because he believes it will reward him, if he pursues it to the limit. He cannot withdraw from it, even if it proves destructive. His whole language is littered with gambling terminology. 'What are the odds?', he asks about everything: about horse-racing; about his friend's mother entering the room and saying certain phrases in a particular order; about jumping fifteen feet across two buildings; about attracting a wife. He is prepared to sacrifice everything on 'one throw of the dice' to prove himself better than anyone else because he is not frightened to take a risk. Key traits in this character are immaturity, obsession, and excess. In order to explain these characteristics we need some background information on the Greek Cypriot community in London, before moving on to contrast Nick with the other characters in the film.

The opening quotation comes from an article by J.G. Peristiany entitled 'Honour and Shame in a Cypriot Highland Village' which refers to the mid-1950s and focuses upon a settlement called Alona. Nevertheless, some of its assertions remain true for second-generation Cypriots in Britain thirty-five years later, as well as for their parents. For the former, brought up in close family units, escape from one's ethnicity remains impossible. Second generation Cypriots are the children of parents born into a traditional rural society, during the inter-war years, and for whom new surroundings in London initially proved a traumatic experience.

The Greek Cypriot community in London, which began to develop in a small way around Soho in the inter-war years, really took off numerically during what we might describe as the 'great migration' of Cypriots to Britain in the 1950s. Between 1951 and 1966 the number of Cypriots in London increased from 7,983 to 45,000, and has continued to expand since then. The main area of settlement moved from Soho to Camden Town and Islington and now focuses upon Haringey and, more recently, Enfield, especially Palmers Green. In these last two areas, as well as Finsbury Park in Islington, Greek Cypriot shops dominate the local economy and Greek is widely spoken.[3]

As I have mentioned, most first generation Greek Cypriot immigrants do not wish to lose their identity. As with other immigrant communities, they have a strong desire to recreate their own homeland which is done by reproducing traditional work patterns and institutions and rituals such as weddings and Easter Saturday, whilst also developing newspapers, shops, coffee shops and schools.[4] Tax evasion, social security and insurance fraud are also practised not only for financial reasons but also as an attempt at the maintenance of ethnicity.

For many men, migration itself represents a major test of their masculinity and after that others must be found: gambling, or opening up a business can compare. Such men illustrate Perestiany's concept of 'true' masculinity, because they are consciously trying to prove themselves in anything they do. Such is the central character of *One Last Chance*. His dress and mannerisms stress his 'up-front' and self confident masculinity: his constant lighting up of cigarettes; his street wise double breasted suits; his leather jacket; his lightly-greased black hair, combed backwards; his Ray-Ban sunglasses. By contrast, his English friend, Terry (Mark Jefferies) looks scruffy, ineffectual and less sexually attractive. Whilst Nick makes himself look sexually attractive, his prospective wife Maria (Marina Sirtis) dresses like a traditional Greek Cypriot woman, with her hair in a bun, emphasising her possible future role as a matriarch. She fits into the traditional role of womanhood described by Peristiany:

> Woman's foremost duty to self and family is to safeguard herself against all critical allusions to her sexual modesty. In dress, looks, attitudes, speech, a woman, when men are present, should be virginal as a maiden and matronly as a wife. If it were possible to combine the concepts of virginity and motherhood the ideal married woman would be, a married mother virginal in sensations and mind.[5]

Thirty-five years later, both in Cyprus and amongst the Greek Cypriots in Britain, we can see that some things have changed. In Haringey, the heart of Cypriot London, Greek Cypriot girls emphasise their 'femininity' and tend to dress extremely fashionably but the concept of virginity before marriage remains important. The siting of Maria primarily within a traditional 'feminine' model rather than one which questions the repression of female sexuality and male double standards, also ensures that the focus of the film remains on Nick and his masculinity.

Nick's masculinity is contrasted with that of Terry. The first scene of the film shows the two friends leaving a casino together. The former cannot believe the bad luck he has just experienced, while the latter simply accepts it. Terry suggests that they should take a break from gambling, to which Nick sharply replies that he could not possibly turn to driving a cab (a common occupation amongst the North

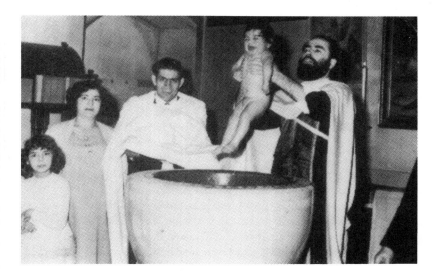

(top right) Young Greek Cypriot males, Lymbia village, Cyprus, 1950s.
(top left) Greek Cypriot migrant, North London, 1966.
(bottom) Greek Cypriot Christening, North London, 1963.
(All from the Panayi Archive)

London working classes) and instantly focuses his mind upon a horse race on the same afternoon. His attitude towards Terry reveals his own pride in his machismo. At one stage he tells his mate, 'You've got no balls' and his own risk-taking is the visible sign that he does have. During the course of the film Terry gives up gambling, admitting that he had no stomach for it. He was a 'fraud', he confesses, but argues that it did not prove his manhood. He turns to antique restoration, a respectable trade though somewhat dull compared with staking everything on one throw of the dice in a smoky casino in central London. One of the most symbolic scenes of the film involves Terry and Nick jumping across a fifteen foot gap between two buildings, pursued by cronies of Nick's main gambling rival, Luka. Nick makes the jump but Terry fails and falls to his death. This seems to prove that Terry was not a man in the fullest sense of the word: after all, he gave up gambling. Flawed by weakness and lacking 'balls', he could not survive. Nick has proved his manhood again while Terry dies physically having died symbolically. He was unable to survive in the world of tough individuals such as Nick and organised groups such as that revolving around Luka.

Luka is a middle-aged man married to a rich woman, which leads Nick to believe he has an unfair advantage over him. One of Luka's bodyguards, Panikos, is, in effect, emasculated because he depends entirely upon Luka for survival. He chases after Nick in order to recover money owed to Luka. He dresses in a leather jacket and greased back hair, not dissimilar to Nick, but his dependence upon Luka means he remains weak. Nick, by contrast, depends on no-one but himself. The relationship between Nick and Luka is intriguing. Does he simply represent a mature Nick who has escaped from the worst aspects of self-destructiveness? He has the security of his wife's fortune, as well as family life, both of which Nick lacks. However, a respectable marriage is also open to Nick. A crucial idea – and one important amongst the Greek Cypriot community in London – put forward at various points throughout the film, is that marriage curbs male excess. We are told that Maria's father, for example, formerly gambled but gave it up when he married her mother. Nick, however, may want marriage but he is not prepared to stop gambling. His role model may be Luka who can have his cake and eat it. He perhaps wants the security of a family without accepting the responsibilities of changing his risky lifestyle.

Another crucial relationship involves Nick and Maria. In the first scene in which they appear together she says to him 'one must grow up before one grows old', and her maturity is used to highlight the immaturity which fuels Nick's obsession with gambling. This contrast between youth and maturity is an important aspect of their relationship. The film presents her as a thirty-five year old, the same age as Nick, a device which gives the appearance of equality, which then serves to further highlight their differences. She has grown old too young in contrast to Nick who has not grown up let alone grown old. She has replaced her dead mother in her father's restaurant and repeatedly tells the male gamblers to behave themselves, as if they were children, suggesting that she is essentially maternal in her relationships with men, including Nick. The boy who refuses to grow up might well need and desire mothering but the film represents this as a desperate and despairing process for both of them. We see her as able at work, making her father's business succeed, through various financial activities which she does well, in contrast to her personal relationship. She wants and needs marriage and she feels the pain more strongly when her marriage does not work out. The wife is depicted as desiring and needing marriage more than the husband, a common enough theme on celluloid as well as in 'real' life.

How does the film show the Greek Cypriot gambler in relation to women and marriage? There are a few references to previous relationships with women and early on Nick fails to keep an appointment to meet a waitress who accuses him of being homosexual: the ultimate insult to the macho Greek Cypriot, especially one proving his masculinity at the gambling table. Nick is shown full of bravado (claiming to have had sex with Panikos's wife) and hot air (he later admits to Terry that it was all lies). Gambling always comes before women and even featured in his decision about marriage, although this again is used to demonstrate the insecurity of Nick's male ego when he claims on one occasion that he decided to marry in order to gain financial backing for his gambling and on another that it was simply for a bet. This suggests that 'real' men in Haringey could never admit to needing or wanting any security other than financial. At one level Maria is a challenge for Nick. She is the same age as him, and can stand up to him to some extent. However, the film touches upon the problems men like Nick, representatives of extreme masculinity, have in finding suitable partners. They might be attracted to women they see as strong and capable yet their egocentricity demands someone passive whose world will revolve around their own wishes.

The film focuses on the wedding night itself to demonstrate the extent of Nick's selfishness. On this night, Nick asserts his freedom, his manhood, by leaving his wife, to attend a casino. He has no knowledge of how to treat women: everything must revolve around his obsession. To surrender to a woman's world might imply a denial of his manhood, constructed as that is on the basis of his independence, his 'free spirit'. He remains true, loyal and devoted to his gambling – the obsession that offers him more excitement than sex or marriage.

Nick provides an example of the Greek Cypriot male obsessive who marginalises women yet, since there is great pressure to get married, takes the easy way out and enters a relationship without thinking through the responsibilities. The film offers no solution to the problematic and destructive elements of such a masculinity. It ends with Nick washing up in Maria's restaurant. She says he will not last the week at this new attempt at stability. He retorts, 'What are the odds?' The film does not answer that question nor does it tell us whether this really was Nick's last chance.

NOTES

I am grateful to Pat Kirkham and Janet Thumim who did much to transform the original paper upon which this article is based.

1 J.G. Peristiany, 'Honour and Shame in a Cypriot Highland Village', in J.G. Perestiany (ed.), *Honour and Shame: The Values of Mediterranean Society*, Weidenfeld and Nicholson, London, 1965, pp187-8.

2 The film was made for BBC TV's 'Screen One' series and shown in September 1990. The script was written by Andrew Kazamia and the film was produced by Andrée Molyneaux.

3 Robin Oakley, *Changing Patterns of Distribution of Cypriot Settlement*, Centre for Research in Ethnic Relations, Coventry, 1987.

4 Pamela Constantinides, 'The Greek Cypriots: Factors in the Maintenance of Ethnic Identity', in James L. Watson, (ed.), *Between Two Cultures: Migrants and Minorities in Britain*, Blackwells, Oxford, 1977, pp269-300.

5 Perestiany, *op. cit.*, p182.

One Hundred and Seventeen Steps Towards Masculinity

Tom Ryall

PRELIMINARY STEPS

The Thirty-nine Steps – John Buchan's espionage 'shocker' – was written around the time of the outbreak of World War One. In the character of Richard Hannay, it constitutes a particular version of masculinity – the heroic adventurer drawn into and troubled considerably by villainy of various sorts but untroubled by the presence of the feminine. Buchan's novel sketches a world which is almost exclusively male, producing a conception of masculine identity in which the presence and implications of the feminine is repressed, displaced and possibly repositioned. It may be termed a consciously 'uncomplicated' version of masculinity although, from another perspective, it may be viewed as a version made complex precisely by the repression and displacement of the world of sexuality.

Subsequently, the novel was the basis for three films. The first and the most celebrated was directed by Alfred Hitchcock and released in 1935 to much critical acclaim and popular success both in Britain and America. The story was filmed once again in 1959 (directed by Ralph Thomas) in a version which owed much to the Hitchcock picture and, in 1978, a version which adhered more closely to the Buchan novel was directed by Don Sharp. The novel emerged from the early years of World War One and the films from Britain during three contrasting and distinctive periods. Hitchcock's picture was made during the depression years and in a period of growing international tension; the Thomas version in a period marked by the development of the consumer society, affluence and emergence of youth cultures of various kinds; and the Sharp film in the context of a popular culture beginning to be marked in various ways (films, television, advertising, magazines) by the contemporary women's movement.

This essay sets out to compare the different constructions of masculinity presented by the three films in the context of the particular delineation of the Hannay character offered by Buchan. It is, in fact, the introduction of the feminine into Hannay's world in the films which marks them off from the novel. This is most evident in the Hitchcock and Thomas films. But even the Sharp version – despite its overall fidelity to the somewhat asexual world of the Buchan novel – does introduce a female partner for Hannay.[1] Raymond Bellour has identified 'the formation of the couple'[2] as the central theme of mainstream cinema and, whilst such a claim runs the risk of appearing somewhat reductive, it is certainly the case that romantic themes and sub-themes are a central ingredient of popular films. The transposition of novel to film accordingly required the insertion of a world of heterosexuality into the world of incident and adventure, although this occurred in different ways in the different versions of *The Thirty-nine Steps*. Identity, in part at least, is a matter of relationships, and the different worlds of relationships set up by the three film versions produce different definitions of masculine identity compared with the one available in the original novel.

Masculine identity is represented in fictional forms in a number of ways: through narrative structure, situation and trajectory, through character role in terms of the initiation of action, the control of the events of the narrative, the determination of the course of action, and the organisation of the resolution. Definitions also emerge from the contrast between different versions of masculinity, different dimensions of maleness, different possibilities of male behaviour, embodied in particular male characters and highlighted through their interrelationships. The Buchan novel attempts to represent masculinity solely in such terms whilst the films add a further layer of contrast by introducing female characters of various sorts. In addition, the film image, the mise en scene, the presentation of maleness by actors both in terms of their physical appearance and of the specific details of their performance, is a key area for scrutiny. Such analysis also offers an insight into historical specificity through details of style, fashion, manners etc. and, crucially, the assumptions about masculinity implied by the performance style of the male star. Finally, from the perspective of psychoanalysis, notions of masculinity and gender can also emerge through the mechanisms of condensation and displacement. In this context, the absence of female characters in the novel attracts attention and prompts a search for displaced signifiers of femininity and sexuality.[3]

NARRATIVE SITUATIONS/TESTS

Buchan's novel is characterised by a narrative in which 'the incidents defy the probabilities, and march just inside the borders of the possible.'[4] Hannay is caught up in a series of events upon which he stumbles and over which he has little control. At the beginning of the Hitchcock film, Hannay is in a music hall when the performance is interrupted by the firing of a pistol. In the ensuing confusion he is 'picked up' by Annabella Smith, later to be revealed as an undercover agent trying to prevent the smuggling abroad of secret information. In the Thomas version, Hannay is walking in Regents Park, witnesses the attempted assassination of 'Nannie Robinson' and picks up her handbag after she has been taken off to hospital for treatment. In both films, the *female* agent figure subsequently goes to Hannay's apartment and is murdered there, leaving him embroiled in the espionage plot and implicated in the murder of the women. In the Sharp version, drawn directly from the novel, Hannay is approached by Scudder – a *male* agent – who informs him about an assassination plot and is subsequently murdered in Hannay's presence in a crowded railway station. In fact, he staggers dying, a knife in his back, into Hannay's arms. As in the other films and the novel, Hannay becomes the one sought for the murder.

From those points of departure, the films proceed at top pace to sketch a series of adventures as Hannay journeys north to Scotland and back again to London, pursued by the police and the enemy agents and in pursuit of the assassination plotters. The flight to Scotland is based upon the novel although Buchan's Hannay simply wishes to disappear for a few weeks and sees the Highlands as the best source of refuge given his Scottish ancestry and his capacity to survive in such an environment. In the films there are specific reasons for going to Scotland, namely, a series of clues concerning the whereabouts of the plotters, scraps of a map and so on.

The novel draws upon definitions of masculinity which belong in the 'Boy's Own Paper adventure category' derived from a nineteenth century British Imperial and colonial ethos. It is an ethos of 'fearless endeavour in a world populated by savage races, dangerous pirates, and related manifestations of the "other" to be encountered on voyages towards dark and unexplored continents.'[5] It presents a masculinity based upon a range of muscular and combative qualities blended with survival skills, ideals of masculinity suited to the demands of adventure, exploration, hunting and survival in a hostile terrain. In addition, it is a masculinity with an economic rationale. As one writer has suggested '[i]n the pages of the Boys Own Paper, manly, intrepid lads wandered around the world, proving their character as plucky Englishmen and, eventually, finding fame and fortune.'[6]

Although *The Thirty-nine Steps* is not a colonial adventure story it is a story about a colonial adventurer and contains 'Boys Own' elements. Richard Hannay, the central character, is an adventurer home from Africa having 'made my pile – not one of the big ones, but good enough for me'.[7] He also refers to his 'veldcraft', his skill in dealing with the problems of rough living in the open country acquired in the course of his unspecified activities in South Africa. The novel provides Hannay with a series of adventures in which he can demonstrate his manly courage and his ingenuity in the face of various adversities provoked by his chance encounter with Scudder. Firstly, there is the response to the initial situation of intrigue – the encounter with Scudder offers Hannay an escape from the boredom of his stay in London, a possibility of adventure and excitement to counter his sense of disillusion with England after his years in South Africa as colonial entrepreneur and adventurer. The masculinity which emerges is based upon a norm of outdoor action and adventure, a combative and muscular masculinity suitable for the Empire builder and coloniser, and one which the novel, in particular, presents as inhibited by urban life. The films have less to say about Hannay's particular background and formation and, if not exactly a tabula rasa when plunged into the series of adventures, the character is, in a more significant sense, defined in terms of masculinity by the adventures and events which unfold through the course of the films.

The adventures constitute various 'tests' of specific human skills and qualities particularly courage, ingenuity and the improvisational skills required to cope with life on the run through the countryside – Hannay's 'veldcraft'. Skills and qualities which one might relate to the 'boy scout' dimensions of colonial expertise. In the Hitchcock and Thomas films, Hannay has to escape from his apartment block in disguise, to evade discovery on a train by leaping onto a bridge and hanging from its supports until the train has moved on, to flee from the police across the Scottish countryside, to pretend to be a speaker at a political rally (Hitchcock) or a guest speaker on botany at a girl's school (Thomas), and to resume his flight handcuffed to a woman whom he has previously alienated. Many of these situations do not appear in the novel yet they function to construct a similar image of masculine ingenuity in the face of seemingly impossible situations. The values involved are that blend of raw, native intelligence matched with physical courage traceable to the upper-middle class English public school ethos of rugged commonsense.

The narrative situations which test Hannay's masculinity and contribute towards its definition, also involve other male characters and other masculinities. In the Hitchcock version, Hannay's identity emerges in part from his encounters with two male figures: the crofter and the Professor (the mastermind of the spy ring). The crofter is a religious and patriarchal figure who represses his wife both by praying at her and beating her. In this context, Hannay emerges as caring and sensitive, almost a vision of refuge and escape for the crofter's wife in whom he confides. The Professor, Hannay's generic adversary, is presented as an upper middle-class English figure and, although their encounter takes place in Scotland, it is in a very English-looking country house and at teatime! The Thomas film also presents the 'evil spy' character in terms of a somewhat bluff, avuncular Englishman in a similar country house setting. However, the structural equivalent to Hitchcock's 'crofter sequence' in the Thomas film – the overnight stay with Mr and Mrs Lumsden at the Gallows Service Station – effectively reverses the power relationship between husband and wife. The Lumsden ménage is clearly a matriarchy, although the husband is kept in a condition of pleasant if celibate servitude compared to the cruel and repressed situation of the crofter's wife. The Sharp film adheres more closely to the novel. Hannay's principal adversary emerges as a rather starkly singleminded villain and conspirator with no redeeming features whatsoever. In this sense the Sharp film retains the melodramatic clarity of the good/evil opposition from the Buchan story.

WOMEN

The Hitchcock and Thomas versions deviate most markedly from the Buchan novel by introducing a number of new incidents into the narrative or by elaborating incidents which appear briefly in the novel. To take one example, the music hall setting, which plays a significant role in both films, is merely mentioned in a two sentence aside in the novel. However, from the perspective of an interrogation of sexuality, the significant additional incidents introduce an array of female characters. The Sharp version, although closer to the original story, does introduce a female character as a romantic partner for Hannay.

There are three female characters in the Hitchcock film; Annabella Smith, the secret agent; Margaret, the crofter's wife; and Pamela, Hannay's romantic partner. Annabella Smith draws Hannay into the espionage plot although he takes her back to his apartment assuming that she is a prostitute. Effectively, after her murder, Hannay replaces her in the narrative and continues the flight from pursuit. She is presented as mysterious, exotic and continental, a presentation of female sexuality which was to become common in later British cinema. Hannay encounters Margaret, the crofter's wife, during his flight through Scotland when he arrives at the remote cottage seeking shelter. In contrast to Annabella Smith, Margaret is open and somewhat unsophisticated, eager for tales of the bright city lights and the excitements of urban life. Her husband, the crofter, is a cruel figure and the presentation of Margaret's entrapment in a violent and repressive marriage is graphic and striking. At one level, the episode – in which the crofter threatens to betray Hannay – is just one of the complicated situations from which he must extricate himself. Yet, it seems to have a greater weight than that, an importance which is comprehensible only within a reading of the film, following Robin Wood's analysis, as a 'A "dramatic poem" on the theme of sexual construction'. In such a context, the episode becomes one of the models of 'sexual/gender organisation' offered by the film.[8]

Hannay's third encounter with the feminine is with Pamela. Whereas the sexual dimensions of the other encounters remain sketched and implied, with Pamela the sexual aspect is central. In their initial encounter on the train in Scotland, Hannay bursts into her carriage and forcibly kisses her in an attempt to mask his identity from the police. She turns him in although he manages to escape. Their second encounter at the political meeting proves more long-lasting. Hannay is 'arrested' by two of the spies and Pamela is asked to accompany them to the police station for identification purposes. They are handcuffed together and, when Hannay escapes from this particular situation, Pamela – now literally attached to him – has to follow and they spend a night of enforced intimacy at a remote Highland inn.

Violence plays a role in all three encounters. Annabella Smith is murdered; Margaret is beaten by her husband for her role in Hannay's escape; Pamela is first forcibly kissed by Hannay, then handcuffed to him and dragged through the Highlands and eventually into the bedroom. As 'models of sexual/gender organisation', the three encounters construct masculinities against the background of prostitution (the smirking assumptions about Annabella Smith – 'actress', 'the chorus'), cruelty and repression in marriage (the crofter's wife), and the forcible taking of a woman (Pamela). It is true that Pamela does warm to Hannay eventually when she learns that he really is trying to break a spy ring but the final shot of the film – a close shot of the couple's joined hands – includes the dangling handcuffs which recalls the coercive nature of the ties that bound them together initially. Robin Wood has suggested that 'the ending is unresolvably ambiguous . . . [a]s the hands of Hannay and Pamela meet, we are reminded that, although the handcuffs no longer bind the couple, they are dangling from Hannay's wrist.'[9]

The Thomas version is based more upon the Hitchcock film than the

Buchan novel and uses the same pattern of the three encounters with different kinds of women. 'Nannie Robinson' the agent figure draws Hannay into the espionage plot first, when he witnesses an attempt to kill her outside Regents Park and secondly, when she accompanies him to his flat to recover her handbag and is murdered by the spies. The episodes are not quite charged with the sexual undertones of the Hitchcock version although 'Nannie' may well be a different kind of English sexual stereotype from her continental forerunner. However, the second encounter – the equivalent of the crofter episode – does have an explicit sexual charge, albeit a comic one. Hannay gets a lift from a lorry driver who directs him to the Gallows Service Station and to Nellie Lumsden, a buxom middle-aged spiritualist. Having established his astrological credentials, Hannay is made welcome and when they realise his predicament both Nellie and her husband help in his escape. Their marriage is constructed in terms of a cheerful bohemianism. Nellie is clearly receptive to entertaining male customers with more than just an account of their stars. In contrast to the repressive marriage in the Hitchcock film, this is a comic marriage based upon a somewhat knockabout, matriarchal relationship. The Pamela figure from the Hitchcock film becomes Miss Fisher, sports mistress at a girls' school, but the incidents – the forcible kiss, the handcuffing, the night at the Inn – are retained and, as in the previous film, Miss Fisher eventually warms to Hannay. However, the Thomas film ends on an unambiguous note with a coda in which Hannay and Miss Fisher walk arm-in-arm in Regents Park.

The third film version of the tale adheres more closely to the original Buchan novel. It contains no equivalents to either the female agent or the married couple and no references to any marriages, either repressed or cheerful. There is, however, an equivalent to the Pamela/Miss Fisher character. Hannay, in the course of his Highland flight, chances upon a hunting party and is invited back to the house for refreshments. Amongst the party is Alexandra Mackenzie who occupies the Pamela/Miss Fisher role although in significantly different ways. In fact, where Pamela/Miss Fisher maintain a sceptical reluctance to help Hannay, Alexandra is clearly 'very taken with him'[10] at first sight. The police call at the home of David Hamilton, her fiancé, and she interrupts him as he is about to mention the stranger (Hannay) who arrived at the hunt. She and Hamilton subsequently meet with Hannay and help to rescue him from the spies. The affinity between Hannay and Alexandra, is established immediately through exchanges of glances supported by appropriate music. It comes as little suprise when her fiancé is killed by the spies leaving the way clear for the 'formation of the couple'.[11] It is an effortless courtship compared with the equivalents in the previous films and, as in the Thomas version, the finale has the couple walking arm-in-arm in a garden setting while the end-credits appear.

In narrative terms Alexandra Mackenzie plays a rather peripheral role although she does intervene at crucial points to help Hannay. Her presence in the film owes more to the conventions of popular cinema, where the romantic couple is an obligatory element, than to any necessities of the actual narrative which, as we have seen, adheres closely to the exclusively masculine world of Buchan. Whereas the women in the previous films (especially the Hitchcock version) pose problems for the hero or serve to define masculinity in various ways, Alexandra Mackenzie remains, rather conventionally, little more than a decorative element of the mise-en-scene set against Hannay's equally conventionally handsome, romantic, leading-man good looks. However, simply including the role of a woman in the film has a transformative effect despite the general closeness of Sharp's picture to the novel. The Hannay character is softened through Robert Powell's matinée idol looks and acquires qualities best alluded to by terms like 'suave' and 'debonair'. As a consequence, the masculinity presented in the Sharp film tends to pull away from the rugged 'Boy's Own' qualities in the original novel, whilst adhering to Buchan's narrative structure and detail.

HEROES/STARS/MEN

Definitions of masculinity emerge from narrative situation and the tests to which the hero is subjected, from contrasts with other male characters, and from the relationships formed with the various female characters encountered in the films. An additional and extremely important element in such definitions comes from the style and performance of the male leading players, from the looks, gestures, the physical playing of the three actors concerned. Robert Donat [Hitchcock], Kenneth More [Thomas] and Robert Powell [Sharp] constitute different versions of masculinity through the contrast in their physical appearances and playing styles, their general star images which interact with the range of narrative situations in which they are placed.

In so far as Donat's star image was defined prior to his appearance in *The Thirty-nine Steps* it was in terms of the costume picture. He had a supporting role in Korda's *The Private Life of Henry VIII* (Alexander Korda, UK, 1933) and played the lead in the Hollywood film *The Count of Monte Christo* (Roland Lee, US, 1938). Subsequently, his soft-spoken and understated playing style was utilised in a variety of roles and, although some were action-orientated, the enduring image of

(top right) Hannay, the 1935 version: Robert Donat.
(bottom left) Hannay, the 1959 version: Kenneth More.
(bottom right) Hannay, the 1978 version: Robert Powell.

Donat probably derives from his performance as a doctor in *The Citadel* (King Vidor, UK, 1930), a schoolmaster in *Goodbye Mr. Chips* (Sam Wood, UK, 1939) and as the tireless and committed British inventor of moving pictures themselves, William Friese-Greene, in *The Magic Box* (John Boulting, UK, 1951). His final leading role as a country parson in *Lease of Life* (Charles Frend, UK, 1954) sums up the somewhat tragic and caring image cultivated in many of his films. The above sketch does not suggest Buchan's Richard Hannay yet the blend of Donat's persona with the Buchan-like adventure trajectory overlaid with Hitchcock's own interests in sexual identity and definition produced the most successful of the three films. By contrast, Kenneth More's sporty, tweedy bluffness is probably more redolent of the literary Hannay yet less amenable to the discourses on sexuality and gender made available by some of the narrative situations preserved from the Hitchcock version. Indeed, as Andy Medhurst commented in an article on the male pin-up, 'how can one seriously make connections between the discourses of sexuality . . . and Kenneth More?'[12] More is associated particularly with comedies such as *Genevieve* (Henry Cornelius, UK, 1953) and *Doctor in the House* (Ralph Thomas, UK, 1954). Whilst 'Happy Go Lucky' the title of his autobiography, probably best captures his star image, some of his films (e.g. *Reach for the Sky* Lewis Gilbert, UK, 1956) do suggest more complexity and seriousness.[13] The final Hannay, Robert Powell, 'a charismatic British leading man'[14], is smooth, sophisticated and unflappable with a sexual identity presented in terms of total security and confidence. His initial encounter with Alexandra Mackenzie produces the first of a number of sequences of gaze and counter-gaze between them which leave no doubts about the eventual outcome of their meeting – the formation of the couple. Twice she mentions her fiancé and on the second occasion betrays the irrelevance of that relationship with a faltering delivery of the line of dialogue. However, there is a real sense in which the female character is grafted onto the basic Buchan tale to satisfy the conventional demand for a heterosexual narrative resolution and no opportunity for complexities of identity and definition have been allowed.

The Sharp version resists analysis in terms of models of sexual identity or in terms of discourses on male/female interrelationships by failing to include a varied set of encounter situations for Hannay. In one sense it presents a Hannay more in keeping with the Buchan prototype despite giving him a partner. Sharp's Hannay is an uncomplicated adventurer whose 'conquest' of Alexandra is achieved by the device of adding an irresistible charm to the literary character, although this in itself does, to some extent, transform the masculinity presented by the film.

The Thomas version, in adopting the narrative pattern of the Hitchcock version should offer a more complex picture of masculinity but fails to do so. Why is this? One answer may lie in authorship and the specific Hitchcockian inflection of the Buchan material which opens onto a range of themes including those of sexual definition and identity. However, another is suggested by Andy Medhurst's rhetorical incredulity when confronted with the idea of Kenneth More as a male pin-up.[15] One crucial difference between the Hitchcock and Thomas versions lies in the performances of the actors, both male and female, and it is this dimension of the Hitchcock film that contributes a great deal to the key deepening of the themes of sexual identity and definition noted by critics such as Wood. This is not simply a matter of Donat versus More, although the playing of the former does incorporate a greater range of tones and moods. It may be more pertinent to examine the playing of the female characters against which the images of masculinity in the two films are defined.

The Hannay image is defined in part by his three encounters with females. Hitchcock's female agent is foreign, glamorous (dressed in black with a fashion hat and veil), and seductive whereas the Thomas equivalent is initially dressed in the uniform of a children's nanny. 'Nanny' Robinson does appear subsequently in a dress when she meets Hannay at the music hall but there is absolutely no sexual hint or implication when she returns with him to his flat. The crofter sequence in the Hitchcock film depicts a young woman somewhat trapped in an oppressive marriage to a rather austere and unsmiling older man whom Hannay initially assumes is her father. It has a weight and depth which marks it off both from the adventure trajectory and from the light sexual banter of the Annabella Smith episode. By comparison, the equivalent episode in the Thomas film – the presentation of the Lumsden marriage – is played for its humorous possibilities. In this marriage the power lies with the woman. Mr Lumsden does not seem oppressed but comes over as a willing junior partner in the Lumsden matriarchy. In contrast to the joyless crofter, Nellie Lumsden is a sensual figure; she propositions Hannay soon after his arrival explaining that 'poor old Lumsden's long past caring about . . . that sort of thing'. Where the Hitchcock episode injected a degree of drama and pathos into the helter-skelter of incident, the passage in the Thomas film sustains the tone of playfulness that marks the film from beginning to end. The final encounters with Pamela/Miss Fisher are identical in both films at the level of incident. They differ markedly, however, in terms of tone and impact due largely to the playing and the contrast between Donat and More and, crucially, between Madeleine Carroll and Taina Elg.

CONTEXTS

The films are very different in terms of tone, mood and the inflection of key elements, especially those that bear upon the exploration of sexuality. Such differences may relate to the rather different historical contexts in which they were made.

The Hitchcock picture was made during the depression years of the 1930s when the cinema was a major feature of the cultural and imaginative life of the bulk of the population. It was also made in the context of the overwhelming popularity of American films which constituted something like seventy per cent of the films screened in Britain during the decade, and was almost certainly conceived of as a film to be directed at American as well as British audiences of the time. In fact, both Donat and Carroll were known to American audiences with previous appearances in American films. The paradigms of masculinity which derive from the American cinema (Fredric March, Spencer Tracy, Gary Cooper, Cary Grant, Douglas Fairbanks) constitute the effective context for a positioning of Donat's Hannay who, in fact, becomes a Canadian in the Hitchcock version.

Kenneth More's Hannay is, perhaps, the most antique of the three and, accordingly, perhaps closer to the Hannay of the novel. As a model of masculinity, he predates by some years the changing patterns of male behaviour circulating in the contemporary culture. Once again, the America cinema supplied the templates and the distance between More and, say, Dean, Brando or Montgomery Clift, Tony Curtis or Burt Lancaster, does seem significant. Yet, as Andy Medhurst has noted, More's persona – 'tweedy', somewhat asexual – does fit into a world of the British star of the 1950s which is to be defined only partly in the context of the American cinema and other aspects of American popular culture notably rock and roll music, Elvis Presley etc. More is the epitome of a masculinity defined by qualities of 'decency, honesty, straightforwardness, steadfastness, manliness, Britishness'[16], associated with the rural middle-classes of the Home Counties and presented most consistently in cinematic terms in the cycle of World War Two pictures made in the 1950s. It contrasts dramatically with the restless, brooding images of masculinity coming from America. However, the image also contrasts with the overtly sexualised masculinities represented by James Mason and Stewart Granger from the 1940s and with the working-class masculinities of Albert Finney and Richard Harris in the British 'new wave' films which began to appear on British screens in the same year as the Ralph Thomas/Kenneth More film.

The third version, from the late 1970s, deploys a more conventional romantic lead in the Hannay character, despite emerging from a context in which the securities of traditional masculinities were being eroded by the proliferation of images of alternative femininities. The film is marked by 'retro' appeal – a precise mise en scene, attentive to period detail in environment, costume, and full of potent icons of nostalgia such as trains and automobiles. It is also marked by a certain self-consciousness in the playing of Robert Powell, especially in the course of his romantic exchanges. This produces a somewhat satirised version of traditional cinematic romantic masculinity of the kind represented by, say, Errol Flynn.

CONCLUSION

Whilst all three film versions of The Thirty-nine Steps and the original novel construct specific forms of masculinity, they do so in different ways. The novel presents a robust, seemingly uncomplicated man's world where adventure is a refuge from the boredom of everyday life. In Buchan's world, in fact, women barely exist and notions of more complicated masculinities would need to be based upon homoerotic interpretations of the adversarial relationships between the males in the story.[17] The Sharp film follows the novel closely but adds a female character in conformity with the demands of conventional narrative cinema for a romantic element. The Thomas version ostensibly copies the Hitchcock picture but lacks the incisiveness of the latter in terms of the discourses of sexuality. One key to this differences lies in performance. Of the three Hannays, only the Donat rendition has the depth to represent the problematics of masculinity; and, in addition, only the playing of Donat's female co-actors provides the strength and depth to push the film towards the probing analysis of sexual construction and sexual relationships, towards those 'realms of experience which never existed for Buchan'.[18] A further key is Hitchcock. It might also be argued that those 'realms of experiences' did not exist for Ralph Thomas or Don Sharp either but that they were very much the central focus for Hitchcock many years before the more overt explorations of such matters in the more prominent American films of the 1950s such as Rear Window (Hitchcock, US, 1954) and Vertigo (Hitchcock, US, 1958). A final irony in the comparison of the three versions of The Thirty-nine Steps is that the film most critically alert to the mechanisms of sexual identity construction is also the earliest and was made in conditions of relatively tight censorship. By contrast, the 1959 film seems untouched by the competing versions of masculinity in the popular culture of the time – Presley, Dean etc. – and the 1978 version, despite a hint of distancing in the playing of Robert

Powell, remains a detailed period piece, and a straightforward adventure tale in the manner of its literary source.

NOTES

Thanks are due to Janet Thumim and Yvonne Tasker for helpful comments on an earlier draft of this article.

1 I shall refer to the films as the Hitchcock, Thomas and Sharp versions for ease of reference rather than for any particular adherence to authorial interpretations.

2 Interview with Raymond Bellour, *Camera Obscura* 3-4, 1979, p88.

3 For comments on such analyses see 'The Divided Gaze: Reflections on the Political Thriller' by Tony Davies, in Derek Longhurst (ed), *Gender, Genre and Narrative Pleasure*, Unwin Hyman, London, 1989.

4 J. Buchan, *The Thirty-nine Steps* Pan Books, 1959, from the dedication.

5 J. Bristow, *Empire Boys*, Harper Collins Academic, London, 1991, p1.

6 J.A. Mangan & J. Walvin, (eds) *Manliness and Morality*, Manchester University Press, Manchester, 1987, p65.

7 Buchan, *The Thirty-nine Steps*, p7.

8 R. Wood, *Hitchcock's Films Revisited*, Columbia UP, 1989, p277.

9 Wood, *op. cit.* p283.

10 From the dialogue of the film.

11 Raymond Bellour interview, *op. cit.*, p88.

12 A. Medhurst, *10/8* No. 17, 1985.

13 K. More, *Happy Go Lucky*, Hale, 1959.

14 D. Quinlan, *Quinlan's Illustrated Directory of Film Stars* Batsford, London, 1986.

15 Medhurst, *op. cit.*

16 *Ibid.*

17 See the Davies article in Longhurst (ed), *op. cit.*

18 P. Wollen, 'Hitchcock's Vision', *Cinema* (UK) No. 3, 1969, p2.

Blood Sweat and Tears: Amitabh Bachchan, Urban Demi-god

Ashwani Sharma

> The fantastic image of a towering universally admired penis is a powerful compensation for the Indian boy's expulsion from the maternal paradise . . .   Sudhir Kakar.[1]

> I feel that there's a bit of anger in all of us and it takes different forms. I had a very nice medium where I could express it and that was cinema . . . Somewhere in the minds and in the hearts of the youth of India there was some kind of suppressed anger, something that they desired and which was not being said . . . There was a tremendous identification by the people and by the youth with characters that I was doing and because of this identification I think they [the roles] became very popular . . .   Amitabh Bachchan.[2]

This article attempts to formulate some ideas about masculinity in Indian Bombay cinema, concentrating on the factors contributing to the construction of the star Amitabh Bachchan, one of the best known and influential stars of recent years. By examining one of Bachchan's recent films *Agneepath* (*Path of Fire*, Mukul Anand, 1990) I will explore the way masculinity is signified and possibly read in an Indian context. Because relatively little is known about Indian culture and cinema in the West, this article is in part an introduction to the topic as well as a critical engagement with Bombay cinema. A major framing argument is that all types of cultural production and construction (of which masculinity is one), are historically and culturally specific, and the ways in which they are read are extremely variable. Different peoples, different cultures at different times, as well as different individuals, will read, identify and interpret the various filmic texts in different ways. This article is offered as a helpful framework for contextualising the manner in which spectators may interpret the multiple readings available.

The dominant Bombay cinema is situated within the polymorphous collection of texts and discourses which is Indian culture.[3] The cinema is a truly hybrid institution, which draws upon a vast array of different cultural sources and reflects the rapidly changing circumstances of twentieth century India. Nothing is 'alien' to the cinematic text; Hindu mythology, Indian folk traditions, Hollywood cinema and Indian history are all reconstituted to create a particular and culturally unique cinematic universe. This incorporation of diverse discourses and ideologies produces significant tensions and contradictions within the film texts. However, in an attempt to continually (re)create an 'Indian cinema world-view', a sense of unity and stability is enforced upon the narrative. An ideologically motivated moral code within a culturally specific mode of signification attempts to simplify the complexity of 'Indian reality' and to create a utopian cinematic fantasy world where forces of 'good' and 'evil' are in perpetual conflict. This is a world where instability and ambivalence are continually suppressed by the re-establishment of moral order. But it is also a world which, in its own way, tries to deal with the complexities of Indian social and political history.

It is in this context of a culturally specific yet still 'contradictory' system of signification that I want to position questions about representation of the male and masculinity. But first a detour through some of the cultural factors bearing on Bombay cinema which will, I hope, illustrate the specificity and differences of Indian masculinity in comparison to other cultural and national formations.

MYTH

Myths have a very strong place in the lives of Indian people. Far more than in the West, mythological narratives are a significant part of the 'reality' of Indian life. It has been argued that Indians have a 'softer' attitude to the distinction between myths, illusions, dreams and so called reality than is the case in many other societies.[4] The myths play an integral part in Indian people's interpretation of the world; all forms of communication are in some sense mediated through the mythical and Bombay cinema must be seen within this context. In their totality the vast collection of narrative/texts from Hindu religious mythology and cinema present a very complex picture of the masculine. The cinema has privileged certain interpretations and has continually reworked the masculine within relatively conservative cultural and ideological historical discourses. Vijay Mishra has argued that all the films are a literal replaying of the 'master' mythological texts of Indian culture; the *Mahabharata* and *Ramayana*.[5] For over 2,000 years, the heterogeneous collection of texts which collectively make up these 'master' epic narratives have continually been reinterpreted and represented. Bombay cinema, therefore, can be seen as a twentieth century urban interpretation of these texts.

Significant for the cinema and for this article is the way in which this hegemonic interpretation of Hindu/Indian religious philosophy places a significant emphasis on *Dharma*/morality and the family. *Dharma* or moral duty is the central metaphysical concept which determines the duties of individuals in society. Cinema translates this concept of *dharma* by allocating particular functions and duties to various members of the family, duties which are strongly demarcated by gender. The male is positioned either as son, brother or father and conversely, the female as mother, daughter, sister or daughter in law. Within the Hindu world view (and Bombay cinema), the male is considered more important and central, females being generally defined in relation to men. The male is expected to follow an 'ideal' path in life thus fulfilling his duty and, in doing this correctly, can overcome the cycle of life/death/rebirth and achieve *moksha* or release.[6] The attainment of *moksha*/release/transcendence is one of the central tenets of Hindu religious philosophy.[7] Classical Indian art and culture is firmly rooted in this philosophy and is based on creating particular emotional states in the spectator which ultimately leads to *moksha*.

The Bombay cinema in its unique way appropriates, draws on and is situated within these philosophical paradigms. In many ways it is a modern, technological, folk form which attempts to affect the spectator by creating particular emotional moods in ways somewhat similar to Western melodrama.[8] The cinema presents the masculine within a 'fantasy' world, a universe in which characters are typical rather than unique, a cinematic world where meaning is articulated through affectivity and, in all of this, the male is crucial in the creation of particular meanings and emotions.

URBAN REALITY AND BACHCHAN THE MEGASTAR

Amitabh Bachchan has been, without question, the leading and most significant star in Bombay cinema in the last twenty years. He has starred in over 200 films, including *Zanjeer* (Prakash Mehra, 1973), *Deewaar* (*I'll Die For Mama*, Yash Chopra, 1975), *Sholay* (*Flames of the Sun*, Ramesh Sippy, 1975), *Amar Akbar Anthony* Manmohan Desai, 1977), *Don* (Naram Irani, 1978), *Naseeb* (*Fate*, Manmohan

Amitabh Bachchan in *Deewaar*, (Chopra, India, 1975)

Amitabh Bachchan in *Agneepath*, (Anand, India, 1990)

Desai, 1981), *Coolie* Manmohan Desai, 1983), *Agneepath* (Mukul Anand, 1990), *Hum* (Mukul Anand, 1991) and *Kudah Gawah* (Mukul Anand, 1992), which have been some of the most popular and commercially successful films in India. Indeed, he has been dubbed a 'one man industry' because of the immense effect he has had on the development of Bombay cinema. The character of the 'angry young man', which Bachchan first played in *Zanjeer* in 1973, has become one of, if not *the* dominant representation of masculinity in that cinema. Although a versatile actor, who has played romantic and comic roles, it is for his roles in action movies that he is best known. The rebellious, anti-establishment characters with which he is associated became extremely popular with both male and female audiences, especially of the working and lower middle classes. Nor is his fame limited to India; he is very well-known in various parts of the Third World, especially Africa, the Arab world and the Caribbean and he also has a very strong following in the diasporan South Asian communities in the West. Within both these contexts, global and Indian, he functions as a hero of the oppressed.

To understand the rise of his popularity and star status we need to place it within the context of Indian social and urban development. India, after Independence in 1947, undertook a major programme of industrialization and urbanization which had significant demographic effects. During the 1960s and early 1970s, there was rapid movement of rural people to the cities in search of employment. Limited housing and inadequate urban welfare led to the formation of an underclass of slum dwellers living on the pavements or in shantytowns and finding work, when they could, in poorly paid casual jobs. This section of the population also constituted a significant element of the rapidly changing cinema-going public. Urbanization radically changed the lives of many Indians, whose world view was traditionally constructed through the myths and rituals of tradition and community. The large scale displacement of rural people brought turmoil to a hitherto relatively stable world. Life in the cities was harsh and alienating; the very fabric of tradition, family and community was put under great strain. Bombay cinema adapted to these changed circumstances and appealed to this growing cinema audience by recreating the traditions of Indian culture within a modern framework which incorporated both urban and national dimensions of experience.[9]

The Bachchan phenomenon is a product of these social changes which were addressed in the Bombay cinematic utopia from the 1970s. He was the first 'real' male working class hero of Bombay cinema, marking a significant break from previous male stars, such as K.L. Saigal, Ashok Kumar, Raj Kapoor, Dev Anand, Dilip Kumar, Guru Dutt, Shammi Kapoor and Rajesh Khanna. The latter were in some degree also critical of Indian society but their critique was much 'softer' and they are best described as romantic heroes. The male romantic hero has deep roots in Indian culture. From the sexual escapades of the god Krishna to the suffering Islamic figure Majnun, there has been a constant rhetoric of male desire in relation to love and romance. This inevitably produced a conflict within a society where the preservation of family and the institution of marriage are far more important than any notions of heterosexual love. Generally, in myth, art and literature, the male figure suffered in his desire for the female and this theme, common also to South Asian poetry and song, is central to the history of Bombay cinema. The figure of the male poet best symbolises this 'soft' side of the masculine in Indian culture, namely the male who suffers and who puts love and romance above all else.

Bachchan represents a significant break from this tradition. He frequently plays an anti-establishment hero who lives on the margins of 'respectable' society, whereas many of the earlier male stars played middle class roles in films whose political critiques were limited to the institution of the family. In these earlier films, conflict was usually personalised and expressed only between members of families. The romantic heroes were ultimately impotent in the face of an unjust society. But the Bachchan hero is productive. This man of action lets nothing stand in the way of getting things done. The sense of achievement conveyed had great audience appeal in the 1970s. The idealism of romance was superceded by the pragmatism of violence. Unlike the more 'passive', romantic heroes, the Bachchan hero externalises his own alienation from the cruel materialist world through anger, action and revenge. In his persona, masculinity became far less ambivalent and much more active and achieving.

The figure of an anti-establishment, good-bad rebel has its roots in a number of diverse narratives. From the mythical texts the character of Karna is an important antecedent.[10] In fact, the *Mahabharata* is a paradigmatic text in the Bachchan cinema; the tension between moral duty, justice and family loyalty, within an environment of conflict, is central to both the mythological text and 1970s cinema. But the Bachchan hero should also be placed in the context of other rebel heroes of world cinema. In the 1970s, male stars such as Clint Eastwood and Bruce Lee had a powerful impact on Indian cinema audiences. The violence of the Hollywood Western and the highly spectacular Hong Kong Kung Fu films found a strong resonance in the construction of the Bachchan star text. He is the result of a particular intersections of masculinity within an increasingly global star system. Bachchan's performances are relatively free of the weight of cultural tradition and he presents a modern and up to date image. Here is a modern man, an 'industrial' man, constructed through the fusion of

Eastern and Western notions of ideal masculinity.

In the Indian context his superstar status has been transformed to a god-like status. Bachchan, the star, is now more significant than the films in which he acts. He has created what has been called his own 'parallel text'. Vijay Mishra, Peter Jeffrey and Brian Shoesmith have persuasively argued that Bachchan has created a text of his own, far more significant than his films; indeed, they go as far as to suggest that he is the 'real author' of these films, since they are subsumed into the larger Bachchan text. Drawing upon theories about Western stars, they argue that in the Indian context Bachchan's popularity goes beyond that usually associated with Western stars. They argue that, through the artificially constructed epic commentaries in newspaper articles and gossip magazines as well as his abortive attempt at a political career, a metatext of Bachchan is created which is read by the audience in conjunction with the filmic texts. They also claim, rather less convincingly, that there '. . . is something symbiotic and emotional, a form of an aesthetic relish in the materiality of the star, something resonating deep in Indian psychology that explains that initial moment of conjunction'.[11] They emphasise that the Bachchan/hero/star plays on previous mythological texts and is a transformation of already known and identifiable, religious, mythical figures. Mishra has stated that through his films Bachchan has become '. . . a complex text in his own right sanctioned by mythology and responding to the need for rebelliousness in the restless lower . . .' class.[12]

AGNEEPATH, THE BACHCHAN METATEXT

Agneepath can be read as the dramatization of the Bachchan parallel text. It's main function is as a vehicle for Bachchan; everyone and everything else is secondary and insignificant. It draws upon his other films and creates a world where the only agency is the mythical, superhuman figure of Bachchan. Stripped of the numerous sub-plots and comic interludes common to most Bombay films and with song and dance numbers reduced to the bare minimum, one is left with a simulation of the core Bachchan text. In effect, this is a Bachchan metatext.

The film has a typically Bachchan revenge narrative, a narrative which, partly because of Bachchan and his action films, has become immensely popular in Bombay cinema. Bachchan, as a young boy Vijay, sees his father, a teacher, needlessly killed by the village mob under the instructions of the feudal landlord, who is working with urban gangsters. The young Bachchan/Vijay, his sister and mother move to the city of Bombay and live on the streets. His mother is sexually abused and he takes revenge by burning the petrol station owned by the leading criminal boss who was involved in the attacks on both his mother and his father. This revenge action is motivated by the total disinterest shown by the corrupt police. The arson attack is the beginning of Bachchan/Vijay's criminalization. A leap forward of twenty years in the film's narrative finds Bachchan/Vijay a leading figure in the criminal underworld. He is called 'brother' by the disenfranchised, shantytown dwellers of the city but his mother is very unhappy with his lifestyle. The 'unscrupulous' gangster bosses attempt to have him killed and they kidnap his wife, baby son, sister and, most importantly, his mother. These events further fuel his desire to reek revenge on the gangsters and the feudal landlord who had previously had his father killed. In the climatic and highly spectacular final confrontation sequence he rescues his family but dies, after suffering great pain, in the arms of his mother. Before this happens, however, there is a highly emotional mother-son reconciliation.

The family which, as we have seen, is central in forming the identity of the individual in Indian culture, is the context within which the film's narrative is situated. *Agneepath* begins with the young Bachchan/Vijay in the family context. His father and mother represent key aspects of the cultural, religious and moral discourses underpinning Bombay cinema. It is the tension between this moral dimension and the individual desires of Bachchan/Vijay that drive the narrative forward. The beginning of the film revolves around the father-son relationship. The father is shown as a good man. As the village teacher he represents possible change and progress in an India where liberals believe that changing feudal and traditional structures and attitudes is best done through education. The father passes his knowledge and understanding to his son. The bond between the young Bachchan/Vijay and the father is strong and clear. The film begins with young Bachchan/Vijay questioning his father about the light in the city and whether the city folk worship this light like the sun. The father replies that '. . . it is wealth that they worship and worshippers of wealth often take the wrong path; the path of truth is the path of fire.' They recite a poem together which Bachchan/Vijay has partially learned:

> The path of fire
> The leafy trees stand tall
> But do not seek the shade of a single leaf
> Never shall you tire
> Never shall you turn back
> The path of fire

A splendid sight: mankind strides ahead drenched in blood, sweat and tears
The path of fire

Crucially, the father explains that '. . . a man drenched in blood, sweat and tears as he seeks his goal cannot be stopped by any obstacles'. Vijay promises to never forget this poem. The son has entered the moral symbolic order of the father.

The path of fire becomes the metaphor for Bachchan/Vijay's life. In the narrative he becomes a 'man' and 'head' of the family when his father is killed. This death is a crucial event in the formation of his identity. The killing of his good but impotent father has a deep effect on Bachchan/Vijay. It marks the death of good and an end to the possibility of progress in the village. A key event for Vijay is the dragging of his father's dead body for cremation. His struggle to move the body, single handedly (none of the villagers would help the young boy) is a recurring flashback in the film and symbolic of Bachchan/Vijay's struggle in later life. The death or withdrawal of the good father early in the film is a common theme in Bombay cinema. It allows the son to become the central male protagonist and it also allows the mother figure to have a greater role both within the family and the film.

If Bachchan/Vijay's father represents one aspect of the (male) symbolic order, the villains effectively represent the other (in psychoanalytic terms), the aggressive father. Ravi Vasudevan, in his analysis of narratives, suggests that Bombay cinema emphasizes the conflict between the aggressive father and the traumatised son.[13] The son is certainly traumatized but that is largely through his father's death and Bachchan/Vijay's role as an active protector of the family is signified early in the film when his father scolds and attempts to strike his sister. Vijay protects her from their father, citing his father's own earlier words regarding justice. Bachchan/Vijay has absorbed the teachings of his father but his father's gentle way of life is replaced by a more aggressive, violent approach based on revenge. The father's moral discourse is continued through the film via the figure of the good but relatively ineffectual chief of police who, in the style of Bombay cinema, is unambiguously a substitute father figure for Bachchan/Vijay. He continually challenges Bachchan/Vijay's methods of achieving justice. There is a scene in which, after Bachchan/Vijay warns him that his life is in danger and when the police chief argues that he nevertheless has duties to perform, Bachchan/Vijay compares him to his own father with his idealism and naïve faith in truth and justice. This conflict between Bachchan/Vijay and tradition and authority, vested in the absent father and the substitute father figure of the police chief, is more intensely and differently played out in his relationship with his mother.

The key familial relationship in this film, as in many other Bombay films, is the mother-son relationship which, as indicated earlier, gains importance after the death of the father/husband. Both the move to the city and the hero's growing criminalization pull him outside the structures of the traditional family and its associated moral dimension. Bachchan/Vijay is torn between his desire to avenge his father's death and to change society, by criminal methods if necessary, and his desire to be accepted and loved by his mother. Throughout the film, the mother is seen to be suffering and enduring great hardship. Sudhir Kakar, an Indian psychoanalyst and cultural theorist, has argued that one of the primary male fantasies in Indian culture is to save the suffering mother from pain and, conversely, the mother's fantasy is to be saved by her son.[14] Bombay cinema continually replays this scenario. There is no doubt that the hero wants to avenge his mother's misfortune as well as the death of his father, but there are a number of highly emotional scenes in the film where his mother rejects him because of his criminal activities. This rejection is source of great pain and anguish for Bachchan/Vijay. Compared to mythology and to earlier cinematic representations of the mother figure, the mother in this film is relatively passive, she acts solely as a preserver of tradition, order and morality. The hero's rejection by her and the lack of mother love form crucial elements in the drama of the film. The final sequence where Bachchan runs through a virtual battlefield in an attempt to save his mother most clearly condenses and articulates their relationship. His saving of her and his death in her arms marks the point of literal and psychic reunion with the mother as well as the death of the rebel and his absorption back into Indian traditional ways, into 'Mother Nature', into Mother India. This transition can also be read as the *moksha*/release from the suffering and pain of life and society.

The other women in the film are very marginal. In relation to his sister Bachchan acts as a father figure, protecting her from his enemies but also concerned, as a father would be, about her romantic attachments. Although Bachchan/Vijay does get married in the film, significantly to a Christian nurse which marks him as being outside sectarian Hindu values, there is nevertheless little hint of romantic or sexual interest. May, his wife, functions like a virginal substitute mother figure. In the hospital, after he had been shot, she looks after him like a mother. Significantly, Bachchan/Vijay visits her on two occasions after he has been in conflict with his mother. On the second he asks her (or more precisely tells her) to marry him. Her marginal role in the film entails looking after Bachchan/Vijay, encouraging him to live up to the dreams of his mother and, last but by no means least, giving birth to their child. This last event re-establishes Bachchan/ Vijay within the family structure and is also the point in the narrative at which he reassesses his criminal actions. His re-entry into the moral structure of the family as a father figure, therefore, is very strongly marked in the film.

EMOTION, MISE EN SCENE AND EXCESS

Bachchan signifies his feelings and emotions to the external world through his actions. The audience is aware of his state of mind through the mise-en-scene. Bombay cinema, as with other melodramatic cinemas, uses *mise en scene* to create powerful meanings and effects. The male figure of Bachchan in *Agneepath* is central in creating meaning; the film's dramatic conflict is played out through the visual representation of him; his figure is the site of conflicts which the narrative must resolve.

A hallmark of the Bachchan text is his superhuman, fighting skills. Fighting has been a signifer of masculinity in all cinema, but in Bombay cinema fighting, and violent action in general, take on an extra significance because masculinity and femininity are not very clearly demarcated, especially in the romantic social films. Many of the Bombay action movies of the last twenty years have used fighting and other violent sequences to dramatise the conflict between good and evil. This violence is central to the Bachchan text. Whereas in previous films he inevitably gets involved in fight sequences, in *Agneepath* the action is less personal but more spectacular. Firearms and explosives offer a grand and flamboyant style of violence; a spectacle of excess. Bachchan/Vijay is the central figure in this pyrotechnic environment. He is at the receiving end of much of the violence but he also perpetuates it. Bachchan's actions are clinical and precise. He shows no remorse or guilt in killing. He acts in a very sadistic way towards his enemies. Yet his very popularity stems in part, from this representation of sadistic violence. The anger and violence that Bachchan displays has a strong effect on viewers. His revenge actions become symbolic and resonate deeply with the oppressed spectators. The pleasures of these scenes lie in their ability to play out the repressed desires and fantasies of the Indian working class and underclasses. *Agneepath's* excessive use of spectacle and its emphasis on mise-en-scene outdoes both Bombay and Bachchan cinema to that date. The film draws upon previous Bachchan scenarios to create meaning in the film but without so fully articulating the moral dimension. It is an audio-visual spectacle of the Bachchan text and the tensions and contradictions of Bachchan in action. Audiences are assumed to be fully aware of the Bachchan text and therefore able to read the various intertextual nuances. The construction of the mise-en-scene and the figure of Bachchan/Vijay are central to the film's signification. Bachchan's boat is blown up – he could not possibly have survived but in the next scene we see a near-Herculean figure dramatically emerge from the sea in slow motion. With such spectacular representations, his dual abilities to defy mortality and confront evil are established; his superhuman capabilities, his status as god-like being are thereby confirmed. Strength and power are central concerns of the Bachchan/Vijay character and referenced throughout the film. But, above all, it is Bachchan's performance which emphasises the importance of strength and endurance in contemporary urban India. Death faces Bachchan continually in his films and it is the absence of fear of death which further signifies his virtually immortal status. It is this ability to defy death and transcend normal humanity which makes him so immensely popular with audiences.

In *Agneepath* it seems that the whole of the Bombay underclass is waiting for news about the health of Bachchan/Vijay after he has been shot; there are riots in the streets and exuberant celebrations on his recovery. This is very similar to the real life event where Bachchan was severely, almost fatally, injured when performing his own stunts during filming. This real life/film intersection adds to the Bachchan metatext, which blurs the difference between 'reality' and the Bachchan character. The media commentary surrounding his accident is crucial to an understanding of a particular type of masculinity, one which had not hitherto been present in Bombay cinema. Furthermore his performance of his own stunts reinforces and is a strong marker of his masculinity.

Linked to the notion of death, and in contrast to the sadism of the Bachchan text, is the agony and hardship he endures. This ability to endure pain, suffer and yet survive is an important aspect of the male star. As noted earlier, the metaphor of his life pattern in this film is blood, sweat and tears. This torment invites empathy for the character and is part of Indian culture's discourse of pain, and the identification with the oppressed; only through suffering, it is said, does one achieve anything. Scenes of this kind in Bombay cinema offer masochistic pleasures to the spectator which are very different in form to the pleasures offered by the sadistic violence emphasised above.[15] The final sequence exemplifies this. The audiences knows that Bachchan/Vijay's final run to save his mother and family will end in death, but he courageously continues to run through the explosions in slow motion, along a 'path of fire'. The highly charged scene is further heightened by his being shot a number of times and yet continuing to run, drenched in blood, towards the villain in order to save his mother.

The construction of Bachchan in this film as meta-Bachchan is particularly highlighted by the deepening of his voice. The tone of the voice is an important factor in the construction of character in Bombay cinema. The deep voice is a key signifier of a particular, authoritative masculinity. The voice of the Bachchan character in *Agneepath* is very deliberately and obviously being deepened and made harsher, further emphasising the excessive and hyperbolic nature of the character and film. But, in line with the complex construction of the male in Indian culture, even in films such as *Agneepath* with its emphasis on excessive violence and revenge spectacle, other emotional states are still present. Bachchan/Vijay also has a sensitive side to him, especially in relation to his mother. He cries in the film after a scene of conflict with her and again at the end when he is dying in her arms. Within the discourses of Bombay action cinema there are no contradictions between these two sides of the male: the co-existence of the sensitive son and the aggressive rebel, particularly within the Bachchan text, poses few difficulties for Indian audiences.

The figure of Amitabh Bachchan has created a persona which floats in and out of cinema. The distinction between his cinematic representation and his life outside cinema is difficult to demarcate. Through the roles and characters he has played he has become a modern demigod, and urban folk hero. He is worshipped and adored in similar ways to Hindu gods. Going far beyond mere fandom, his audiences see him as the symbol of utopian hope. He is a new type of god, a figure who questions traditional values and also challenges the corruption of modern society. His appeal lies in the apparent ability to go beyond the limitations of traditional justice. He signifies many of the conflicts in contemporary Indian society. His masculinity is the site which signifies the various conflicting social and historical forces. Bachchan the text is 'real' in the context of Indian cultural conceptions of reality and representation. Though he very clearly represents a male figure, masculinity itself is not limited to the male body. The Bachchan text oscillates between Bachchan the male star, Bachchan the demigod, Bachchan the fantasy figure and Bachchan the political text.

NOTES

This article is dedicated to Sangeeta, without you there is nothing. I'd especially like to thank Pat Kirkham and Janet Thumim for their help, support and encouragement during the writing of this article.

1 Sudhir Kakar, *The Inner World: A Psychoanalytic Study of Childhood and Society in India*, Oxford University Press, Delhi, 1978, p156.

2 Nasreen Munni Kabir, *Indian Cinema on 4*, booklet produced by Channel Four Television, 1984, p34.

3 Less than one fifth of current Indian film production (approximately 800 films per year), are made in Bombay. But, nevertheless, the Hindi Bombay cinema, with its pan-Indian audience, is dominant in terms of audiences. Significant industries exist in the south of the country but these films are limited in appeal by language to the regional states. See (eds) Paul Willemen and Behroze Gandhi, *Indian Cinema*, British Film Institute Dossier no 5, BFI, London, 1980, for an overview of the regional film industries.

4 Wendy Doniger O'Flaherty, *Dreams, Illusions and Other Realities*, University of Chicago Press, Chicago, 1984.

5 Vijay Mishra, 'Towards a Theoretical Critique of Bombay Cinema', *Screen* 26, May-August 1985, pp133-155.

6 See Misra, *op.cit.*, p139. He argues that there are two types of men in Hindu India-The renouncer and Man-of-the-World. Although this argument is relevant to the representation of masculinity in Bombay cinema, it is not clear to me how this ahistorical reading transfers to the cinema in the 1970s.

7 See Kakar, *op.cit..*, chapters 1 and 2, for a good overview of the concept of *Mokhsa* and general Hindu religious philosophy and its relationship to the individual.

8 The historical and philosophical roots of Bombay cinema are very different to the roots of Western melodrama. See Peter Brooks, *The Melodramatic Imagination: Balzac, Henry James, and the Mode of Excess*, Yale University Press, New Haven, 1976, for a clear outline of the roots of Western melodrama.

9 Bombay cinema has always been highly nationalistic and emphasised the creation of an Indian national, cultural identity.

10 See Vijay Mishra, Peter Jeffery, Brian Shoesmith, 'The Actor as Parallel Text in Bombay Cinema', *Quarterly Review of Film and Video*, vol. 11, 1989, pp49-67, for a detailed examination of the character Karna, his role in the *Mahabharata* and the archaeology of the Bombay film hero.

11 See Mishra *et al.* 'The Actor as Parallel Text in Bombay cinema', *op.cit.* p57. This article is the most thorough study of the Bachchan phenomenon to date.

12 *Ibid.*, 'Parallel Text', p57.

13 Ravi Vasudevan, 'The Melodramatic Mode and the Commercial Hindi Cinemas,' *Screen*, vol.30 no.3, Summer 1989, pp29-50.

14 See Sudhir Kakar, 'The Cinema as Collective Fantasy' in Aruna Vasudev and Phillipe Lenglet, (eds), *Indian Cinema Superbazaar*, Vikas Publishing House, New Delhi, 1983 pp89-97, for a psychoanalytical interpretation of the mother-son relationship.

15 See Gaylyn Studlar *In the Realm of Pleasure*, University of Illinois Press, Urbana and Chicago, 1988, for a strong argument about the difference in form of sadistic and masochistic pleasures and for a more general thesis regarding the centrality of masochism in cinema. Her arguments seem particularly pertinent to the study of Bombay cinema.

The Invisible Man: Shrinking Masculinity in the 1950s Science Fiction B-Movie

Paul Wells

'Roger, I could bop that monster over the head with my handbag!'[1]

Spiders, Saucermen and Satellites!; Monsters, Madmen and Machines!. Aliens, alternative worlds and alliterative publicity slogans screamed from billboards and trailers as the science fiction B-movie entered into the 1950s zeitgeist. Looking back from our new age perspective, what exactly is it that we are watching? Thinly disguised tracts about the atomic threat? Warnings about the infiltration of Communists? The revenge of nature? Yes, but beware another kind of reading. It came from beneath the sub-text . . .! What we are witnessing, I would suggest, in anything from the best of the Bs (*The Thing from Another World* (Christian Nyby/Howard Hawks, US, 1951), *The Incredible Shrinking Man* (Jack Arnold, US, 1957)) to the worst of the Zs (*The Amazing Colossal Man* (Bert I. Gordon, US, 1957), *Attack of the Fifty Foot Woman* (Nathan Hertz, US, 1959)) is a systematic destabilization of movie-made masculinity.

It is important to recognise that, although these films were valuable in constructing metaphors around the nuclear threat or the fear of Communism, they also served as a distraction from the more mundane issues of the period, which ironically they also reflect. In *Communism, Conformism and Civil Liberties*, Samuel Stouffer's research revealed that, in the 1950s, the American public was more concerned with domestic and financial problems than Communism or the issue of civil liberties.[2] Similarly, in David Reisman's important post-war study of the changing American character, *The Lonely Crowd*, it is suggested that, despite increased personal mobility and the cultural and national imperative to expand and grow, the tendency of social character was 'inner-directed',[3] a concept I will return to in discussing the figure of the scientist in the sci-fi B-movie. This shift away from the external, global and universal at the social level makes the study of personal relationships and gender roles depicted in science fiction even more fruitful. The real subject of these narratives is the fantastic as a projection of inner concerns. The science fiction B-movie of the 1950s works on a number of levels; it prioritises the fantastic above the contextual realism from which it emerges, thus initially distracting the viewer from its assumptions and re-definitions of domestic bonds and the roles of men and women. As Dale Carter suggests:

> In 1938 Orson Welles' radio dramatization of *The War of the Worlds* revealed the ways in which the intersections of economic and social conditions, media codings, technical change, and historical events constituted what Hadley Cantril termed 'a pattern of circumstances providing a matrix for high suggestibility' – and therefore, exploitation, however exciting. Between 1950 and 1957 no less than 133 Science Fiction films – beginning, predictably, with *The Flying Saucer* – tapped the same vein. They used an expanding stockpile of mythological apparatus to dramatise contemporary existence as an extreme extension of established frontier myth.[4]

What becomes clear, and what I wish to address in this essay, is the fact that, time and again, men in the sci-fi B-movie demonstrate ineptitude in their attempt to secure power and take control of their circumstances. They have inherited the frontier myth and its patriarchal lore but they find themselves in a society where these values are subject to change and re-definition. Men can no longer trust their status and position. The world is in flux, and the promise of the future is destabilization – a condition suggested by certain advertisements of the time in which:

> . . . technological utopias stretch off into a distance that is the visible symbol of the intangible, invisible and distant future. They are bathed in the same cold sunlight that illuminates de Chirico's metaphysical puzzles – a sunlight whose clarity does little to reveal the true meaning of the objects upon which it falls. While advertisers intended these images to convey a positive sense of scientific progress, the effect, more often than not, is a bit alienating. Those clean orderly utopias, impressive and idealised though they are, ultimately seem unin-habitable.[5]

Central to this tension between the old and the new, the past and the present, the mythic and the real, is the figure of the scientist, a key protagonist in most sci-fi movies of the period. As Andrew Tudor remarks:

> In the 1930s and 1940s, the actions of individual mad scientists were all-important – whether they were evil men pursuing their own ends or good men corrupted by their overwhelming commitment to science. In the 1950s that changes; although it is still scientific knowledge that routinely causes mayhem, scientists are more often portrayed as our saviours than as our executioners.[6]

We readily recognise the scientists who use knowledge in order to benefit humankind. Deemer, in *Tarantula* (Jack Arnold, US, 1955), for instance, is trying to provide a solution to the world's food shortage by nurturing animals of abnormal size until an accident kills him and his assistants, releasing a giant tarantula to terrorise the locals. (Luckily, the beast is later napalmed by pilot Clint Eastwood in one of his early roles, anticipating perhaps the uncompromising outlaw machismo of the 1970s movie male.) Strains of the latter breed can, to a certain extent, be found in the film *Dr Cyclops* (Ernest Schoedsack, US, 1940) where jungle explorers are captured and minimalised by the psychopathic meglomaniac of the same name. But in his obsession with world domination, the doctor more properly echoes the mad scientist of the 1930s. Other models of the scientist include the cold, rational empiricist, embodied for example, by Dr Carrington in *The Thing from Another World* and the old style, benevolent paternalist personified by Dr Medford in *Them!* (Gordon Douglas, US, 1954). However, in focusing on these characters as metaphorical figures which interpret a variety of socio-cultural imperatives, we neglect their position as men and fail to properly define their masculinity. The scientist is largely perceived as an isolated figure, single-mindedly pursuing his research, sometimes at great personal cost, but with an unbridled energy and intensity that sometimes borders on the obsessive. This stereotype has, of course, been partly created and perpetuated by movie narratives themselves, in turn influenced by literary models and the proliferation of news items of the time.

In the 1950s, science and technology entered the public domain. The public became increasingly aware of technology through its very presence in their homes; commercial colour television was available in the United States in 1950. In 1951, Mauchly and Eckerts pioneered the UNIVAC 1, the first commercially available electronic computer; Watson and Crick developed a model for DNA in 1953; Edward Teller and his associates created the first thermonuclear device in 1952. In the wake of innovations such as the artificial sweetener, TV dinners and Velcro, the scientist passed into the popular imagination as an instrumental figure in modern life. The sci-fi B-movie played on the fascination with this figure; I would argue that it also revealed him to be an example of 'the inner-directed man', a definition I have culled from David Riesman's *The Lonely Crowd*. Riesman suggests;

> The over-steered men of the period, unable either to throw off or accept their inhibitions, were not always able to guard them by withdrawal into privacy. Where there was pressure to prove oneself a good fellow in tavern or brothel, their bodies sometimes betrayed them into nausea or impotence – in the effort to be competent weakness of the flesh gave away unwillingness of the spirit.[7]

He continues:

> It is as if his character, despite its seeming stability, did not feel stable, and indeed, the puritan, in the theological projection of this inner feeling, had constantly to fight against doubts concerning his state of grace or election.[8]

These views reveal the psycho-sexual confusion of men in the post-war period, a set of complexities which inform the figure of the scientist and, indeed, the male hero, in the sci-fi picture. The desire to adopt a puritanical stance is undermined by the emergence of drives and imperatives he has not previously encountered or acknowledged. The inhibitions imposed by a social role (i.e. the limits of legitimate behaviour within the professional context) can produce effects within the private and apparently self-determined sphere. Time and again in sci-fi 'B' features of the period, the male body collapses into nausea when confronted by the alien, or impotence when faced with women. The alien exposes the man in his socio-cultural brief and the woman threatens him in his social and familial role. I would suggest that the weakness of the flesh (the redefinition of the body) reveals the confusion of a spirit unwilling to relinquish its historically determined status and sense of control.

Jack Pollexfen, writer/producer of cult classics including *The Man from Planet X* (Edgar Ulmer, US, 1951) and *Captive Women* (Stuart Gilmore, US, 1952), has pointed out that

> sci-fi does not give the male player too many opportunities and less to the girl – unless each is lucky enough to have two heads.[9]

As I have shown, there is clearly a psychological/emotional dimension to the sci-fi B-movie but it is played out in terms of fantastic scenarios and monstrous apparitions, rather than at a level available to the talents of an actor. Thus the onus passes to the non-human characters and special effects. Whilst not having two heads, many of our heroes are left uncharacteristically in two minds, gripped by uncertainty, powerlessness and a tendency to behave absurdly. Kenneth Tobey, playing Captain Pat Hendry in Hawks' *The Thing from Another World*, for example, is only keen to visit an Arctic base, not because his curiosity has been aroused by the possible landing of an extraterrestial but because it offers the opportunity of rekindling a romance with a woman whom he cannot believe did not want him in the first place! His military chums tease him remorselessly about affairs of the heart, and we gather that he is supposedly professionally competent but not very successful with women. 'You know better than to fool our captain', says one wag, 'only dames can do that'. The men are rather in awe of women; tellingly, they recall a situation in which an 'army nurse has caused the same kind of disturbance as this guy from Mars has here'. Equating women with the alien is merely one manifestation of the vulnerability and remoteness men experience in these narratives.

Hendry is the typical hard-drinking, hard nosed Hawksian hero, but in the course of the film he is revealed as deeply flawed. His pride makes him reticent about the jokes made at his expense; he has clearly made mistakes with Nikki Nicholson, the object of his romantic attentions; he lacks knowledge about arctic conditions; he is criticised for incompetence in losing the alien; he doesn't comprehend anything technically or intellectually taxing. Hendry also takes decisions that endanger his men: he orders the kerosening of the alien *within* the building, thus burning down half the base! It becomes clear that whilst ostensibly reinforcing a masculine rhetoric, the film also mounts a critique of macho complacency.

Dr Carrington, the film's de-sexualised rationalist, in defining and defending the alien, coincidentally highlights the reason for Hendry's inadequacy. The alien ('the intellectual carrot', played by Gunsmoke's James Arness) is 'our superior in every way' claims Carrington, because his development is not hindered by 'emotional or sexual factors'. Hendry's actions are ill-considered. He is driven by an intense sense of his own rightness and jurisdiction, which means that he goes as far as to disobey the orders of his superiors back in Washington. He doesn't want to capture The Thing. He wants to destroy it. The Thing is the embodiment of all that proves him inadequate in his own eyes, in the eyes of his men, and in the eyes of women. The Thing is the physical manifestation of Hendry's confused and repressed emotional state, a psychic doppelganger on the loose. Men like Hendry are literally and metaphorically threatened by the monster, both from without and within.

In narrative terms, Hendry's central role in determining the 'action' is also in many ways usurped by 'The Thing'. It is the alien who initiates, the hero merely reacts. This has the knock-on effect of re-defining the traditional female position in the narrative, which further de-stabilises the heroic norm. For example, there is an absurd scene where Nikki ties up Hendry. This is not some kinky escapade, but rather Nikki's attempt to literally civilize the Captain and cure him of wandering hand trouble. She then delivers the knock-out blow: 'The trouble is, you don't know anything about women'. If 'The Thing' is the manifestation of the monster from without, this criticism provokes the monster within.

The motif of the monster emerging from within finds its most famous expression in Robert Louis Stevenson's *Dr Jekyll and Mr Hyde*, borrowed by director/producer, Robert Clarke for his 1959 monster masterpiece, *The Hideous Sun Demon*:

> We just did a flip-flop of the Robert Louis Stevenson plot – instead of the Jekyll and Hyde thing, where the man drinks the potion, we made it a scientist working with the fissionable materials who has an accident with radioactive isotopes. That upsets the chromosome balance so that he reverts, in the sun's rays to a reptilian type of monster.[10]

Clarifying this pseudo-scientific nonsense for any potential audience, posters raged that 'The blaze of the sun made him a monster'. While the Jekyll and Hyde plot makes the monstrous the manifestation of the libidinous and the violent, the *Sun Demon* plot takes the notion of transformation and lets it become metamorphosis. Hyde is always a primitive version of humanity. The sun demon is a reptile, a symbol of the primordial, but specifically, *not* human and most significantly, not a man. This development results, not in the revelation of violent or sexual passions latent in the repressed male, but in the exposure of dormant forces in a supposedly extinct creature. The sheer energy and presence of dominant masculinity, which is normally so crucial in the dramatic conflict of cinematic narratives, is here translated into the actions of a mythical demon. Physical potency, normally the domain of the male hero, is distanciated and consigned to the past. This displacement legitimises the monster and emasculates the man.

Harry Essex, screenwriter of Jack Arnold's *Creature from the Black Lagoon* (Jack Arnold, US, 1954), whilst also exploring the displacement of the masculine heroic onto 'the monster', attempts to reduce the coldness, remoteness and alienation inherent in the public perception of the reptilian. He states:

> It's pretty much formula for the kind of horror stories we used to do in those days, except in this particular case I added 'the Beauty and the

Beast' theme. The whole idea was to give the creature a kind of humanity – all he wants is to love this girl, but everybody's chasing him![11]

Unfortunately for B-movie regular, and ostensible hero of the film, Richard Carlson, audience sympathy thus shifts to the Gill man (played by Ben Chapman). The sexuality of Carlson, the hero, is largely ignored in favour of watching the Gill man's attraction to swimming beauty, Julie Adams; as John Baxter describes it:

> Gliding beneath her, twisting lasciviously in a stylised representation of sexual intercourse, the creature, his movements brutally masculine and powerful, contemplates his ritual bride, though his passion does not reach its peak until the girl performs some underwater ballet movements, explicitly erotic poses that excite the Gill man to reach out and clutch at her murmuring legs.[12]

Baxter continues:

> This conflict continues throughout the film, the Gill man being presented as a force of elemental power, not maliciously evil but 'other directed', a fragment of a world where our ideas of morality have no relevance.[13]

The idea that the creature is 'other directed' is particularly significant in the reading of masculinity. In embodying another social and moral code, the creature's physicality, however much it echoes the brutally masculine, recognises *difference* and therefore establishes a distance from the socio-cultural constructions of the male. In these films, the male character normally defines his sexuality through the status of his role and the effective action he takes. The 1950s sci-fi hero is often a military man, like Hendry, or a scientist, a policeman, a doctor: a professional with professional standards and disciplines to uphold. Their standards come under assault in these movies from an assemblage of creatures who redefine the narrative space. The creature in *Black Lagoon* operates outside the norms and parameters of men within their professional environment. The creature exists in itself, for itself, without social dimension. It violates the space of the hero who is confined by his circumstances and the limitations of his role, and made inadequate by his lack of physical prowess.

The most eloquent and touching expression of these conditions occurs in another of Jack Arnold's films, *The Incredible Shrinking Man*, scripted by Richard Matheson from his own novel. In the film,

Scott Carey, vacationing with his wife, Louise, on his brother's boat is suddenly overwhelmed by an atomic cloud.

The film opens by establishing that the Carey marriage is characterised by playful bonhomie, and that six years of togetherness 'seems like six minutes'. Some six months later, Louise puts some milk out for the cat as normal, but Scott realizes that something is wrong. His clothes are too big. This is no mix up at the laundry; Scott Carey is shrinking. The doctor tries to convince him that it is stress related but he knows different. Scott remembers that he has passed medicals for the draftboard, the navy, the insurance company – he could have been a soldier, a sailor, he could have been a contender, he could have been somebody, and indeed he is: he is a writer. He is (temporarily) assured by the knowledge that 'People just don't get shorter' but his first reaction upon telling Louise, his wife, the news is to insist that she kiss him. 'You think that's going to fix it, huh?' she says; an off-the-cuff whimsy which alerts the audience to the first signs of Scott's sexual anxiety, especially since she no longer has to stretch to kiss him they way she used to. Literally, she no longer has to look up to him; metaphorically, the domestic cat anticipates the role played by Jonesy, Ripley's feline companion in *Alien* (Ridley Scott, US, 1979).

Tests confirm that Scott is a few inches short of the heroic stature with which he started the movie. A freak combination of tree spray insecticide and radioactivity are put down as the cause. Scott quickly realises that his marriage is in jeopardy. He tells Louise that under these circumstances 'There's a limit to your obligation', and continues:

> You loved Scott Carey. He has a size and a shape and a way of thinking. All that is changing now.

Scott begins the process of self-denial, distancing himself from what he used to be and what he is becoming. He no longer represents what he once did and when his wedding ring slips from his finger his marriage is doomed. Once Scott stops perceiving himself as a husband (clearly, in his own mind the embodiment of proper manhood), an important transition takes place within the story. From being mild-mannered, married and manly, Scott becomes frustrated, freakish and famous. Unemployed, Scott keeps the wolf from the door by submitting to the lucrative notoriety that attends the press relevation of his condition. But with this, he loses the final vestige of his masculinity. He publicly admits that he is 'A child that looks like a man'. He is impotent and, though temporarily encouraged by the discovery of an anti-toxin which arrests the degenerative process of the disease, he concludes 'my relationships with the world has ceased'. Poignantly, he then confronts his sexual crisis by admitting his 'desperate need' for Louise, as she goes to bed, followed by the cat. Feeling 'puny and absurd', Scott sums up his diminished status by saying, 'Easy to talk of soul and spirit and essential worth but not when you're three feet tall. I loathed myself'. Enough to stop any of us being sizeist ever again.

Significantly, it is at this point that Scott sees one last hope of reviving his sexuality, and with it, notions of himself as a man. Running from the family home, he comes upon a circus show featuring Tiny Tina: 'Thirty six inches of feminine pulchritude'. Initially he sees this freakish display as yet another embodiment of his fate. Utterly maudlin he goes to a cafe for a coffee, only to meet glamourous dwarf, Clorice Bruce, who chattily insists 'You're not alone now', and muses that, for them 'The sky is as blue as it is for the giants'. This scaled down 'brief encounter' visibly cheers Scott Carey. Being taller than the object of his affection once more, he suddenly takes a grip on his life again, committing himself to completing a book about his experience. Not for the first time, a filmic text suggests that libidinal drives liberate creativity and lend purpose and identity to a man who operates as an individual outside the group (the army etc.). This happy interlude is short lived because the relationship collapses when Scott realises that he is shrinking again. This aversion to taller women is something to which I will return later.

Ensconced in a doll's house, Scott becomes ever more irrational claiming that he is becoming 'more monstrous in my domination of Louise'. Although distressed about her husband, Louise's reaction is as much about frustration as pity (a characteristic shared by Marge in *I Married a Monster from Outer Space* (Gene Fowler Jnr., US, 1958). Whilst feeling powerless to alter Scott's fate, Louise is empowered to pursue her own existence, knowing that she cannot be challenged. She leaves the house one day and the cat terrorises Scott in his tiny living room. Following a struggle of lounge dimensions, the cat is instrumental in making Scott run towards the cellar, whereupon Louise returns, the door opens and the draught blows Scott to a prison below stairs. Louise assumes that Scott has been eaten by the cat. The cat purrs contentedly, perhaps even conspiratorially. The man of the house is gone.

Consigned to the cellar, Scott becomes an urban Crusoe, constructing a lifestyle within an environment in which the ordinary is made strange. A matchbox is a home. A crate is a canyon-like abyss. A spider is a key adversary in the pursuit of food: 'More than a spider it was every known terror in the world, every fear fused into one night black horror'. However, Scott finally decides to engage in the 'death struggle' with the spider in the belief that he will win because he has 'a man's intelligence'. More importantly, he has reclaimed his pin-sword and hook and, once again, the possession of weapons signifies

Shrinking masculinity: man meets arachnid adversary, (*The Incredible Shrinking Man*, Arnold, US, 1956). (Courtesy of BFI Stills, Posters and Designs with the kind permission of MCA Television.)

masculinity: 'With these bits of metal I was a man again'. With the lancing of the spider, Scott Carey dramatises the return of the phallus. His victory signals his acceptance that his sexuality is in some way intact but recontextualised through a deeper knowledge of the limits of the natural order. He recognises within himself a heightened sensitivity and a spiritual understanding of the infinite and the infinitesemal. He has experienced the fullest engagement with, and understanding of, the possibilities of being human and of being a man. He has known the extremities of its pleasures and pains, and most significantly, its relativity. He poses himself the question, 'Was I the Man of the future?' We can only answer that this reconstituted hero has at least come to terms with the idea that his own notion of what it is to be a man is subject to redefinition. Moving beyond the limitations of his physicality and egocentricity, he has attained spiritual growth by seeing his masculinity within the natural rather than sociocultural order. The relativity of being in this more universal dimension at once creates and annihilates any one sense of the masculine. To be reduced is not to be diminished, rather it is to be enhanced.

Such philosophic positions did not underpin subsequent movies modelled on *The Incredible Shrinking Man* but other views of masculinity proved to be just as challenging, if moving dangerously towards the absurd. Bert I. Gordon ('Mr B.I.G.'), the Z-picture auteur, was evidently hung-up on size. Bert couldn't seem to see beyond the notion that big was beautiful: bugs, monsters and men were all overblown with the Gordon touch. Discussing *The Amazing Colossal Man* Dean Chambers charts the limits of largesse, which echo in all but scale, the difficulties of Scott Carey:

> What good is having the strength to squash a Sherman tank if you must spend the rest of your life hiding from more artillery than you can handle? And where would you hide? What would you eat? Where would you rest your tired back? Imagine what answering the call of nature would do to the immediate ecology (on second thought, don't). Other than masturbation you could forget about sex.[14]

Unlike Scott, the appositely named Glenn Manning, does not properly confront his condition. He remains embittered, having survived the Korean War, come through a nuclear blast (which surprisingly invests plutonium with regenerative healing powers) and come to terms with his doting fiance, Carol, only to find himself grown enormous. He is left wondering:

> What sin can a man commit in a single lifetime to bring this upon himself?

Glenn's particular circumstances are even more difficult to accept because his heroic deeds have been of A-feature quality. Selflessly, he had attempted to save a pilot who had crash-landed in the middle of a plutonium bomb test. During his time in Korea, Glenn had avenged the death of his platoon sergeant, by shooting the guerrilla fighter who had stabbed his buddy in the back. Normally, such film bravery would result in congressional medals and getting the girl, not abnormal growth and having to wear an expandable sarong. Looking ridiculous when you are of normal build is standard fare in this kind of movie but being dressed in a nappy when you are fifty foot tall can prove embarrassing. This, however, is central to the film's concerns. Glenn looks like an overgrown baby. The bigger he gets, the more childish he seems to be. Glenn perceives his predicament as the consequence of some terrible sin that he has committed in his past. He is overwhelmed by guilt – a guilt made manifest by his overbearing size and the obviousness of his exposure. He cannot redeem himself nor can he cope with the new conditions of his masculinity. Like Scott Carey, he moves from being the embodiment of movie ordained heroism to an abstract, alienated figure. The disruption and redefinition of the body is instrumental in delineating an interrogation of manhood as it moves through the process of sexual and social estrangement.

Only when these characters are distanced from the functional orthodoxy of their bodies do they actually address the spiritual and emotional aspects of their identity, previously only defined by the efficiency of their physicality. This not merely places them in closer contact with the traditionally feminine qualities within their own sensibilities, but makes them more fully acknowledge the influence of the feminine in the roles played by their wives. As Scott and Glenn feel more and more betrayed by their bodies, they recognise the need to be with their respective partners, Louise and Carol, who have effectively legitimised the masculine body through the sexual bond. As 'sex' recedes as an issue, the women gain greater independence, born out of a liberation from their partners and, by extension, by their release from the limitations imposed by marriage (an issue I will explore further in relation to *I Married a Monster from Outer Space*). One might go as far as to suggest that if the physical re-definitions that Scott and Glenn experience are indeed a punishment for some past sin, it is probably the sin of patriarchy in its oppression and devaluation of women. Through the collapse and humiliation of the male body, the limitations of the patriarchal body politic are revealed and female affectivity and power recognized.

Men in the sci-fi B-movie are deeply fearful of this latent power in women. They seek to negate or ignore it but the fantastic machinations of the sci-fi narrative essentially undermine the status quo of masculine experience and liberate alternatives, both in the men themselves, and for the women who have the patience to endure them. In Nathan Hertz's *Attack of the Fifty Foot Woman*, Nancy Archer is confronted by a giant, bald alien in a satellite who tries to take 'The Star of India' which dangles provocatively around her neck. (We later learn that these Cosmic Kojaks use diamonds as a life source. We also learn that they wear medieval tee-shirts with adjustable elbow-pads, but enough of these fashion niceties.) Nancy survives the attack but of course, sheriff and townsfolk alike don't believe her story and she is dismissed as a crackpot, a view reinforced by the fact that she doubles as town lush and has done the odd stint at the local sanitarium. Not short of a dollar or two, she commands a degree of tolerance, especially from husband, Harry, a thorough cad: even as his wife experiences her alien assault, he is dancing the night away at Tony's cafe with mistress and fellow golddigger, Honey Parker.

Nancy, for some obscure reason remains enthralled by Harry, even though she knows him to be a 'miserable parasite'. She is abused by him, she is abused by the rest of the community, she is even abused in a TV news broadcast. This kind of oppression is bound to have serious consequences; we are about to witness the return of the repressed.[15] Sedated in her bedroom, Nancy swells to enormous proportions as a result of the radioactivity she was exposed to in her close encounter. Taking this 'astounding growth' in their stride, doctors order in a delivery of chains, plasma, meathooks and an elephant syringe! This is an attempt to cope with the doctor's diagnosis that: 'When women reach the age of maturity, Mother Nature sometimes overworks the frustration to the point of irrationalism.' If for Mother Nature, one reads 'womanhood', then the point is not so much about menopause but rather a statement about women's liberation. The Feminine, in the shape of the fifty foot Nancy, mobilises itself, literally and metaphorically destroying the marital home; plunging Tony's den of sexist sin into darkness, killing Honey in the process and, in a *tour de force* of assertion, crushing Harry in a Kong-like fist. Floored only by exploding electricity pylons, Nancy has addressed and challenged masculine complacency in small town America. Though ostensibly cast as the 'monstrous feminine', echoing movie monsters like Godzilla, or later, the predator of *Alien*, Nancy has been instrumental in the exposure of the 'monstrous masculine' as it has been absorbed into the dominant ideology of this small town culture. Nancy's actions make the smug, ignorant and insensitive men recognise dimensions of femininity beyond their understanding.

Stereotypically, women are only perceived as sex objects (Honey) or marital bores (Nancy); the liberators and inhibitors of masculine passion. Harry, for example, is willing to tolerate Nancy's tantrums as long as he benefits sexually or financially. He accepts material domination in his marriage so long as it has no effective power. Enlarged, Nancy demonstrates effective power and makes the masculine ludicrous. Harry, the sheriff, his deputy, Nancy's butler and the doctors are seen to be inept, selfish, petty and weak. It is the very irony of this kind of feature that the apparently ridiculous concept which informs the narrative – the attack of a fifty foot woman – both offers extraordinary narrative possibilities and yet also trivializes the gender issues raised and explored within the film. Nevertheless, the movie itself questions the commonplace expectations of gender politics through the actions of its main protagonist and this may count as a limited radicalism.

Similarly, it can be argued that a film like *I Married a Monster from Outer Space* extends the critique of men within relationships, and exposes the restrictions of the marital agenda for women. The film starts ominously enough when Bill Farrell's pre-nuptials 'boys' night out' offers the collective view that the proper alternative to marriage is 'mass suicide'. Bill drives off planning to call in on bride to be, Marge, prior to turning in for a good night's sleep before the big day. Unfortunately, Bill knocks down a pedestrian on the way, or at least thinks he does, until the accident is revealed as an alien ruse to lure him from the car and take over his body. Damn clever these aliens; this trick was performed in many a movie of this period, most famously, in *Invasion of the Body Snatchers* (Don Siegel, US, 1956), and placed identity crisis firmly on the agenda.

Bill is late for his wedding. This is passed off as a stag night hangover, but soon there are signs that all is not well. Bill (now an alien), becomes distant, absent minded and self-absorbed. He forgets to put the car headlights on when driving at night, and more significantly he omits to carry Marge across the threshold, prompting her rather plaintive cry that 'You can't have a honeymoon without a bride'. Scriptwriter Louis Vittes, keen to milk the nuance of his script, sat beneath the camera mouthing each line that his characters had to say. Charitably, one might say that this inhibited the actors. Conversely, one might suggest that Tom Tryon (Bill) and Gloria Talbott (Marge) embody the kind of woodenness that make my bookcase seem like Robert De Niro. Nevertheless, well acted or no, the implications are clear; Vittes uses the device of the alien takeover to highlight masculine complacency within marriage. Bill's remoteness is only the first sign. He doesn't talk, he doesn't emote, he doesn't make love. Soon Marge realises that 'Bill isn't the man I fell in love with'. Childless after a year, Marge follows the lead of Louise in *The Indredible Shrinking Man* and buys a pet for comfort and companionship. Unlike Scott, Bill doesn't take this lying down; he strangles the dog. Marge's devastation is more centrally concerned with her despair that she may not have children. Marge has married with the expectation of becoming a mother. Ironically, Bill, in alienating Marge, has caused her to distance herself from the very idea of marriage itself. Marge for the first time questions and challenges the disciplines and boundaries that constitute marriage and, though she still desires a successful marriage, she enters into a new understanding of what it means by experiencing a new independence. Estranged from Bill, she considers life alone, as did her friend Helen, before finally accepting a proposal from Sam, one of Bill's friends. Helen comments that, before deciding to marry Sam, she 'was reading books about Florence Nightingale, Joan of Arc, Madame Du Barry – you know, career women.'

While Marge is undergoing a painful transition into new womanhood, the aliens provide a commentary on the limitations of being a man: 'The design's pretty lousy' says alien Sam. 'I find human beings disgusting' chirps another. Then the grand plan is revealed: the aliens have come to have children by earth women. Chillingly, one of the aliens obliterates a prostitute when she approaches it, as it stares through a toy shop window, at a doll, suggesting thoughts of its future offspring. Even aliens, it seems, perpetuate the virgin/whore dichotomy and allow it to inform their choice of partners. But by this time Marge is challenging these tired antitheses, confronting Bill with her suspicions and standing against the male community which is increasingly colonised by aliens. Marge is standing firm against the indifference and assumed superiority of a dead patriarchy. At the same time, however, Bill begins to develop an affection towards Marge and that makes him vulnerable.

Ironically, just at the moment when the narrative appears to be rounding on its male characters, it remobilises patriarchy in the guise of men whose wives have recently become pregnant (i.e. obviously potent men); their wives safely impregnated, they are not prime targets for alien takeover. Dr Wayne realises this and takes these men into the woods to confront the aliens. Having used Marge and the aliens as a device to expose the inadequacies of patriarchy, Vittes' script effectively concludes with the transition from an old, dead patriarchy to a new, vibrant one, perpetuating old codes and conventions, but freshening them with the energy of youth. Interestingly, though, despite being armed to the teeth, it is not the representatives of this new patriarchy who kill the aliens but a pack of dogs who have the ability to rip flesh. (Once again, animals get a greater chance to shine in these epics than the men do!) The men who have been taken over by aliens hang suspended in the space ship, mere husks of manhood, passive and powerless, kept alive by an electrical charge. Once the circuits are disconnected the aliens die and the original men revive. Completing the transition from old to new, alien Bill admits that he has come to terms with being human, but as he dies (soap suds emerging from every orifice), earthly Bill returns in a check jacket ready to resume his matrimonial duties. One can only hope that this salutory experience teaches him not only to improve as a husband but to cultivate a better dress sense.

Challenging patriarchal dominance is central to the role of women, especially when they appear as monsters. Men fear the unpredictability and power of these monsters and double their efforts to control, oppress and destroy them. In *The She Creature* (1956) the authorities must face the 'materialisation of the prehistoric female' which embodies a spirit which 'comes from the beginning of time, huge and indestructible'. Here is a case of patriarchal fear stretching back to a pre-gendered state of being with the emergence of a woman 'into her first body'. Patriarchal infrastructures are still traumatised by this 'body', of creative and destructive potency. We have already seen how this informs *Attack of the Fifty Foot Woman*, but it is also fundamental to *She Demons* (Richard E. Cunha, US, 1958), *Jungle Woman* (R. Le Borg, US, 1944) and *The Wasp Woman* (Roger Corman, US, 1959).[16] Actress Susan Cabot, said of playing 'The Wasp Woman':

> The Wasp woman was totally isolated from a normal kind of feeling, and that was a wonderful experience for me; I think that was the most fun part I've ever had. To be able to go from a forty year old character to a twenty one year old was a challenge. Then, to be a monster, one of the very few female beasties in movies – was great fun. The wasp woman is very special.[17]

Very special indeed. The Wasp Woman has the maturity of experience, the ability to become younger *and* she can fly. Acts of intimacy with men become vampiric bloodbaths. Men are denied emotional security with the forty year old Janice Starlin, sexually alienated from her twenty-one year old incarnation, and stung to death by the embodiment of 'the monstrous feminine'. In destabilising and controlling her relationships with men, Janice undermines dominant sexual orthodoxies and reflects the increased attention given to women's sexual practices as evidence in the 1953 Kinsey Report.[18]

The powerful and mobile 'flying female' in *The Wasp Woman* is also of major concern in *Them!*. The giant Queen ant, inflated by radioactive fall-out, has flown from her desert nest to lay eggs in the Los Angeles drains. Even the patriarchs of Washington are worried about this one. As Biskind suggests:

... it implicitly presents, in slightly disguised form, a paranoid fantasy of a world dominated by predatory females. The ant society is, after all, a matriarchy presided over by a despotic queen. The Queen it seems strikes only at patriarchy. Not only does she kill the male drones, but all her human victims are male (one man's phallic shotgun is bent like a paper clip), including two fathers.[19]

The film also presents a woman of intelligence, strength and versatility in Pat Medford, daughter of Dr Medford, who is in charge of the investigation into the presence of giant mutant ants in the desert. She challenges the heroic centre assumed by Agent Graham, by insisting that she, 'A trained observer must go into the nest'. Arresting masculine doubt and catapulting it straight into complete insecurity, she says, 'Let's stop all the talk and get on with it'. Seconds later, she has ordered the torching of the Queen's chamber; it is quite clear who is in charge here. It is only with the full scale mobilisation of patriarchal military power at the end of the film that men temporarily regain their position of dominance.

In addressing a situation beyond the patriarchal agenda, the men in the films discussed above have had to recognise the inability of their own identities in texts which interrogated the ideological and political status quo. The sense of 'otherness' in the alien and the feminine inevitably dislocates masculine assumptions. Although these images of 'otherness' have been perceived as warnings about incipient Communism or the nuclear threat, they can also be read as signs of personal redefinition and the emergence of new socio-cultural options. To be 'taken over' is not so much about being absorbed by another more dominant ideology, as about being given new psychic and physical space in which to demonstrate difference and address fresh alternatives. As John Baxter describes in his analysis of *It Came From Outer Space* (Jack Arnold, US, 1953):

> All those people who have been 'taken over' behave in a way slightly but eerily out of key: the two truck drivers, glimpsed in town by Putnam and cornered in an alley, emerge from the shadows holding hands ... When Putnam faces his girl on a windy hillside at dawn, she stands untroubled by the chill desert wind while he must pull up his collar and flinch against its bite.[20]

Here it becomes clear that the destabilised hero, with his identity rendered confused and inadequate, must recognise other kinds of relationships: the gentle yet assured connectedness of the aliens with its homoerotic overtones; and the strength, confidence and power of woman as she insists on proper recognition with regard to sexual identity and social position. This does bring panic and paranoia. Miles, in *Invasion of the Body Snatchers*, says: 'A moment's sleep and the girl I loved was an inhuman enemy bent on my destruction'. Miles, like Putnam, and like many a sci-fi hero, mistakes the strange, the unorthodox, the alien as 'inhuman' simply because it operates beyond the narrow confines of patriarchally defined notions of 'humanity' which have excluded, marginalized or repressed alternative notions of being. The 1950s sci-fi B-movie starts to engage with these issues, anticipating some of the more radical stances of the 1960s.

NOTES

1 Beverley Garland, star of *It Conquered The World*, registers her disappointment to Roger Corman that her monstrous adversary looks a bit cheap and ineffectual; quoted in Tom Weaver, *Interviews with B-Science Fiction and Horror Movie Makers*, McFarland and Co, North Carolina, 1988, p158.
2 Samuel Stouffer, *Communism Conformism and Civil Liberties*, John Wiley and Sons, London, 1966, p59-60.
3 David Riesman, *The Lonely Crowd*, Yale University Press, New Haven 1961.
4 Dale Carter, *The Final Frontier*, Verso, London, 1988, p94.
5 Richard Horn, *Fifties Style*, Columbus Books, London, 1985, p48.
6 Andrew Tudor, 'Seeing the worst side of science', *Nature* Vol. 340 24/8/89, p589.
7 Riesman, *op. cit.*, p123.
8 Riesman, *op. cit.*, p124.
9 Weaver, *op. cit.*, p275.
10 Weaver, *op. cit.*, p82.
11 Weaver, *op. cit.*, p148.
12 John Baxter, *Science Fiction in the Cinema*, Tantivy Press, London, 1970, p121.
13 *Ibid.*, p121.
14 Dean Chambers, 'The Amazing Colossal Glenn Manning', *Midnight Marquee*, Issue 37, Autumn 1988, p164.
15 For a discussion of this concept see Robin Wood's essay, 'The American Nightmare: Horror in the seventies' in Robin Wood, *Hollywood: From Vietnam to Reagan*, Columbia University Press, New York 1986.
16 *She Demons* was produced by Richard Cunha and Arthur Jacobs and showed a woman moving from 'Beauty to Beast', while *Jungle woman*, featured Acquenetta as half-ape, half-housewife. In *The She Monster*, the monster was played by Shirley Kirkpatrick in a silver suit, so that according to Robert Clarke, 'she would appear to be a monstrous yet appealing type of alien'.
17 Weaver, *op. cit.*, p259.
18 Kinsey's report included among its conclusions that almost fifty per cent of

women had sexual relations before marriage, twenty-five per cent were unfaithful afterwards, and twenty-five per cent of those who remained unmarried had lesbian relationships. From Hellemans and Bunch, *The Timetables of Science*, Sidgwick and Jackson, London, 1989, p516.

19 Biskind, *op. cit.*, p133.
20 Biskind, *op. cit.*, p119.

No Room For Uncertainty: Gridiron Masculinity in *North Dallas Forty*

Garry Whannel

Sport + Masculinity

Sport has been a significant component of one dominant form of masculinity in western cultures for the last hundred years and, not surprisingly, has featured in many contemporary films. I will discuss one of these films, *North Dallas Forty* (Ted Kotcheff, US, 1979) in detail but before that I will comment on the relationship between sport and masculine culture. To be involved in sport as player or spectator both confers and confirms masculine status while to be indifferent to or hostile to sport poses a question mark about one's masculinity. Masculinity is not innate but has to be learned and in any particular social and historical context, there are a range of masculinities on offer. Particular educational and familial practices will privilege certain forms of masculinity while others may be labelled deviant or merely marginalised. Since the mid nineteenth century, the world of sport has constituted a cultural domain in which a particularly rigid and intolerant form of heterosexual hegemony has been constructed.[1] In both British and American society, an interest in active muscular physical sporting activity has been an important component of the most dominant form of masculinity. One major strand of this masculinity was forged in the nineteenth century British public schools, with their muscular Christianity and commitment to team games, and exported from there into the Church, the Civil Service, the Officer class and hence to the Empire.[2] The working class masculinity forming in the same period extended the values of the work-place physical self-reliance, toughness and endurance – into leisure activities such as football.[3] Similar processes were also at work in North America.

If masculinity has to be learned, there is clearly also the possibility of failing to learn the norms. The construction in language of a terminology associated with homosexuality or effeminacy – nancy boy, pansy – carries both a negative portrayal of femininity and the connotations of inadequacy and failure, that is, failure to be a 'real man'. If sport confirms masculinity it problematises femininity. Sportswomen endlessly find themselves having to assert, defensively, that they are still women despite their sporting involvement. To enter into the domain of physicality, muscularity and competitiveness is to cross a divide, to invade and challenge an area of culture that has been a closely policed male domain.[4]

Clearly this sharp distinction has been undergoing a degree of transformation in recent years with the rapid expansion of women's sport. Masculinity too has undergone changes. When footballer Paul Gascoigne (Gazza) shed tears of frustration during the World Cup, it was not taken as a sign of deficient masculinity. On the contrary, the moment has been mythologised in the form of a tee shirt showing Gascoigne in tears and the slogan 'there'll always be an England'. This patriotic frame of reference within which Gascoigne's tears were legitimised is significant. No-one turned Olympic athlete Steve Ovett into a popular icon after he burst into tears on live television, as a result of stress generated by the forces of commerce. Seemingly it is now, in certain circumstances, alright for men to cry, if not over personal matters, at least over sport, particularly where the fate of the nation is involved.

The range of masculine positions available in the 1990s is qualitatively different, and, arguably, quantitatively greater than, the range available at the start of the 1960s. The sight of men shopping, holding babies, wearing pink sweaters, or crying (not all at once!) may or may not represent meaningful or measurable sociological change. But such sights are no longer considered remarkable, exceptional or aberrant as they would have been in 1960. However, despite changing attitudes, it is still the case that sport offers, in discursive terms, a system of difference that serves to buttress and underpin gender difference.

SPORTING MASCULINITY, AMERICAN FOOTBALL AND AMERICAN LIFE

There are a number of distinct components of sporting masculinity: toughness, aggression, and physicality, competitiveness and combativeness, loyalty, discipline, self sacrifice and commitment, and endurance and ability to withstand pain without complaint. It is precisely these qualities that are prominently foregrounded in most representations of American football, and this needs to be understood in relation to the close homology between the sport and American life. In the era of industrial capitalism, in both the sport and American society, corporate structures with an advanced division of labour attempt to boost productivity at the cost of pain suffered by producers. There are specialist teams for attack and defense, other experts only come on for the punt or kick. Every player has precisely defined roles in any one of a hundred moves that have to be memorised. There are specialist coaches for every aspect of the game, and nowadays specialist spotters who watch the opponents moves. The work process has been fragmented and de-skilled in ways that echoes broader social processes.[5] A winning team achieves its goal, but only through disciplined adherence to leadership and corporate planning. Winning is everything, losing is nothing, and American sport has devised structures which make a draw impossible.

Productivity is closely monitored; every move in a game can be reduced to a set of figures, an abstract system of equivalence which makes it possible to compute the effectiveness of the sporting labour power. There is a constant pressure to increase productivity, to perform better and more efficiently. This has been called a Taylorisation of the body, an attempt to wring maximum productivity from the human frame;[6] sportsmen are constantly encouraged to cross the pain threshold, both in training and in performance. Indeed it is precisely pain that signals that the body is being pushed hard enough to produce an improvement, a concept that has entered into popular common sense with the phrase 'no pain, no gain'. Pain becomes a signifier of success, and athletes come to adopt an almost masochistic pursuit of excellence.

SPORT AND THE MOVIES: NORTH DALLAS FORTY

Sport is not an ideal topic for mainstream cinema because many sports have a relatively local appeal. Major American sports like baseball and American football are not that popular elsewhere, British sports like soccer and cricket are shunned in the USA and, above all, there is always the danger of failing to appeal to an audience of both men and women. Despite this, many films featuring sport have been made, although few have achieved either commercial or creative success.[7]

The discursive field through which the ideologies of sport performance are represented is articulated in cinematic form in two distinct narrative structures: 'triumph over obstacles' and 'decline and fall'. The classic celebratory sport film (eg *Chariots of Fire* (Hugh Hudson, GB, 1981), *Rocky* (John Avidsen, US, 1976) follows an athlete, several athletes or a whole team on the path to victory. In achieving success the star has to overcome a series of obstacles and the final triumph sets the seal on a celebration of those qualities (persistence, commitment, dedication) necessary for such success.[8] The rather more cynical and critical 'decline and fall' structure portrays athletes on the downhill slope, approaching retirement, becoming disillusioned, and therefore in structural terms it is more likely to re-articulate the elements of sporting ideology around a critical principle. *The Harder They Fall* (Mark Robson, US, 1956) is an archetypal example, although *Raging Bull* (Martin Scorsese, US, 1980) also fits the pattern.[9]

North Dallas Forty contains elements of both these plot structures, but ultimately the 'decline and fall' theme dominates, with the 'triumph over obstacles' theme being immediately followed by double disaster. The hero scores the potentially winning touchdown, but the winning kick is missed, and the hero subsequently quits when faced with evidence of his drug-taking and other misdemeanours.

The film, based on a novel by ex-Dallas Cowboys player Peter Gent, follows a week in the life of Phil Elliott of the North Dallas Bulls.[10] We first see him waking up after a game, wincing with pain and remembering the moments that caused it, together with the moments that gave him pleasure. Three fellow players arrive to go hunting, Elliott's close friend, quarterback Seth Maxwell, and the neanderthal Jo Bob and O.W. Meadows. Later, at a party, Elliott meets Charlotte, a wealthy young woman who is disgusted by the loutish macho swaggering of the footballers. He subsequently turns up, somewhat stoned, at her apartment and falls asleep on the couch.

Elliott is called in by the owner and the coach for a pep-talk about his undisciplined attitude and begins a hard week of training, during which it revealed that he is having an affair with the boss' brother's fiancee, smokes dope, and takes all manner of drugs to deaden the pain of his injuries. He also begins a rather uneasy affair with Charlotte.

He is told he will play in the crucial game at Chicago, but it turns out that this is a ruse to persuade black player Delma to agree to have a pain killing injection. However, Delma hurts his knee, and tackled while limping, is badly injured. Elliott comes on as substitute, and in the closing seconds catches a touchdown pass to give North Dallas the chance of victory. But the punt is missed and the game lost. The following day, Elliott is confronted with a private detective and evidence of his dope smoking and his private life. Furious at the invasion of his privacy he resigns and storms out. Outside, his friend Maxwell waits, concerned only to confirm that he has not been implicated.

While Elliott is not different from many of the other players in his enthusiasm for drink, drugs and casual sex, his indulgences are of a different character. Other players use drugs in a more rational instrumental and calculating manner (speed to psych themselves up, mild narcotics to kill the pain) but Elliott gobbles drugs down in an indiscriminate and hedonistic manner. Fellow players Jo Bob and O.W. Meadows share Elliott's hedonistic approach to drink and sex, but they compartmentalise their lives along the lines of that classic male business/pleasure axiom, 'work hard, play hard'. Elliott's confused and inchoate search for a more humane way of life admits no such easy resolutions. In their various ways the other players all ultimately accept and inhabit a particular form of dominant sporting masculinity that calls for them, when the whistle blows, to be disciplined, careerist, and motivated. Elliott transgresses against this corporate masculinity, but can find no comfortable alternative position to inhabit.

Through Elliott' eyes we see a grotesque world. On the hunt that opens the film, the drunken Jo Bob and O.W. Meadows fire their guns at cows, mailboxes and anything that moves. Jo Bob gropes at women at the party and throws television sets into the pool while another player hammers this hand repeatedly against a table, in the belief that blood and wounds will turn the women on. The team coach behaves like a cold-blooded automaton as he bullies the team, quoting statistics to reveal their inadequacy, while the assistant coach recites vacuous pseudo-religious tracts. Elliot's friend Maxwell details his previous night's experiences at an orgy. Elliott himself is constantly bothered by pain and consumes drugs indiscriminately, breaking into the team medicine cabinet to replenish his supply.

This grotesque world has a number of distinct components.

- Power and violence are closely related. The drunkenness, destruction, lechery and sado-masochism are all in the end related to the need to establish power relations. Jo Bob can only deal with the world by imposing his power upon it; hence his violent reaction when Elliott teases him about his aspirations to open a restaurant, mischievously suggesting the slogan, 'Jo Bob's Fine Foods – Eat here or I'll kill you!'
- Rationalist automatons: the players are required to fit without question into a playing system completely dependent on computer-generated statistics. They are in effect subjected to that process Brohm dubbed the 'Taylorisation of the body', the attempt to obtain maximum productivity.[11]
- Christian morality and the work ethic intersect to provide the underpinning for this ultra-rationalised, performance-centred regime.

- Sex constantly appears as a substitute for human relations rather than an element of a relationship.
- Pain is a confirmation of a job well done. Just as in more recent years the aphorism 'no pain, no gain' has become popular, the footballers in *North Dallas Forty* come to associate pain so closely with the successful performance of their role that it comes to signify fulfilment and success.

The characters offer various routes through the madness. Jo Bob and O.W. Meadows have little critical distance and participate fully in all the rituals of the gridiron world. Elliott by contrast rejects the rituals; he cannot play along. Maxwell advises him to learn how to fool them ('learn how to play the game') and while Maxwell shares much of Elliott's deviance, he knows how to pass, how to conform. Team owner Conrad Hunter calls Elliott in and tells him, 'seeing through the game isn't the same as winning the game'.

Clearly 'the game' functions as metaphor – it is not just about football but the American way. It can also be read as referencing the particular form of masculinity that is hegemonic in the football world. Elliott – with his refusal to take training seriously, his tendency to clown and coast on his undoubted ability; his rejection of the macho swaggering, and his rather ill-defined search for a more substantial relationship with women – emerges as a character not settled in his world. He is unable to engage fully with the 'game'.

Elliott and Maxwell sustain each other in a classic buddy movie relationship. Watching a replay of a pass he throws to Elliott, Maxwell comments 'the things I do for love'. Later coach B.A. Struthers decries 'this buddy buddy stuff'; the closeness between Elliott and Maxwell threatens the power of the coach, which is, in a sense, the authority of a father over his 'children'. It undermines the ability of the coach to impose strategy and is seen as irrational, defying the 'law' of the statistics. The coaches prefer to encourage hostilities and rivalries between the players, believing that this encourages aggression and competitive performance: Emotional warmth is a threat to their patriarchal authority.

But Maxwell is ultimately unable to give Elliott emotional support. He constantly prioritises the team and himself above his loyalty to friends. When Elliott confronts Jo Bob over his physical assault on Charlotte, Maxwell grumbles that he does not want Jo Bob upset, he needs him to be 'up' for the sake of the team. As Elliott is increasingly disturbed by aspects of the game. Maxwell is less and less willing to listen and when Elliott comments on Delma's smashed face during the final game, Maxwell snaps back 'I can't worry about that now'. The friendship seems to have soured by the time Elliott finally realises

Maxwell has known all along about the drug investigation, and that his main concern has been that his own involvement is not exposed. The film ends with Maxwell in a position of knowledge: 'you know everything' Elliott says to him, suggesting he has a way of handling the system, whereas Elliott is still left with his uncertainties. But the price of Maxwell's knowledge is a partial loss of humanity: 'I ain't never loved no-one' he has earlier confided to Elliott.

Elliott is paired romantically with Charlotte, whom we first see at the party. Right from the start she, like Elliott, is represented as a non-participant in the general debauchery – but, unlike Elliott, she is openly appalled, and thinks Jo Bob should be stopped. On her way out, she is grabbed by Jo Bob, and this pushes Elliott, against his better judgement into a old style chivalrous act, confronting Jo Bob. But he cannot pull it off, and needs to shout to Maxwell for help.

To Jo Bob, Charlotte is just one more female body, whose very presence at the party signifies her availability to him. Consequently he cannot understand her unwillingness to 'play' – that is, to submit to his assault. Maxwell can see that she is not part of the hedonistic world of casual sex, but to him she does not represent a challenge or a threat. He is more settled in his position, inhabiting a more multi-faceted masculinity than Jo Bob, without committing himself to any one particular facet. Both professionally and socially he is an adept player of 'the game', burying his emotions so deeply beneath the various social roles, that he can no longer easily make contact with his own feelings. To Elliott, Charlotte represents difference; unlike the other women at the party she does not simply accept the dominant masculinity of Jo Bob and the football world nor does she allow it to control her. She represents possibility; confirmation that there is a world outside football in which different standards apply and where a different sort of masculinity may be possible. She also represents a problem: he is not sure how to respond to her. He feels it is his responsibility to rescue her from Jo Bob, but lacks the strength to do so without Maxwell's help. Elliott's growing interest in Charlotte is precisely because she seems to offer a route to a new masculine position; one not rooted in the football culture.

For Elliott, Charlotte comes to represent the further possibility of leaving the game entirely but this merely heightens his dilemma: while distanced from the rituals surrounding the game, he loves the act of sport performance. During the course of the film the conflict between the de-humanised world of the sport and his fumbling search for a fuller humanity comes to crisis. Charlotte then, represents difference, contrasting the football world with the world outside, masculinity with femininity, the de-humanised with the humanised. But in her affluent self-sufficiency she also represents yet another form of settled life with which Elliott is unable fully to connect, even by the end of the film.

Elliott lives for the pleasure of the well caught pass which compensates for all the travails of the game. He is seen as being in constant pain, which makes for problems in making love and in sleeping. When he and Maxwell discuss pain, it is clear that Elliott has recognised the paradox that the pain signifies fulfilment, work well done, an insight that comes as a disturbing revelation to Maxwell. While Elliott rejects many of the other rituals of the game, he freely uses pain-killing injections but fully realises the absurdity when he is unwittingly used by the coach to lever the anti-drug Delma into having a jab to deaden his wounded knee.

NO ROOM FOR UNCERTAINTY

The particular form of masculinity required to survive in the game is clearly demarcated in a post-mortem discussion early in the film. A defender's error is cruelly exposed in action replay and the coach asks what he thought he was doing. The player, Stallings, confesses that he was not sure. The coach bitingly replies, 'there's no room for uncertainty in this game'. Stallings is fired and when Elliott later comments on his dismissal with disbelief, Maxwell merely says blankly, 'who's Stallings?'

However, the film is not about Stallings' uncertainties, but about Elliott's. In a world where hierarchies are clearly defined, authority rigidly enforced, roles understood and social convention conformed to, Elliott is the one uncertain character. He is unable to reconcile his love of the game itself with his distaste for its rituals and for authority. He can't follow Maxwell's advice to 'learn how to fool them'. All he has left are his own uncertainties: how to conduct himself, how to relate to the game and whether to stay within it. It is therefore, significant that when, days before the big game, Charlotte tries to engage him in a discussion about leaving the sport he brushes her off, saying, 'I can't get confused now.' There is in coach B.A.'s words, no room for uncertainty: no room for improvisation, impulse, flair, idiosyncrasy, non-conformism or deviance. So it is in the gridiron-solid world of masculinity of American football. When Elliott suggests to another player at training that it would be preferable to be at home in front of the fire with a good book, the player snaps back the one word rebuke, 'faggot!' It is a token of the profound anti-intellectualism etched into that strand of dominant masculinity most closely linked to sport that we readily recognise this typical linking of literary-cultural pretensions and homosexuality. Reading, and especially a preference for reading over sport is signified here to be profoundly non-masculine.

Coach B.A. confronts Elliott over his attitude and quotes Corinthians on putting away childish things and acting like a man. By implication the childish things Elliott must 'put away' are promiscuity, drugs, flippancy, anti-authoritarianism, and lack of commitment. Acting like a man, for B.A., is being disciplined and committed, bowing to the patriarchal authority of the coach and the rationality of his computer, and becoming, in the full corporate sense, a team player. But by the end of the film Elliott has re-interpreted 'childish things' to refer to the game itself, and his closing line to B.A. as he resigns from the team is 'you are right, B.A. It's time to put away childish things'. In both Elliott's and the film's re-ordering of things, it is American Football which becomes a childish immature form of masculinity. Childish things here are the rigid corporate discipline, authoritarianism, masochism and dehumanised attitudes of the sport. 'They're the team, we're just the equipment,' Elliott asserts towards the end of the film, referring to the corporate owners of the Dallas Bulls. In the final image, Maxwell throws Elliott a pass on the street outside the glass skyscraper in which he has just resigned. Shaping to catch it, Elliott at the last moment throws his arms wide in a crucified image, letting the ball bounce off his chest. The camera freezes as Elliott gazes at Maxwell, having demonstrated to him that he has left the game.

The ending is somewhat ambiguous. Has Elliott grown up and matured, in leaving the game, or has he been crucified by the authoritarian Christianity of the football world? He is left on the outside, with Charlotte to go to, but no other obvious direction. Maxwell is left inside with his ability to fool them and in his position of knowledge, whilst Elliott is marginalised.

NEW MAN, OLD MAN OR MAN OF THE PAST

So, in terms of the definitions of masculinity proposed in or offered by, the film, who is Elliott? In some senses he is the classic hedonistic individual of the 1960s, rebelling against the rigid conservatism of the corporate America of the 1950s. Elliott in this sense is from the 1960s generation who refused to become the man in the grey flannel suit, and turned instead to sex, drugs and rock and roll. The dress codes in the film constantly counterpose Elliott's brown outdoor/frontier casualness with the charcoal grey suits of corporate America.

But by the time the film was released in 1979 Elliott was already starting to look a little anachronistic. The laid-back dope smoker was as dead as sideburns and flared trousers, and corporate America was being reshaped in the guise of the enterprise culture. It was all too easy to imagine Seth Maxwell with his multi-faceted ability to 'play the game' reborn into the era of Gordon Gecko as enterprise man, but there would be no place for Elliott in the world of *Wall Street* (Oliver Stone, US, 1987).

But, seen from the perspective of 1990, now that the *Wall Street* world of red braces, power dressing and pre-breakfast deals is also in eclipse, Elliott seems in some ways a precursor of the 'new man' in his rejection of the obsessive combative and sado-masochistic world of corporate sport. The term 'new man', is notoriously awkward to define. Used as a term of abuse as well as of approval, it means different things to different people in different contexts and has the complexity of all terms that draw upon and retread that multi-layered ground of popular common-sense.[12] I use the term here to refer to the emergence in popular public discourse of a set of ideas associated with the concept of a restructuring of traditional gender roles. The term, even in its confused form, appears to suggest that traditional masculinity is open to criticism, and, prompted by feminism and the women's movement, that such a criticism has been mounted. It also suggests that men in traditional masculinity cannot easily express emotion, are formed by their dominant position in power relations, are not able to be adequately caring or supporting, and do not play a full or significant role in child care or domestic labour. The 'new man' has responded to these critiques by attempting to forge a new, reconstructed masculinity. Whether such a figure exists, sociologically, in the real world, in significant numbers or whether it is principally a figure in representation, conjured up by advertisers, is well beyond the scope of this article. However, a cluster of images, that could be grouped under the new man heading unquestionably does exist. *North Dallas Forty*, like any other movie, does not ultimately have a fixed set of meanings, for this depends also on the position of the spectator. The character of Elliott is essentially rooted in the late 1960s, the date of the book on which the film is based, and some of this might have appeared dated to a 1980s audience. Yet in the twelve years that have elapsed since the release of the film, the opening up of questions about masculinity make new readings possible in which Elliott, originally the focal point for a humanistic-bohemian critique of corporate America, now becomes the focal point for a critique of a dominant form of masculinity, which is rooted in top level competitive sport.

Elliot himself is not a 'new man'. There is no sense, in the construction of his character, of masculinity being redefined in terms of caring, nurturing or taking responsibility for domestic labour. But Elliott is unable to inhabit comfortably either the blue suited corporate world of Conrad Hunter, or the ultra macho swaggering world of Jo Bob, Nor, unlike Maxwell, can he don a series of masks in order to play along. In some senses he is in the mould of the classic frontier individualist (he owns some land in the country and dreams of building a ranch one day.) But even this gives him no basis for a real reconstruction of his identity. When Charlotte challenges him about building the ranch, he says that maybe he prefers it as a fantasy. He is left with nothing but uncertainties. (Though it could be argued that part of the process of a critical reconstruction of masculinity is precisely a rejection of the old certainties).

In this sense the discursive organisation of the film categorises a range of masculinities in a negative light, without offering alternative models. The blue-suited business world of owner Conrad Hunter is shown as exploitative and hypocritical. The Christian moralism of the padre, the assistant coach, and one or two of the players is shallow and irrelevant: the assistant coach offers vacuous homespun slogans; the padre is a gridiron junkie whose role echoes that of the army chaplain, blessing the troops before battle; and the Christian footballer is just plain naive. Set against these two aspects of shallow and hypocritical Texan respectability is the more working class macho swagger of Jo Bob and O.W. For the most part this is shown as grotesque, yet at the end of the picture, in an impassioned, semi-coherent monologue, O.W. to the surprise of Elliott, exhibits a genuine passion for the game, in contrast to the soulless efficiency of the coach. Naivete, in the form of genuine love for the game, confronts cynicism in the shape of commercial management. Naive enthusiasm is losing out, a fact Elliott realises from the start of the film, and by the end even O.W. is beginning to understand.

The film leaves us with the final image of Elliott on the street, arms spread wide. He does not, in true 1950s fashion, get the girl, although he may be off to see her. He does not become the rugged individual frontiersman on his ranch, though he may be off to build it. Too late to be a hippy and too early to be a 'new man'. Elliott is left at the end of the 1970s in his uncertain limbo, with the 1980s and Gordon Gecko lurking just around the corner. Twelve years on, masculinity itself can arguably be said to have entered an age of uncertainty, some of the gridiron-solid rigidity of earlier positions rusting towards decay without the construction or even design of any reworked version having yet taken clear shape.

NOTES

1 See Eric Dunning 'Sport as a Male Preserve', in *Quest for Excitement Sport and Leisure in the Civilising Process*, by Norbert Elias and Eric Dunning, Basil Blackwell, Oxford, 1986; and Joe Maguire 'Images of Manliness and Competing Ways of Living in Victorian and Edwardian England', in the

British Journal of Sports History, Vol. 3, No. 3 for a more elaborate and nuanced account.

2 See Mangan, J.A. (1981) *Athleticism in the Victorian and Edwardian Public School*, Cambridge UP, London, and McIntosh, Peter (1952) *Physical Education in England Since 1800*, Bell, London.

3 Critcher, Charles, 'Football Since the War', in *Working Class Culture*, Clarke, Critcher and Johnson (eds), Hutchinson, London, 1979.

4 See Jennifer Hargreaves, 'Playing Like Gentlemen while Behaving like Ladies', in the *British Journal of Sports History*, Vol. 2, No. 1, Frank Cass, London, 1985, Helen Lensky, *Women Sport and Sexuality*, Womens' Press, 1986, Toronto, and the following three articles, all from *Theory Culture and Society*, Vol. 3, No. 1, Sage, London, 1986; Eric Dunning, 'Sport as A Male Preserve'; John Carroll, 'Sport, Virtue and Grace'; Jennifer Hargreaves, 'Where's the Virtue? Where's the Grace? Social Production of Gender'.

5 Harry Braverman, *Labour and Monopoly Capital*, Monthly Review Press, New York, 1974.

6 Jean-Marie Brohm, *Sport, A Prison of Measured Time*, Ink-Links, London, 1978.

7 Ronald Bergan, *Sports in the Movies*, Proteus, New York, 1982.

8 Alan Tomlinson, 'Situating Chariots of Fire', *British Society of Sports History Bulletin* N8, British Society of Sports History, 1988. See also: Steve Neale (1982) Chariots of Fire: Images of Men, in *Screen*, Vol. 23, Nos. 3-4, 1982.

9 Pam Cook, 'Masculinity in Crisis?', in *Screen*, Vol. 23, Nos. 3-4, 1982.

10 Peter Gent, *North Dallas Forty*, Michael Joseph, London, 1974.

11 See Brohm, *op. cit.*

12 Gramsci, Antonio, *Prison Notebooks*, Lawrence and Wishart, London, 1971.

Notes on Contributors

Richard DYER teaches film at Warwick University and is the author of *Heavenly Bodies* (BFI/Macmillan 1987) and *Now You See It* (Routledge 1990).

Joe FISHER is a writer, producer and literary critic. He is the author of *The Hidden Hardy* (Macmillan 1992) and *The American Marriage* (Macmillan, forthcoming). He is currently co-editing, with Beverly Skeggs, a collection of essays about genre breakdown in contemporary communications *Hybrid Media*.

Mike HAMMOND lectures in film studies at Southampton Institute of Higher Education. He is currently writing a book on memory and American cinema to be published by Manchester University Press.

Leon HUNT is a freelance lecturer, currently teaching courses in film and in popular music at Coventry University. He is researching a book on the Italian horror film, and has contributed to *Early Cinema: Space, Frame, Narrative* ed. Thomas Elsaesser (BFI 1990).

Peter HUTCHINGS lectures in film studies at the University of Northumbria at Newcastle. He is the author of *Hammer and Beyond: The British Horror Film* (Manchester University Press, forthcoming).

Pat KIRKHAM is a Principal Lecturer at De Montfort University, Leceister, where she teaches design history and film studies. She has published widely in the fields of design history and women's studies co-editing with Judy Attfield *A View From the Interior: Feminism, Women and Design* (The Women's Press, 1989). She is currently completing a book on the film makers and designers Charles and Ray Eames, and researching another on Saul and Elaine Bass.

Andy MEDHURST lectures in media studies at the University of Sussex where he teaches courses on film, television, popular culture and sexuality. He is a frequent contributor to *Sight and Sound* and *Gay Times*.

Walt MORTON is currently writing a book on intermedia adaptation theory using *Tarzan of the Apes, The Invisible Man* and *She* as examples. He has recently completed the PhD programme in film and literature at the School of Cinema-Television. University of Southern California.

John NEWSINGER teaches history at Bath College of Higher Education specialising in Irish, British and Imperial history. He has published on a variety of topics including Tarzan (the novels), British Imperialism, science fiction, counter insurgency, the Irish labour movement and *Judge Dredd*.

Ken PAGE is Senior Lecturer in film and cultural studies at the University of Wolverhampton. He is currently working on a book, 'The Moment of Horror: Masculinity and Horror in 1950s British Cinema'.

Panikos PANAYI lectures in history at De Montfort University, Leicester. He is the author of *The Enemy in Our Midst: Germans in Britain during the First World War* (Berg 1991) and editor of *Racial Violence in Britain 1840-1950* (Leicester University Press, forthcoming) and *Minorities in Wartime: National and Racial Groupings in Europe, North America and Australias during the Two World Wars* (Berg, forthcoming).

Tom RYALL is Principal Lecturer in film studies at Sheffield Hallam University. He has written on various aspects of British and American commercial cinema including *Alfred Hitchcock and the British Cinema* (Croom Helm, 1986), and has just completed a study of *Blackmail* for the BFI Film Classic series.

Ashwani SHARMA teaches film and media studies freelance, currently at De Montfort University, Leicester and at the University of Derby where he is completing his MA thesis on gender, sexuality and performance in films starring Sridevi. He is also involved in film and video production.

Janet THUMIM teaches film and television studies at the University of Bristol. She is the author of *Celluloid Sisters: Women and Popular Cinema* (Macmillan 1992).

Paul WELLS lectures in media studies at De Montfort University, Leicester. He has made a number of series for BBC radio including *America – The Movie, Britannia – The Film* and *Calling the Shots* profiling British film directors. He is currently preparing a series on the horror film, and is writing a book on animation.

Garry WHANNEL is senior lecturer in sports studies at Roehampton Institute. He is the author of *Fields in Vision: Television Sport and Cultural Transformation* (Routledge 1992) and has co-edited books on television studies, the World Cup and the Olympic Games. Having completed his doctorate, he was relaxing in a bar when a woman approached him and asked him to contribute to a book on masculinity.

Film Index

Films discussed in detail in the text are listed in the main index

215

Subject Index